Creative Solutions to Global Business Negotiations

Creative Solutions to Global Business Negotiations

Second Edition

Claude Cellich

Subhash C. Jain

BEP BUSINESS EXPERT PRESS

First published in 2016 by
Business Expert Press, LLC
222 East 46th Street, New York, NY 10017
www.businessexpertpress.com

ISBN-13: 978-1-63157-309-5 (paperback)
ISBN-13: 978-1-63157-310-1 (e-book)

Business Expert Press International Business Collection

Collection ISSN: 1948-2752 (print)
Collection ISSN: 1948-2760 (electronic)

Cover and interior design by S4Carlisle Publishing Services
Private Ltd., Chennai, India

First edition: 2016

10 9 8 7 6 5 4 3 2 1

Printed in the United States of America.

Abstract

Making deals globally is a fact of life in modern business. To successfully conduct deals abroad, executives need skills to negotiate with counterparts who have different backgrounds and experiences. *Creative Solutions to Global Business Negotiations* provides international executives with the savvy they need to negotiate with finesse and ease, no matter where they are. It offers valuable insights into the fine points of negotiating, and guidelines on delicate issues that can influence a promising deal.

This book is an indispensable tool that provides know-how and expert strategies for striking favorable deals. The book emphasizes the importance of preparation and offers basic rules and checklists for staying on top in negotiations.

The frameworks introduced in *Creative Solutions to Global Business Negotiations* are relevant in conducting business negotiations anywhere in the world in any type of business. Executives will be prepared for the real-life situations they face in international deal making. Pinpointing the importance of developing a global mindset, this book examines how to handle crucial cross-cultural differences in negotiating styles; deal with unfamiliar aspects of punctuality, manners, and gift giving; and emerge victorious as a successful international negotiator.

The book is divided into five parts. Part 1 deals with the global business negotiations framework. Part 2 focuses on the role of culture in negotiations and on choosing an appropriate negotiation style. The negotiation process is examined in Part 3 comprising prenegotiation planning, making the first move, concession trading, price negotiating, closing the deal, and understanding renegotiations. Part 4 is devoted to negotiation tools, such as communication skills, role of power in negotiations, managing negotiating teams and developing organizational capability. Part 5 covers miscellaneous topics such as negotiating intangibles, negotiating on the internet, gender issues in global negotiations, how small firms can effectively negotiate with large firms and negotiating via interpreters.

Drawing on their own experiences, the authors explain how to overcome problems such as the instability of the international marketplace and differences in culture, economy, ideology, law, politics, and currencies that may arise when negotiating with businesses abroad. Clear and comprehensive, the authors outline the hallmarks of strengthening and maintaining a strong bargaining position for negotiating deals even under adverse conditions.

Keywords

Culture and negotiations, global negotiations, negotiation styles, negotiation process, negotiation on the Internet, renegotiations

Contents

Preface

Today's globalization requires professionals to deal with their counterparts in countries with different economic, cultural, legal, and political environments. You may need to resolve a dispute with a supplier, finalize a counterproposal for a state-owned enterprise, or lead a multicultural team. Thus in a globalized market, few subjects are as critical as negotiating across cultural boundaries. When negotiators are from diverse cultures, they often rely on quite different assumptions about social interactions, economic interests, and political realities. Consequently, culturally sensitive negotiating skills are necessary for managing in an international setting.

Creative Solutions to Global Business Negotiations has been prepared for all those who negotiate globally: managers, lawyers, government officials, and diplomats. The book provides an insightful, readable, highly organized tour de force of both the conceptual and practical essentials of international business negotiation.

Negotiation is a lifelong activity. In business, you can do much better by negotiating successfully. Those not skilled in negotiation will get less than they deserve, perhaps significantly less. Surprisingly, it is often easier to sharpen your negotiating skills by simply trying. To do this, you must acquire proven negotiation strategies and tactics as well as the latest techniques of dealing with the challenges and opportunities of today's complex global alliances and quickly forming partnerships. At the same time, you must know how to navigate across national, organizational, and professional cultures at the negotiating table.

The book provides a clear framework to guide global negotiators around diverse cultural boundaries to close deals, to create value, to resolve disputes, and to reach lasting agreements in a constantly changing competitive context. In other words, this book will help managers and professionals acquire knowledge and develop indispensable skills in today's global business environment.

The book emphasizes the hardheaded sense of reality at its core. It makes negotiators feel how it will likely be at the international negotiating table. It tells you how to avoid mistakes and how to optimize your goals.

It helps you strengthen the skills that are keys to success in conducting business in a multicultural environment. The strength of your agreements and the development of lasting relationships can be the difference between success and failure. Poor agreements with overseas companies result in frequent and endless disputes affecting the profitability of the outcome. Mutually beneficial agreements help you reach and exceed your objectives and give the other party greater satisfaction at the same time. This is true whether you are (a) determining the price and terms of the deal, (b) closing with a key customer, (c) persuading others to work with and not against you, (d) setting or meeting budgets, (e) finalizing and managing complex contracts, (f) working on a project with someone important to you, or (g) breaking or avoiding a serious impasse.

While brief, our acknowledgments express our deep gratitude to all who have helped us to design and shape this book over the last several years. Many concepts are grounded on the work of others and are intended as a tribute to those found in the bibliography—a dedicated group of authors recognized for their research on cross-national negotiations. Some of them may agree or disagree with this book, and that reaction is to be expected.

Closer to home, we wish to acknowledge the support of colleagues Eric Willumsen at the International University in Geneva and John Elliott at the University of Connecticut. We are thankful to our students at the International University in Geneva and at the University of Connecticut who read drafts and provided excellent feedback. The staff at the International University in Geneva and the University of Connecticut have been extraordinarily gracious in supporting the project and providing help in numerous ways. We owe a special word of thanks to the talented staff at Business Expert Press for their role in shaping the book.

Finally, we are thankful to our wives for their gracious support and inspiration in countless ways.

Claude Cellich, Geneva, Switzerland
Subhash C. Jain, Storrs, Connecticut, United States
March 2016

PART 1

Introduction

CHAPTER 1

Overview of Global Business Negotiations

In business you don't get what you deserve, you get what you negotiate.
—Chester L. Karras

Business requires undertaking a variety of transactions. These transactions involve negotiations with one or more parties on their mutual roles and obligations. Thus, negotiation is defined as a process by which two or more parties reach agreement on matters of common interest. All negotiations involve *parties* (i.e., persons with common interests who deal with each other), *issues* (i.e., one or more matters to be resolved), *alternatives* (i.e., choices available to negotiators for each issue to be resolved), *positions* (i.e., defined response of the negotiator on a particular issue: what you want and why you want it), and *interest* (i.e., underlying needs a negotiator has). These should be identified and stated clearly at the outset.

In the post-World War II period, one of the most important developments has been the internationalization of business. Today companies of all sizes increasingly compete in global markets to seek growth and maintain their competitive edge. This forces managers to negotiate business deals in multicultural environments.

While negotiations are difficult in any business setting, they are especially so in global business because of (a) cultural differences between parties involved, (b) business environments in which parties operate differently, and (c) gender issues in global business negotiations. For these reasons, business negotiations across borders can be problematic and sometimes require an extraordinary effort.[1] Proper training can go a long way in preparing managers for negotiations across national borders. This book provides know-how and expertise for deal making in multicultural environments.

The book is meant for those individuals who must negotiate deals, resolve disputes, or make decisions outside their home markets. Often managers take international negotiations for granted. They assume that if correct policies are followed, negotiations can be carried out without any problems. Experience shows, however, that negotiations across national boundaries are difficult and involve a painstaking process. Even with favorable policies and institutions, negotiations in a foreign environment may fail because individuals are dealing with people from a different cultural background within the context of a different legal system and different business practices. When negotiators have the same nationality, their dealing takes place within the same cultural and institutional setup. But where negotiators belong to different cultures, they have different approaches and assumptions relative to social interactions, economic interests, legal requirements, and political realities.

This book provides business executives, lawyers, government officials, and students of international business with practical insights into international business negotiations. For those who have no previous training in negotiations, the book introduces them to the fundamental concepts of global deal making. For those with formal training in negotiation, this book builds on what they already know about negotiation in the global environment.

Negotiation is interdependent, since what one person does affect another party. It is imperative, therefore, that a negotiator, in addition to perfecting his or her own negotiating skills, focus on how to interact, persuade, and communicate with the other party. A successful negotiator works with others to achieve his or her own objectives. Some people negotiate well, while others do not. Successful negotiators are not born; rather, they have taken the pains to develop negotiating skills through training and experience.

Negotiation Architecture

There are three aspects to the architecture of global negotiations: negotiation environment, negotiation setting, and negotiation process. Negotiation environment refers to the business climate that surrounds the negotiations; this is beyond the control of negotiators. Usually, negotiators have influence and some measure of control over the negotiation setting. Negotiating process refers to the events and interactions that take place between parties to reach an agreement. Included in the process are the verbal and nonverbal communication among parties, the display of bargaining strategies, and the endeavors to strike a deal. Figure 1.1 depicts the three aspects of negotiation architecture.

Negotiation Environment

Negotiation environment can be thought of having the following components: legal pluralism, political pluralism, currency fluctuations and foreign exchange, foreign government control and bureaucracy, instability and change, cultural differences, ideological differences, and external stakeholders.[2]

Legal Pluralism A multinational enterprise in its global negotiations must cope with widely different laws. A U.S. corporation not only must consider U.S. laws wherever it negotiates, but also must be responsive to the laws of the negotiating partner's country. For example, without requiring proof that certain market practices have adversely affected competition, U.S. law, nevertheless, makes them violations. These practices include horizontal price fixing among competitors, market division by agreement

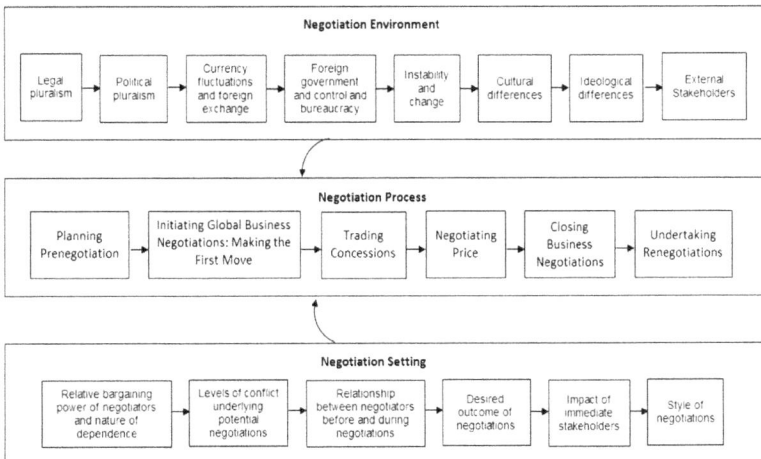

Figure 1.1 Negotiation architecture

among competitors, and price discrimination. Even though such practices might be common in a foreign country, U.S. corporations cannot
engage in them. Simultaneously, local laws must be adhered to even if
they forbid practices that are allowed in the United States. For example,
in Europe, a clear-cut distinction is made between agencies and distributorships. Agents are deemed auxiliaries of their principal; distributorships
are independent enterprises. Exclusive distributorships are considered re-
strictive in European Union (EU) countries. The foreign marketer must
be careful in making distribution negotiations in, say, France, so as not to
violate the regulation concerning distributorship contracts.

Negotiators should be fully briefed about relevant legal aspects of the
countries involved before coming to agreement. This will ensure that the
final agreement does not contain any provision that cannot be implemented
because it is legally prohibited. The best source for such briefings is a law
firm with in-house expertise on legal matters of the counterpart's country.

Political Pluralism A thorough review of the political environment of
the party's country with whom negotiation is planned must precede the
negotiation process. An agreement may be negotiated that is legal in the
countries involved and yet may not be politically prudent to implement.
There is no reason to spend effort in negotiating such a deal. Consider the
following example.

The U.S. federal government officially discourages cigarette smoking
in the United States. But if people in other countries are going to smoke,
why shouldn't they puff away on American tobacco?

Thailand, with a government tobacco monopoly of its own, has
been fighting U.S. pressure to open up, and U.S. tobacco companies
approached the Bush administration to take up trade sanctions against
Thai authorities. That raises the question about U.S. trade policy, such as:
Should Washington use its muscle to promote a product overseas that it
acknowledges is deadly? The U.S. should first examine this question before deciding to negotiate with the Thai authorities to open their cigarette
market.[3]

A thorough review of the political environment of a country must
precede the negotiation exercise. A rich foreign market may not war-
rant entry if the political environment is characterized by instability and
uncertainty.

Political perspectives of a country can be analyzed in three ways: (1) by visiting the country and meeting credible people; (2) by hiring a consultant to prepare a report on the country; and (3) by examining political risk analysis worked out by such firms as the Economist Intelligence Unit (EIU), a New York-based subsidiary of the Economist Group, London, or the Bank of America's country Risk Monitor or BERI S.A.'s Business Risk Service.

Currency Fluctuations and Foreign Exchange A global negotiation may involve financial transfers across national lines in order to close deals. Financial transfers from one country to another are made through the medium of foreign exchange. Foreign exchange is the monetary mechanism by which transactions involving two or more currencies take place. It is the exchange of one country's money for another country's money.

Transacting foreign exchange deals presents two problems. First, each country has its own methods and procedures for effecting foreign exchanges—usually developed by its central bank. The transactions themselves, however, take place through the banking system. Thus, the methods of foreign exchange and the procedures of the central bank and commercial banking constraints must be thoroughly understood and followed to complete a foreign exchange transaction.

A second problem involves the fluctuation of rates of exchange that occurs in response to changes in supply and demand of different currencies. For example, in 1992, a U.S. dollar could be exchanged for about three Swiss francs. In early 2001, this rate of exchange went down to as low as 1.3 Swiss francs for a U.S. dollar, and in early 2016 the U.S. dollar further declined such that a dollar fetched less than one Swiss franc. Thus, a U.S. businessperson interested in Swiss currency must pay much more today than in the 1990s. In fact, the rate of exchange between two countries can fluctuate from day to day. This produces a great deal of uncertainty, as a businessperson cannot know the exact value of foreign obligations and claims.

Foreign Government Controls and Bureaucracy An interesting development of the post-World War II period has been the increased presence of government in a wide spectrum of social and economic affairs it previously ignored. In the United States, concern for the poor, aged, and minorities, as well as consumers' rights and the environment has spurred government response and the adoption of a variety of legislative measures.

In a great many foreign countries, such concerns have led governments to take over businesses to be run as public enterprises. Sympathies for public-sector enterprises, successful or not as businesses, have rendered private corporations suspect and undesirable in many countries. Also, public-sector enterprises are not limited to developing countries. Great Britain and France had many government corporations, from airlines, to broadcasting companies, to banks and steel mills. Thus, in many nations, negotiations may take place with a government-owned company, where profit motive may not be as relevant as for a private company.

Some nations look upon foreign investment with suspicion. This is true of developed and developing countries. Take, for example, Japan, where it is extremely difficult for a foreign business to establish itself without first generating a trusting relationship that enables it to gain entry through a joint venture. Developing countries are usually afraid of domination and exploitation by foreign businesses. In response to national attitudes, these nations legislate a variety of controls to prescribe the role of foreign investment in their economies. Therefore, a company should review a host country's regulations and identify underlying attitudes and motivations before deciding to negotiate there. For advice on legal matters, the company should contact a law firm, who may know an expert in the host country. Furthermore, the company should examine the political risk analysis of firms such as the Economist Intelligence Unit, mentioned previously.

The government of a country sometimes imposes market control to prevent foreign companies from competing in certain markets. For example, until recently, Japan prohibited foreign companies from selling sophisticated communications equipment to the Japanese government. Thus, AT&T, Hewlett Packard, and Cisco could do little business with Japan.

Obviously, in nations with an ongoing bias against homegrown private businesses, a foreign company cannot expect a cordial welcome. In such a situation, the foreign company must contend with the problems that arise because it is a private business as well as a foreign one. Sound business intelligence and familiarity with the industrial policy of the government and related legislative acts and decrees should provide clarification of the role of the private sector in any given economy. This type of information should be fully absorbed before proceeding to negotiate.

Instability and Change Many countries have frequent changes of government. In such a climate, a foreign business may find that by the time it is ready to implement an agreement, the government with whom the initial agreement was negotiated has changed to one that is not sympathetic to the commitment by its predecessor. Consequently, it is important for international negotiators to examine, before making agreements, whether the current government is likely to continue to be in office for a while. In a democratic situation, the incumbent party's strength or the alternative outcomes of the next election can be weighted to assess the likelihood of change. To learn about the political stability of a country, a company should contact someone who has been doing business in the host country for some time. A company may also gain useful insights on this matter from its government agencies. For example, in the U.S., a company may contact the International Trade Administration (U.S. Department of Commerce) in its area for advice; they may even put the company in touch with a representative in the host country.

More than anything else, foreign companies dislike frequent policy changes by host countries. Policy changes may occur even without a change in government. It is important, therefore, for foreign businesses to analyze the mechanism of government policy changes. Information on the autonomy of legislatures and study of the procedures followed for seeking constitutional changes can be crucial for the global negotiator.

An example of policy change is provided by China. A few years ago, China ordered all direct-sales operations to cease immediately. Alarmed by a rise in pyramid schemes by some direct sellers and uneasy about big sales meetings held by direct sellers, Beijing gave all companies that held direct-selling licensing six months to convert to retail outlets or shut down altogether. The move threatened Avon's China sales, of about $75 million a year, and put Avon, Amway, and Mary Kay Inc.'s combined China investment of roughly $180 million at risk. It also created problems for Sara Lee Corporation and Tupperware Corporation, which had recently launched direct-sales efforts in China.[4] (China withdrew the order after a little arm-twisting from Washington and because over 20 million Chinese were involved in direct sales, with more turning to the businesses as unemployment rose.)

Sovereign nations like to assert their authority over foreign business through various sanctions. Such sanctions are regular and evolutionary and, therefore, predictable. An example is increase in taxes over foreign operations. Many developing countries impose restrictions on foreign business to protect their independence. (Economic domination is often perceived as leading to political subservience.) These countries are protective of their political freedom and want to maintain it at all costs, even when it means proceeding at a slow economic pace and without the help of foreign business. Thus, the problem posed by political sovereignty exists mainly in developing countries.

The industrialized nations, whose political sovereignty has been secure for a long time, require a more open policy for the economic realities of today's world. Today, governments are expected simultaneously to curb unemployment, limit inflation, redistribute income, build up backward regions, deliver health services, and avoid abusing the environment. These wide-ranging objectives make developing countries seek foreign technology, use foreign capital and foreign raw materials, and sell their specialties in foreign markets. The net result is that these countries have found themselves exchanging guarantees for mutual access to one another's economies. In brief, among developed countries, multi-nationalism of business is politically acceptable and economically desirable, which is not always true of developing countries.

A basic management reality in today's economic world is that businesses operate in a highly interdependent global economy and that the 200-plus developing countries are significant factors in the international business area. They are the buyers, suppliers, competitors, and capital users. To successfully negotiate in developing countries, a company must recognize the magnitude and significance of these roles.

Cultural Differences Doing business across national boundaries requires interaction with people nurtured in different cultural environments. Values that are important to one group of people may mean little to another. Some typical attitudes and perceptions of one nation may be strikingly different from those of other countries. These cultural differences deeply affect negotiation behavior. International negotiators, therefore, need to be familiar with the cultural traits of the country with which they want to negotiate. International business literature is full of instances where stereotyped notions of countries' cultures have led to insurmountable problems.

The effect of culture on international business ventures is multifaceted.[5] The factoring of cultural differences into the negotiating process to enhance the likelihood of success has long been a critical issue in overseas operations. With the globalization of commerce, cultural forces have taken on additional importance. Naivety and blundering in regard to culture can lead to expensive mistakes. And although some cultural differences are instantly obvious, others are subtle and can surface in surprising ways.[6]

Successful negotiators advise that in Asian cultures, a low-key, nonadversarial, win-win negotiating style works better than a cut-and-dried businesslike attitude. A negotiator should listen closely, focus on mutual interests rather than minor differences, and nurture long-term relationships.

Four aspects of culture are especially important in negotiating well. They are spoken language, body language, attitude toward time, and attitude toward contracts.[7]

Ideological Differences There are always ideological differences between nations, which influence the behaviors of their citizens. Ideologies that are attributed to traditional societies imply that they are compulsory in their force, sacred in their tone, and stable in their timeliness. They call for fatalistic acceptance of the world as it is, respect for those in authority, and submergence of the individual in collectivity. In contrast to this, the ideologies of Western societies can be described as stressing acquisitive activities, an aggressive attitude toward economic and social change, and a clear trend toward a higher degree of industrialization.

For example, many feel that having a contract with the Chinese does not have the same meaning because Chinese do not view contracts as binding. Even if a contract was negotiated in good faith with Mr. Chu, when Mr. Lin comes in to replace Mr. Chu, he might say, "Well, you signed the contract with Mr. Chu, not me. So to me this contract is void. So what you can do is to sue the Chinese government." While keeping their ideological differences intact, traditional societies want to be economically absorbed in Western ways, having a strong emphasis on specificity, universalism, and achievement. Thus, if matters are handled in a delicate fashion, problems can be averted.

Negotiators should be familiar with and respect each other's values and ideologies. For example, a fatalistic belief may lead an Asian negotiator to choose an auspicious time to meet the other party. The other party should be duly sensitive to accommodate the ideological demands of his or her counterpart.

External Stakeholders The term *external stakeholders* refers to different people and organizations that have a stake in the outcome of a negotiation. These can be stockholders, employees, customers, labor unions, business groups (e.g., chambers of commerce), industry associations, competitors, and others. Stockholders welcome the negotiation agreement when it increases the financial performance of the company. Employees support the negotiation that results in improved gains (financial and in-kind) for them. Customers favor the negotiation that enables them to have quality products at a lower price. Thus, if a foreign company that is likely to provide good value to consumers is negotiating to enter a country, the consumers will be excited about it. However, the industry groups will oppose such negotiation to discourage competition from the foreign company.

Different stakeholders have different agendas. They support or oppose negotiation with a foreign enterprise depending on how it will affect them. In conducting negotiation, therefore, a company must examine the likely reaction of different stakeholders.

Negotiation Setting

Negotiation setting refers to factors that surround the negotiation process and over which the negotiators have some control. The following are the dimensions of negotiation setting: the relative bargaining power of the negotiators and the nature of their dependence on each other, the levels of conflict underlying potential negotiation, the relationship between negotiators before and during negotiations, the desired outcome of negotiations, impact of immediate stakeholders, and style of negotiations.

Relative Bargaining Power of Negotiators
and Nature of Dependence

An important requisite of successful negotiations is the mutual dependence of the parties on one another. Without such interdependence, negotiations do not take place. The degree of dependence determines the relative bargaining power of each side. The style and strategies adopted by a negotiator depend on his or her bargaining power. A company with greater bargaining power is likely to be more aggressive than one with weaker bargaining power. A company with other equally attractive alternatives may apply a "take it or leave it" posture, while a company with no other choice to fall back upon may adopt a more submissive stance.

Levels of Conflict Underlying Potential Negotiations Every negotiation situation has a few key points. When both parties agree on essential issues, the negotiation is concluded with supportive attitude. On the other hand, differences over the key points may cause the potential negotiation to conclude in a hostile environment.

Where the goals of two parties depend on each other in such a way that the gains of one party have a positive impact on the gains of the other party, the negotiations are concluded in a win-win situation (also called a nonzero-sum game, or integrative bargaining). If, however, the negotiation involves a win-lose situation (i.e., the gains of one side result in losses for the other party), the negotiation will proceed in a hostile setting.

Suppose a U.S. women's fashion company is interested in manufacturing some of its goods in a developing country to take advantage of low wages. The developing country, on the other hand, is interested in increasing employment. This presents a win-win situation, and the negotiation will take place in a friendly setting. Assume a European company is negotiating a joint venture in a developing country. The company desires majority equity control in the joint venture, while the government of the developing country is opposed to it (i.e., the government wants the foreign company to have a minority interest in the joint venture). This case represents a win-lose situation (or a zero-sum game, or distributive bargaining) since the gains of one party come at the cost of the other.

Relationship between Negotiators before and during Negotiations The history of a positive working relationship between negotiating parties influences future negotiations. When previous negotiations establish a win–win situation, both sides undertake current negotiation with a positive attitude, hoping to negotiate another win-win agreement. However, when the previous experience is disappointing, the current negotiation setting may begin with a pessimistic attitude.

Even during the current negotiation, what happens in the first session sets the stage for the next session and so on. Usually, a negotiation involves several sessions over a period of time. When, in the first session, relationships are less than cordial, future sessions may proceed in a negative atmosphere. Therefore, a company should adopt a positive, friendly, and supportive posture in the initial session(s). Every effort should be made to avoid conflicting issues.

Desired Outcome of Negotiations The outcomes of global business negotiation can be tangible and intangible. Examples of tangible outcomes are profit sharing, technology transfer, royalty sales, protection of intellectual property, equity ownership, and other outcomes whose values can be measured in concrete terms. Intangible outcomes include the goodwill generated between two sides in a negotiation, the willingness to offer concessions to enhance the relationship between parties (and the outcome through understanding), and give-and-take. The tangible-intangible outcomes can be realized in the short term or long term.

One basic precept of global business negotiation is to compromise for tangible results to happen in the long run. Business deals are long-term phenomena. Even when a company is interested in negotiating with a foreign company only for an ad hoc deal, the importance of a long-term relationship and its positive impact should be remembered. The situation may change in the future such that the company with whom a person negotiated in the past on a minor project may not be a major player for which he or she is currently negotiating. Relationship is an important criterion for conducting successful negotiations. And it takes time to establish a relationship.

Often, developing countries want multinational companies to transfer technology to the country. But technology is a very important and unique asset of the company, which it does not want to fall into the wrong hands. Negotiators from developing countries should, in the short term, be willing to live with intangible benefits from the current negotiation, in the interest of realizing the tangible gain of technology transfer in the long run. Similarly, a multinational corporation might initially accept a minority position in a developing country if the latter is willing to reconsider the equity ownership question a few years later. When goodwill is created, the government may approach the company's desire to have equity control in the venture with an open mind.

Impact of Immediate Stakeholders The immediate stakeholders in global business negotiation refer to employees, managers, and members of the board of directors. Their experience in global negotiations, their cultural perspectives, and their individual stakes in negotiation outcomes have a bearing on the negotiating process.

Long-term experience in negotiating deals with Japanese, for example, teaches a U.S. manager that the Japanese do not mean yes when they say "okay" to some point. Experience also teaches about the rituals of a culture and the meaning of gestures, jokes, gifts, and so on. Such experience comes in handy in the planning of negotiating tactics and strategies. Likewise, the cultural background of negotiators influences the outcomes. In Russia and Eastern European countries, the emphasis on profits by Western managers is not easy to grasp. In many cultures, people like to deal with their equals. Thus, a lower-ranking Western manager may have a problem negotiating with the CEO of an Indian company. The ranks of the people involved in negotiation are a consideration in the successful outcome. Other cultural traits such as outside interests, emphasis on time, etc. also impact negotiations.

Different stakeholders have different stakes in the negotiation. Labor in a developed country does not want global negotiation to transfer jobs overseas or to use pressure to institute lower wages. Managers do not like to negotiate an agreement that counters their personal stakes, such as financial gain, career advancement, ego, prestige, personal power, and economic security. Members of a board of directors may be interested in an agreement for prestige sake rather than any financial gain. This means they might compromise on an agreement in terms of profit as long as it ensures the prestige they are seeking.

Style of Negotiations Every person has certain traits that characterize his or her way of undertaking negotiation. Some people adopt an aggressive posture and hope to get what they want by making others afraid of them. Some people are low-key and avoid confrontation, hoping their counterparts in negotiations are rational and friendly. Different styles have their merits and demerits.

With regard to negotiations, the best style is the one that satisfies the needs of both parties. In other words, a negotiator should embrace a style that helps in a win-win outcome, i.e., adopt a style that makes the other party feel comfortable and helps in minimizing any conflict.

Negotiation Process

Although companies of all sizes run into negotiation problems, managers of small- and medium-sized firms often lack the business negotiation skills needed to make deals in the international marketplace. These companies may also need negotiation skills for discussions with importers or agents when the firm is exporting its products. Such skills are also necessary when the firm is exploring joint-venture possibilities abroad or purchasing raw materials from foreign suppliers. As mentioned previously, negotiating with business partners located in other countries, where the customs and language of the counterpart are different from those at home, is more difficult than dealing with local companies. Such cultural factors add to the complexities of the transaction.

Assume the export manager of a small manufacturing company specializing in wooden kitchen cabinets wants to find an agent for the firm's products in a selected target market and has scheduled a visit there for this purpose. The manager has never been to the country and is not familiar with the business practices or the cultural aspects. The manager realizes the need for a better understanding of how to conduct business negotiations in the market before meeting several potential agents.

The negotiation process introduced in this book (see Figure 1.1) can be of real help to managers who do not have any formal training on the subject. The negotiation begins with prenegotiation planning and ends with renegotiation, if necessary. In between are stages of initiating negotiation, trading concessions, negotiating price, and closing the deal.

After completing prenegotiation planning, negotiation begins with contention; i.e., each party starts from a different point concerning what he or she hopes to achieve through negotiation. In the example above, when the export manager meets the potential agents in the target market, he or she has certain interests to pursue in the business dealings that may not necessarily coincide with those of the counterpart. The manager may want the agent to work for only a minimal commission so the extra profits can be reinvested in the company to expand and modernize production. Furthermore, the manager may wish to sign up several other agents in the same country to increase the possibility of export sales; he or she may also want to limit the agency agreement to a short period in order to test the market. The potential agent, on the other hand, may demand a higher percentage of sales than is being offered as commission, may insist on exclusivity within the country concerned, and may call for a contract of several years instead of a short trial period. In this situation, the exporter needs to know how to proceed in the talks to ensure that most of the firm's interests are covered in the final agreement.

The terms clarification, comprehension, credibility, and creating value are basic phrases in the negotiating process between the initial starting position and the point where both parties develop a common perspective. By applying each concept in sequence, one can follow a logical progression during the negotiation.

Clarification and comprehension are the first steps away from the situation of confrontation. In the case above, the exporter and the potential agent should clarify their views and seek the understanding of the other party about matters of particular concern. For instance, the parties may learn that it is important for the exporter to obtain a low commission rate and for the agent to have exclusivity in the territory concerned.

The next stages in business negotiation concern the concepts of credibility and creating value; i.e., the attitudes that develop as both parties discuss their requirements and the reasons behind them. In the example above, this may mean that the agent accepts as credible the exporter's need to reinvest a large portion of profits in order to keep the company competitive. The exporter, on the other side, has confidence that the agent will put maximum efforts into promoting the product, thus assuring the exporter that a long-term contract is not disadvantageous. As the negotiation proceeds, the two gradually reach a convergence of views on a number of points under discussion.

Following this is the stage of concession, counterproposals, and commitment. In this phase, the final matters on which the two parties have not already agreed are settled through compromises on both sides.

The final stage is conclusion; that is, agreement between the two parties. In the case of the exporter, this means a signed agreement with a new agent, incorporating at least some of the exporter's primary concerns (such as a low commission on sales) and some of the agent's main considerations (for instance, a two-year contract). The negotiation process, however, is not complete as circumstances may change, particularly during the implementation phase, requiring a renegotiation, a possibility both parties should keep in mind.

Negotiation Infrastructure

Before proceeding to negotiate, it is desirable to put negotiation infrastructure in place. It makes the lives of negotiators easier and makes their jobs more rewarding. The infrastructure consists of assessing the current status of the company and establishing the BATNA; i.e., best alternative to a negotiated agreement.

Assessing Current Status

The current status can be assessed using the strengths, weaknesses, opportunities, and threats (SWOT) analysis, a technique often used to assess business management situations. Although this is a well-known business management tool, insufficient attention has been given to linking the results of a SWOT analysis with the development of a business negotiation strategy.

The SWOT method as used for business management purposes consists, in simple terms, of looking at a firm's production and marketing goals and assessing the company's operations and management policies and practices in the light of these goals. The framework for this analysis consists of four key words: strengths, weaknesses, opportunities, and threats. All aspects of the company's activities are reviewed and classified under one of these terms.

This analysis is taken a step further when the results of SWOT analysis are applied to a negotiating plan. The strengths, weaknesses, opportunities, and threats identified are used to plan the negotiating strategy and tactics. Applying the SWOT technique to cross-border negotiations helps executives optimize their companies' strengths, minimize their weaknesses, be open to opportunities, and be ready to neutralize threats. On the basis of his or her company's strengths, a negotiator can obtain more support for the firm's proposals during the discussions. Similarly, to offset weaknesses, the negotiator can minimize their importance by focusing on other aspects of the talks or broadening the range of issues. With regard to opportunities, specific plans can be incorporated into the negotiating strategy for capitalizing on them. Finally, any threats to the company's business operations identified through the SWOT analysis can be countered in the negotiations through specific measures or proposals.

For example, if a company, through the SWOT analysis, finds that one of its weak points is a lack of consumer familiarity with its products, the negotiator might overcome this weakness in negotiation with prospective agents in the target market by offering promotional allowance. At the same time, the negotiator may use one of the company's strength identified through the SWOT analysis, that of the high quality of the firm's wooden cabinets, to convince the prospective agents to work with the firm on favorable terms.

Assessing BATNA

By assessing its BATNA (i.e., the best alternative to a negotiated agreement), a party can greatly improve the negotiation results by evaluating the negotiated agreement against the alternative.[8] If the negotiated agreement is better, close the deal. If the alternative is worse, walk away.

The BATNA approach changes the rules of the game. Negotiators no longer see their role as that of producing agreements, but rather as making good choices. If an agreement is not reached, negotiators do not consider that a failure. If a deal is rejected because it falls short of a company's BATNA, the net result is a success, not a failure.

BATNA is affected by several elements; namely, alternatives, deadlines, interests, knowledge, experience, negotiator's resources, and resources of the other party. Any change in these elements is likely to change the BATNA. If, during the discussions, the negotiator obtains new information that influences the BATNA, he or she should take time to review the BATNA. BATNA is not static, but dynamic, in a negotiation situation.

The BATNA should be identified at the outset. This way an objective target that a negotiated agreement must meet is set, and negotiators do not have to depend on subjective judgments to evaluate the outcome. As the negotiation proceeds, the negotiator should think of ways to improve the BATNA by doing further research, by considering alternative investments, or by identifying other potential allies. An attempt should be made to assess the other party's BATNA as well. The basic principle of BATNA is this: Never accept an agreement that is not at least as good as the BATNA.

Going into Negotiations

When conducting business negotiations, executives should keep in mind certain points that may arise as the discussions proceed.

- Situations to avoid during the negotiations: conflict, controversy, and criticism vis-à-vis the other party
- Attitudes to develop during the talks: communication, collaboration, and cooperation
- Goals to seek during the discussions: change (or, alternatively, continuity), coherence, creativity, consensus, commitment, and compensation

In business negotiations, particularly those between executives from different economic and social environments, introducing options and keeping an open mind are musts for establishing a fruitful, cooperative relationship. Experienced negotiators consider the skill of introducing options to be a key asset in conducting successful discussions. Giving the other party the feeling that new ideas proposed have come from both sides also contributes greatly to smooth negotiations.

The goal in such negotiations is to reach an agreement that is beneficial to both parties, leading to substantive results in the long run, including repeat business. To negotiate mutually beneficial agreements requires a willingness to cooperate with others. The discussions should, therefore, focus on common interests of the parties. If the negotiations come to an impasse for any reason, it may be necessary to refocus them by analyzing and understanding the needs and problems of each party.

The approach to business negotiations is that of a mutual effort. In an international business agreement (whether it concerns securing an order, appointing a new agent, or entering into a joint venture), the aim is the creation of a shared investment in a common future business relationship. In other words, a negotiated agreement should be doable, profitable, and sustainable.

Plan of the Book

In today's global business environment, you must negotiate with people born and raised in different cultures. Global deal making has become a key element of modern business life. To compete abroad, you need skills to negotiate effectively with your counterparts in other countries. This book provides insightful, readable, and well-organized material about the conceptual and practical essentials of international business negotiations.

The book is divided into five parts. Part 1 covers an overview of global negotiations. Discussed in Chapter 1 are a number of variables relative to negotiation environment and negotiation setting. Of these, one environmental factor and one setting factor stand out as having the biggest effect in global negotiations. These are influence of culture and choice of proper negotiating style. Part 2, made up of Chapter 2 and Chapter 3, is devoted to the negotiation environment and setting. Chapter 2 examines the important role of cultural differences in global negotiations, and Chapter 3 discusses the appropriate negotiation style for successful results.

The negotiation process is examined in Part 3. The subject is covered in Chapters 4 to 9. Chapter 4 deals with prenegotiation planning. Initiating global business negotiation and making the first move are covered in Chapter 5. In Chapter 6, trading concessions are examined. Chapter 7 explores price negotiations. Closing negotiations is covered in Chapter 8. Chapter 9 focuses on renegotiations.

The four chapters, Chapter 10, 11, 12, and 13, in Part 4 deal with negotiation tools. The subject of Chapter 10 is communication skills for effective negotiations, while Chapter 11 is devoted to demystifying the role of power in negotiations. Chapter 12 examines management of negotiating teams. Chapter 13, the last chapter in Part 4, focuses on developing organizational capabilities for negotiations. Finally, Part 5 includes five chapters: Chapter 14 is devoted to negotiating intangibles; Chapter 15 explores online negotiations; Chapter 16 examines gender role in cross-cultural negotiations; Chapter 17 focuses on negotiations by smaller firms; and Chapter 18 deals with negotiating via interpreters.

Summary

For most companies, global business is a fact of life. That means executives must negotiate with people from two or more different cultures. This is more difficult than simply making deals with people who share one's own culture. Therefore, it is important to learn fundamental principles of global business negotiations.

This chapter introduces the global business negotiation architecture and its three aspects: negotiation environment, negotiation setting, and negotiation process. The environment defines the business climate in which negotiation takes place. The setting specifies the power, style and interdependence of the negotiating parties. The negotiation process involves planning prenegotiation, initiating global business negotiation, negotiating price, closing negotiations, and renegotiating.

The next topic concerns negotiation infrastructure, which includes assessing the current status of a company from the viewpoint of global negotiation and assessing the BATNA (i.e., best alternative to a negotiated agreement).

PART 2

Negotiation Environment and Setting

CHAPTER 2

Role of Culture in Cross-Border Negotiations

Credibility is essential in cross-cultural negotiations

—Anonymous

In a globalizing world, companies operate in a multicultural environment. Even when people from other nations may seem to present a similar perspective, they are different in many ways, defined by their cultures. Even if they speak English, they view the world differently. They define business goals, express thoughts and feelings, and show interest in different ways. Culture is a deep-rooted aspect of a person's life that is always present. No manager can avoid bringing his or her cultural assumptions, images, prejudices, and other behavioral traits into a negotiating situation.

Culture includes all learned behavior and values that are transmitted through shared experience to an individual living within a society. The concept of culture is broad and extremely complex. It involves virtually every part of a person's life and touches on virtually all human needs, both physical and psychological. A classic definition is provided by Sir Edward Taylor: "Culture is that complex whole which includes knowledge, belief, art, morals, law, custom, and any other capabilities and habits acquired by individuals as members of society."[1]

Culture, then, develops through recurrent social relationships that form patterns that are eventually internalized by members of the entire group. It is commonly agreed that a culture must have these three characteristics[2]:

It is learned; that is, people over time transmit the culture of their group from generation to generation.

It is interrelated; that is, one part of the culture is deeply connected with another part, such as religion with marriage or business with social status.

It is shared; that is, the tenets of the culture are accepted by most members of the group.

Another characteristic of culture is that it continues to evolve through constant embellishment and adaptation, partly in response to environmental needs and partly through the influence of outside forces. In other words, a culture does not stand still, but slowly, over time, changes.

Effect of Culture on Negotiation

Culture is non-negotiable. Deal or no deal, people do not change their culture for the sake of business. Therefore, it behooves negotiators to accept the fact that cultural differences exist between them and try to understand these differences. Cultural differences can influence business negotiations in significant and unexpected ways. Summarized below are the major effects of culture on cross-border negotiations.[3]

Definition of Negotiation

The basic concept of negotiation is interpreted differently from one culture to another. In the United States, negotiation is a mechanical exercise of offers and counteroffers that leads to a deal. It is a cut-and-dry method of arriving at an agreement. In Japan, on the other hand, negotiation is sharing information and developing a relationship that may lead to a deal.

Selection of Negotiators

The criteria for the selection of negotiators vary from culture to culture. Usually, the criteria include knowledge of the subject matter, seniority, family connections, gender, age, experience, and status. Different cultures assign different importance to these criteria in choosing of negotiators. In the Middle East, for example, age, family connection, gender, and status count more; while in the United States, knowledge of the subject matter, experience, and status are given more weight.

Protocol

The degree of formality used by the parties in the negotiation is affected by their cultures. Culturally, the United States is an informal society, such that Americans like to address other people by their first name upon first meeting. Europeans, on the other hand, are highly title conscious. While in the United States, graduate students call their professor by his or her first name, in Germany, a professor with a Ph.D. has to be addressed as Professor or Doctor.

Presentation of business cards at the beginning of a first meeting is normal protocol in Southeast Asia. As a matter of fact, the cards must be presented in a proper manner. In the United States, cards may or may not be exchanged and there is no cultural norm of presenting the cards. In many traditional cultures, a man placing the other person's business card in his wallet and then putting the wallet in his back pocket is considered an insult. (Women negotiators do not have this problem.) Likewise, methods of greeting as well as dress codes are impacted by one's culture. The way a person greets the other party or dresses for the occasion communicates his or her interest and intentions relative to the negotiation.

Communication

As noted in Chapter 1, culture plays a significant role in how people communicate, both verbally and nonverbally. Language as a part of culture consists not only of the spoken word, but also of symbolic communication of time, space, things, friendship, and agreements. Nonverbal communication occurs through gestures, expressions, and other body movements.

The many different languages of the world do not translate literally from one to another, and understanding the symbolic and physical aspects of communication in different cultures is even more difficult to achieve. For example, the phrase *body by Fisher* translated literally into

Flemish means "corpse by Fisher." Similarly, *Let Hertz put you in the driver's seat* translated literally into Spanish means "Let Hertz make you a chauffeur." *Nova* translates into Spanish as "it doesn't go." A shipment of Chinese shoes destined for Egypt created a problem because the design on the soles of the shoes spelled *God* in Arabic. Olympia's Roto photocopier did not sell well because *roto* refers to the lowest class in Chile, and *roto* in Spanish means "broken."[4]

In addition, meanings differ within the same language used in different places. The English language differs so much from one English-speaking country to another that sometimes the same word means something entirely different in another culture. *Table the report* in the United States means "postponement" while in England, it means "bring the matter to the forefront."

A case of nonverbal communication is body language. A certain type of body language in one nation may be innocuous, while in another culture, the same body language may be insulting. Consider the following examples.

Never touch a Malay on the top of the head, for that is where the soul resides. Never show the sole of your shoe to an Arab, for it is dirty and represents the bottom of the body, and never use your left hand in Muslim culture, for it is the hand reserved for physical hygiene. Touch the side of your nose in Italy, and it is a sign of distrust. Always look directly and intently into your French associate's eye when making an important point. Direct eye contact in Southeast Asia, however, should be avoided until the relationship is firmly established. If your Japanese associate has just sucked air in deeply through his teeth, that's a sign you've got real problems. Your Mexican associate will want to embrace you at the end of a long and successful negotiation; so will your Central and East European associates, who may give you a bear hug and kiss you three times on alternating cheeks. Americans often stand farther apart than their Latin associates but closer than their Asian associates. In the United States, people shake hands forcefully and enduringly; in Europe, a handshake is usually quick and to the point; in Asia, it is often rather limp. Laughter and giggling in the West indicates humor; in Asia, it more often indicates embarrassment and humility. Additionally, the public expression of deep emotion is considered ill-mannered in most countries of the Pacific Rim; there is an extreme separation between one's personal and public selves. The withholding of emotion in Latin America, however, is often cause for mistrust.[5]

Time

The meaning and importance of time vary from culture to culture. In Eastern cultures, time is fluid and circular; it goes on forever. Therefore, if delay occurs in negotiation, it does not matter. In the United States, time is fixed and valuable. Time is money, which should not be wasted. For this reason, North Americans like to begin negotiation on time, schedule discussions from hour to hour to complete the day's agenda, and meet the deadline to close the negotiation. To a Chinese, however, the important thing is to complete the task, no matter how long it takes.

Risk Propensity

Cultures differ in their willingness to take risks. In cultures where risk propensity is high, negotiators are able to close a deal even if certain information is lacking but the business opportunity otherwise looks attractive. Risk-prone cultures suggest caution. Negotiators belonging to risk-averse cultures demand additional information to carefully examine all sides of a deal before coming to a final agreement.

Groups Versus Individuals

In some cultures, individuality is highly valued. In others, the emphasis is on the group. In group-oriented cultures, negotiation takes more time to complete since group consensus must be built. For example, in a negotiation in China, a U.S. negotiator had to meet six different negotiators and interpreters, going over the same material until the deal was completed. Compare that to the United States, where individuals can make decisions without getting approval from the group.

Nature of Agreement

The nature of agreement also varies from culture to culture. In the United States, emphasis is placed on logic, formality, and legality of the agreement. For example, when a deal can be completed at a low cost, when all details of the agreement are fully spelled out, and when the agreement can be enforced in a court of law, it is satisfactory. In traditional cultures, a deal is struck depending on the family or political connections, even when certain aspects of the agreement are weak. Furthermore, an agreement is not permanent and is subject to change as circumstances evolve.

Understanding Culture

The first step in gaining cultural understanding is to identify the group or community whose culture you want to know more about. Culturally, the world can be divided into a large number of groups, with each group having its own traditions, traits, values, beliefs, and rituals. People often speak in generalities, such as Asian culture, Latin culture, Western culture, and so on. With regard to negotiations, having a broad perspective about Asians is not sufficient since a Japanese negotiator may hold different values than a Chinese or a Korean. Similarly, a culture and a nationality are not always the same. In India, for example, Southern Indians may represent a different culture than Northern Indians. Indian Muslims are a different cultural group from Hindus. That is, a country may have several distinct cultural groups.

Once a negotiator knows the cultural group to which the other party belongs, he or she should attempt to understand the history, values, and beliefs of the culture. The best way to learn the culture of another group is to devote many years to studying the history, mastering the language, and experiencing the way of life by living among the people. For a prospective negotiator, however, this commitment is inconceivable. As an alternative, therefore, you should gain as much insight into the culture of the group as possible by reading books, talking to people who are knowledgeable about the group, and hiring consultants who specialize in conducting business deals with the group.

As you undertake to understand the culture of the group, you may wonder what particular aspects you should concentrate on. This is important since culture per se is a broad field, and you may not learn much even after reading many books if you do not know what you are trying to achieve.[6] For negotiators, the relevant cultural knowledge can be divided into two categories: (1) traditions and etiquette, and behavior of the group (which can be further split into protocols and deportment, and deeper cultural characteristics), and (2) players and the process.

Before elaborating further on these categories, understand that cultural knowledge should be used with caution. You should avoid forming stereotypical notions about a group and considering them as universal truths. For example, not all Japanese avoid giving a direct negative answer. Not all Mexicans mind discussing business over lunch. Not all Germans make cut-and-dry comments about proposals. As a matter of fact, people are offended when you use stereotypes to describe their culture. A Latin executive would be offended if you said to him, "Although we plan to start the meeting at 9 a.m., I know you won't be here before 9:30 since Latinos are always late."

In addition to national cultures, negotiators need to be aware of professional and corporate cultures. Professional cultures refer to individuals who have studied a specific discipline, such as accounting, economics, engineering, and chemistry. As a result of their studies, these professionals have developed analytical skills, have acquired technical jargon, and tend to look at problems through their own professional interest (which sets them apart from their typical national culture).

Corporate cultures play a significant role in business negotiations. All companies over the years develop their own business culture, values, rules, and regulations. For example, an official from a state-owned enterprise or from a public utility has a different style than a manager from a high-tech start-up. An entrepreneur is likely to have a negotiating style different from that of a CEO of a multinational (see Figure 2.1).

Experience shows that these cultural traits are only indicative and must be dealt with cautiously in view of two other factors that influence the behavior of negotiators. One is age, and the other is multiculturalism. Today, young professionals have more affinity among themselves. It is not uncommon to meet young executives who have studied abroad, who speak one or more foreign languages, and who have traveled extensively. These executives feel comfortable working outside their cultural environment and are no longer representatives of their own culture.

Similarly, executives with overseas experience have, over the years, developed greater understanding of foreign cultures while acquiring new values and tolerance for cultural diversity. Such executives are more multicultural oriented. For these reasons, the wise negotiator finds out as much as possible about the background of the other party to avoid committing cultural blunders that can derail the discussions as well as lead to inferior outcomes.

Cultural Trait	Type of Company		
	Entrepreneurs/ Executives from Start-Ups	Managers from Multinationals	Senior officials from Public/ State Enterprises
Believes in	risk taking	calculated risks	avoiding risk
Seeks	high returns	high and sustainable profits	stable returns
Makes decisions	rapidly	decisively	after lengthy meetings
Sees himself or herself as a	doer	decision maker	policy maker
Concerned with	fast growth	reputation	stability continuity
Responsible to	self/partners	stakeholders	public at large
Negotiates in	small teams/alone	multidisciplinary teams	large teams
Appreciates	self-realization	power	status/reputation
Communicates	using direct/ technical jargon	directly but cautiously	indirectly/ conservatively

Figure 2.1 Cultural differences among managers belonging to different types of companies

Protocol and Deportment

Hundreds of articles, and numerous books and manuals have been written about cultural traits of different groups, advising global businesspeople what to do or not to do in different matters. Consider the following cross-cultural negotiating behavior ascribed to different societies:

- English negotiators are very formal and polite and place great importance on proper protocol. They are also concerned with proper etiquette.
- The French expect others to behave as they do when conducting business. This includes speaking the French language.
- Protocol is important and formal in Germany. Dress is conservative; correct posture and manners are required. Seriousness of purpose goes hand in hand with serious dress.

- The Swedes tend to be formal in their relationships; dislike haggling over price; expect thorough, professional proposals without flaws; and are attracted to quality.
- Italians tend to be extremely hospitable but are often volatile in temperament. When they make a point, they do so with considerable gesticulation and emotional expression.
- The Japanese often want to spend days or even weeks creating a friendly, trusting atmosphere before discussing business.
- In China, the protocol followed during the negotiation process should include giving small, inexpensive presents. As the Chinese do not like to be touched, a short bow and a brief handshake are used during the introductions.
- Business is conducted in a formal yet relaxed manner in India. Having connections is important and one should request permission before smoking, entering, or sitting.
- Emotion and drama carry more weight than logic does for Mexicans. Mexican negotiators are often selected for their skill at rhetoric and for their ability to make distinguished performances.
- For Brazilians, the negotiating process is often valued more than the end result. Discussions tend to be lively, heated, inviting, eloquent, and witty. Brazilians enjoy lavish hospitality to establish a comfortable social climate.
- Russian executives tend to distrust executives who are consumed with business issues only. They are extremely cautious when dealing with parties for the first time.

Such a list—about the cultural differences between different groups—can go on and on. While such information might help a negotiator avoid certain mistakes, it is too general to be useful in negotiations. Further, while culture does have a role in negotiation, other factors, such as personality of the negotiator and the culture of the organization to which the negotiator belongs influence negotiation behavior. As a guide, therefore, a negotiator should seek answers to the questions about protocol and deportment shown in Figure 2.2. Sensitivity to these issues allows a negotiator to avoid being offensive, to demonstrate respect, to enhance cordial relationship, and to strengthen communication.

Greetings	How do people greet and address one another? What role do business cards play?
Degree of Formality	Will my counterparts expect me to dress and interact formally or informally?
Gift Giving	Do businesspeople exchange gifts? What gifts are appropriate? Are there taboos associated with gift giving?
Touching	What are the attitudes toward body contact?
Eye Contact	Is direct eye contact polite? Is it expected?
Deportment	How should I carry myself? Formally? Casually?
Emotions	Is it rude, embarrassing, or unusual to display emotions?
Silence	Is silence awkward? Expected? Insulting? Respectful?
Eating	What is the proper manner for dining? Are certain foods taboo?
Body Language	Are certain gestures or forms of body language rude?
Punctuality	Should I be punctual and expect my counterparts to be as well? Or are schedules and agendas fluid?

Figure 2.2 Cross-cultural etiquette

Source: James K. Sebenius, "The Hidden Challenge of Cross-Border Negotiations," *Harvard Business Review*, March 2002, pp. 80.

Deeper Cultural Characteristics

Two frameworks are presented for gaining deeper behavior knowledge of a culture: Hall's "Silent Language" and Hofstede's Cultural Dimensions.

Hall's Framework

According to Hall, the following aspects drive surface behavior, and their understanding can be of immense help in seeking cultural knowledge of a group.[7]

- Relationship: *Is the culture deal-focused or relationship-focused?* In deal-focused cultures, relationships grow out of deals; in relationship-focused cultures, deals arise from already developed relationships.
- Communication: *Are* communications *indirect and "high-context" or direct and "low-context"?* Do contextual, nonverbal cues play a significant role in negotiations, or is there little reliance on contextual cues (see Figure 2.3). *Do communications*

Cultures can be predominantly verbal or nonverbal. In verbal communications, information is transmitted through a code that makes meanings both explicit and specific. In nonverbal communications, the nonverbal aspects become the major channel for transmitting meaning. This ability is called context. Context includes both the vocal and nonvocal aspects of communication that surround a word or passage and clarify its meaning—the situational and cultural factors affecting communications. High context or low context refers to the amount of information that is given in communication. These aspects include: the rate at which one talks, the pitch or tone of the voice, the fluency, expressional patterns, or nuances of delivery. Nonverbal aspects include eye contact, pupil contraction and dilation, facial expression, odor, color, hand gestures, body movement, proximity, and use of space.

The greater the contextual portion of communication in any given culture, the more difficult it is for one to convey or receive a message. Conversely, it is easier to communicate with a person from a culture in which context contributes relatively little to a message. In high-context cultures, information about an individual (and consequently about individual and group behavior in that culture) is provided through mostly nonverbal means. It is also conveyed through status, friends, and associates. Information flows freely within the culture although outsiders who are not members of the culture may have difficulty reading the information.

In a low-context communication, information is transmitted through an explicit code to make up for a lack of shared meaning—words. In low-context cultures, the environment, situation, and nonverbal behavior are relatively less important and more explicit information has to be given. A direct style of communications is valued and ambiguity is not well regarded. Relationships between individuals are relatively shorter in duration and personal involvement tends to be valued less. Low-context countries tend to be more heterogeneous and prone to greater social and job mobility. Authority is diffused through a bureaucratic system that makes personal responsibility difficult. Agreements tend to be written rather than spoken and treated as final and legally binding.

Low-context countries include the Anglo-American countries, and the Germanic and Scandinavian countries.

High-context cultures can be found in East Asia (Japan, China, Korea, Vietnam), Mediterranean countries (Greece, Italy, Spain, to a lesser extent France), the Middle East, and to a lesser extent Latin America.

Figure 2.3 Low-context versus high-context communication

Source: Excerpted from Donald W. Hendon, Rebecca A. Hendon, and Paul Herbig, *Cross-Cultural Business Negotiations* (Westport, CT: Quorum Books, 1996), pp. 65–67.

require detailed or concise information? Many North Americans prize concise, to-the-point communications. Many Chinese, by contrast, seem to have an insatiable appetite for detailed data.

- Time: *Is the culture generally considered to be "monochronic" or "polychronic"?* In Anglo-Saxon cultures, punctuality and schedules are often strictly considered. This monochronic orientation contrasts with a polychronic attitude, in which time is more fluid, deadlines are more flexible, interruptions are common, and interpersonal relationships take precedence over schedules. For example, in contrast to the Western preference for efficient deal making, Chinese managers are usually less concerned with time.

- Space: *Do people prefer a lot of personal space, or are they comfortable with less?* In many formal cultures, moving too close to a person can produce extreme discomfort. By contrast, a Swiss negotiator who instinctively backs away from his up-close Brazilian counterpart may inadvertently convey disdain.

Hofstede's Cultural Dimensions

According to Hofstede, the way people in different countries perceive and interpret their world varies along four dimensions: power distance, uncertainty avoidance, individualism versus collectivism, and masculinity. Hofstede drew his conclusions based on his interviews with 60,000 employees of IBM in over 40 countries.[8]

Power Distance (Distribution of Power): Power distance refers to the degree of inequality among people the population of a country considers acceptable (i.e., from relatively equal to extremely unequal). In some societies, power is concentrated among a few people at the top who make all the decisions. People at the other end simply carry out these decisions. Such societies are associated with high power distance levels. In other societies, power is widely dispersed and relations among people are more egalitarian. These are low power distance cultures. The lower the power distance, the more individuals expect to participate in the organizational decision-making process. With reference to negotiations, the relevant questions are these: Are significant power disparities accepted? Are organizations run mostly from the top down, or is power more widely and more horizontally distributed?

Uncertainty Avoidance (Tolerance for Uncertainty): Uncertainty avoidance concerns the degree to which people in a country prefer structured over unstructured situations. At the organizational level, uncertainty avoidance is related to such factors as rituals, rules orientation, and employment stability. As a consequence, personnel in less structured societies face the future as it takes shape without experiencing undue stress. The uncertainty associated with upcoming events does not result in risk avoidance behavior. To the contrary, managers in low uncertainty avoidance cultures abstain from creating bureaucratic structures that make it difficult to respond to unfolding events. But in cultures where people experience stress in dealing with future events, various steps are taken to cope with the impact of uncertainty. Such societies are high uncertainty avoidance cultures, whose managers engage in activities such as long-range planning to establish protective barriers to minimize the anxiety associated with future events. With regard to uncertainty avoidance, the United States and Canada score quite low, indicating an ability to be more responsive in coping with future changes. But Japan, Greece, Portugal, and Belgium score high, indicating their desire to meet the future in a more structured and planned fashion. The pertinent question for cross-cultural negotiations is this: How comfortable are people with uncertainty or unstructured situations, processes, or agreements?

Individualism Versus Collectivism: Individualism denotes the degree to which people act as individuals rather than as members of cohesive groups (i.e., from collectivist to individualist). In individualistic societies, people are self-centered and feel little need for dependency on others. They seek the fulfillment of their own goals over the group's goals. Managers belonging to individualistic societies are competitive by nature and show little loyalty to the organizations for which they work. In collectivistic societies, members have a group mentality. They subordinate their individual goals to work toward the goals of the group. They are interdependent on each other and seek mutual accommodation to maintain group harmony. Collectivistic managers have high loyalty to their organizations and subscribe to joint decision making. The higher a country's index of individualism, the more its managerial concepts of leadership are bound up with individuals seeking to act in their ultimate self-interest. Great Britain, Australia, Canada, and the United States show high ratings on individualism; Japan, Brazil, Colombia, Chile, Costa Rica, and Venezuela exhibit very low ratings. A negotiator should determine whether the culture of the other party emphasizes the individual or the group.

Masculinity (Harmony Versus Assertiveness): Masculinity relates to the degree to which "masculine" values such as assertiveness, performance, success, and competition prevail over "feminine" values such as quality of life, maintenance of warm personal relationships, service, care for the weak, and solidarity. Feminine cultures value "small as beautiful" and stress quality of life and environment over materialistic ends. A relatively high masculinity index for the United States, Canada, and Japan is prevalent in approaches to performance appraisal and reward systems. In low-masculinity societies such as Denmark and Sweden, people are motivated by a more qualitative goal set as a means to job enrichment. Differences in masculinity scores are also reflected in the types of career opportunities available in organizations and associated job mobility. For cross-cultural negotiations, a negotiator should know if the culture emphasizes interpersonal harmony or assertiveness.

Years later, Hofstede added a fifth cultural dimension, namely long-term orientation versus short-term orientation. Long-term orientation societies value perseverance, thrift, large savings, and face-saving, among others. In contrast, short-term orientation societies value mainly quick results: spending, low savings, and social obligation by "keeping up with the Joneses". The long-term orientation index for East Asian countries is high while most Western societies have lower ratings. This cultural dimension allows negotiators to adapt their initial proposals and counterarguments in light of the other party's long-or short-term orientation.

Managers negotiating in cross-cultural settings can use either of the two frameworks mentioned previously to gain deeper cultural understanding of the society in which they negotiate. Hall's and Hofstede's books, referred to here, are easy to read and are highly recommended for those who are negotiating globally.

Players and Process

Negotiators are the people who represent their organizations in striking business deals. While it is important to learn about culture and negotiating style, it may be more crucial to know about the organization that negotiators belong to and the process they must follow in seeking final approval of the agreement. A meaningful business agreement goes through a hierarchy of individuals in an organization before it is finalized. Therefore, it is useful to find out who the individuals who might influence the negotiation outcome are, what role each individual plays, and what the informal networking relationships between the individuals that might affect the negotiation are.[9]

Key Individuals

Key individuals refer to those people inside and outside the company whose approval must be sought before a negotiated deal is finalized.

It is essential that the attitude of key individuals toward particular types of agreements be thoroughly examined before beginning to negotiate. For example, in the United States, any large deal must be approved by the company's top officers and the board, as well as the Securities and Exchange Commission, the Federal Trade Commission, the Justice Department, and others. Similarly, in Germany, labor unions must be taken into confidence before a deal goes through. In Europe, the European Union can become a stumbling block in many cases. For example, General Electric's management was shocked by the concerns raised by the EU about competition relative to the company's acquisition of Honeywell.

In developing countries, different government departments must clear a business deal before it is approved. In some cases, even nongovernment organizations (NGOs) can derail a deal. Thus, a negotiator should compile a list of all individuals who have a say in an agreement.

Decision Process

Equally important is the need to understand the role each individual is likely to play in the approval process. What particular aspects of the deal is an individual concerned with? Who has the authority to override the concerns a person might raise? What kind of information can be used to generate a favorable response from different individuals?

Informal Influences

Many countries have webs of influence that are more powerful than the formal bosses. These influences may not have formal standing, but they can make or break negotiations. A negotiator should determine the role of such influences and factor them into his or her negotiation approach.

The following illustration shows the significant role informal influences can play. A U.S. electrical goods manufacturer entered a joint venture with a Chinese company and hired a local manager to run the Chinese operation. The company tried to expand its product line, but the Chinese manager balked, insisting there was no demand for the additional products. The U.S. management team tried to resolve the dispute through negotiations. But when the Chinese manager would not budge, the team fired him; however, he would not leave. The local labor bureau refused to back the U.S. team, and when the U.S. executives tried to dissolve the venture, they discovered they could not recover their capital because Chinese law dictates that both sides need to approve a dissolution. A foreign law firm, hired at great expense, made no headway. It took some behind-the-scenes negotiation on the part of a local law firm to finally overcome the need for dual approval—an outcome that demanded local counsel well versed in the intricacies of Chinese culture.[10]

Simply knowing the individuals who are involved in the process is not enough. When negotiating with people, a negotiator is typically seeking to influence the outcome of an organizational process. The process takes different shape in different cultures. Besides, different processes call for radically different negotiation strategies. This means a negotiation approach should be carefully crafted depending on the individuals involved and the process they follow.

Traits for Coping with Culture

Knowledge about the culture of one's counterpart helps a negotiator to communicate, understand, plan, and decide the deal-making aspects effectively. But culture is a broad field, and there are hundreds of cultures in the world. No executive who negotiates internationally can cope with the cultural challenge no matter how skilled and experienced he or she is. To make the job easier, the following discussion presents the traits that are commonly faced in cross-cultural negotiations.[11] When a negotiator learns to deal with them, he or she can gain sufficient cultural training for negotiating.

Negotiating Goal: Contract or Relationship

In some cultures, negotiators are more interested in short-term deals, such as in the United States. Therefore, for them, a signed contract is the goal. In other countries, the emphasis is on building long-term relationships. A case in point is Japan, where the goal of negotiation is not a signed contract, but a lasting relationship between the two parties.

A negotiator must determine if his or her goals match the goals of the other party. It is difficult to close a deal if the goals differ.

Negotiating Attitude

Basically, there are two approaches to negotiations: win-win and win-lose. If both parties view the negotiation as a win-win situation, it is easier to come to an agreement since both stand to gain. If one party sees the negotiation as a win-lose situation, it may be difficult to strike a deal because the weaker party believes its loss is the other party's gain. The stronger party can take the following steps to soften the attitude of the opponent: (1) Explain the perspectives of the transaction fully since the other party might lack the sophistication to understand the nitty-gritty of the business deal being negotiated. (2) Determine the real interest of the other party through questioning. This may require the negotiator to understand the other's history and culture. (3) Amend the proposal to satisfy the interest of the other party.

Personal Style: Informal or Formal

The negotiating style of the individuals can be informal or formal. Style here refers to the way a negotiator talks, uses titles, and dresses. For example, North Americans believe in informality, addressing people by their first name in an initial meeting. Germans, on the other hand, maintain a formal attitude. In this matter, the guest should adapt his or her attitude to be in line with the host.

Communication: Direct or Indirect

In cultures where communication is direct, such as Germany, a negotiator can expect direct answers to questions. In cultures that communicate indirectly (Japan, for instance), it may be difficult to interpret messages easily. Indirect communication uses signs, gestures, and indefinite comments, which a negotiator must learn to interpret.

Sensitivity to Time: High or Low

Some cultures are more relaxed about time than others. For North Americans, time is money, which is always in short supply. Therefore, they like to rush through a negotiation to obtain a signed contract quickly.

Mexicans, as an example, are more relaxed about time. Thus, a Mexican dealing with a North American may view the latter's attempt to shorten the time as an effort to hide something. Thus, negotiation sessions should be planned and scheduled such that the pace of discussions is appropriate.

Emotions: High or Low

Some negotiators are more emotional than others. A negotiator should establish the emotional behavior of the other party and make appropriate adjustments in negotiation tactics to satisfy such behavior.

Form of Agreement: General or Specific

Culture often influences the form of agreement a party requires. Usually, North Americans prefer a detailed contract that provides for all eventualities. Chinese, however, prefer a contract in the form of general principles. When a negotiator prefers a specific agreement while the other party is satisfied with general principles, the negotiator should carefully review each principle to make sure it is, in any event, not interpreted in such a manner that he or she stands to lose significantly.

Building an Agreement: Bottom-Up or Top-Down

Some negotiators begin with agreement on general principles and proceed to specific items, such as price, delivery date, and product quality. Others begin with agreement on specifics, the sum of which becomes the contract. It is just a matter of style. If a negotiator prefers a bottom-up approach and the other party is satisfied with general principles (i.e., a top-down approach), the negotiator should seek specific information about various aspects before closing the deal.

Team Organization: One Leader versus Consensus

In some cultures, one leader has the authority to make commitments. In other cultures, group consensus must be sought before agreeing to a deal. The latter type of organization requires more time to finalize an agreement, and the other party should be prepared for the time it may take.

Risk Taking: High or Low

A negotiator must examine the attitude of the other party about risk. If the negotiator determines that the other party is risk-averse, he or she should focus the attention on proposing rules, mechanisms, and relationships that reduce the apparent risks in the deal.

Summary

When people negotiate with someone outside their home country, culture becomes a significant factor. It is because people from different cultures present a different perspective in everything they do. Thus, their negotiating style, skills, and behavior vary. More specifically, culture affects the definition of negotiation, the selection of negotiators, protocol, communication, time, risk propensity, group versus individual emphasis, and the nature of agreement.

From the viewpoint of cross-cultural negotiator, the necessary cultural knowledge is grouped into two categories: (1) traditions and etiquette, and group behavior (or protocols and deportment, and deeper cultural characteristics), and (2) players and process.

Protocols and deportment deal with greetings, degree of formality, gift giving, touching, eye contact, emotions, silence, eating, body language, and punctuality. Two frameworks are suggested for deeper cultural understanding: one by Edward Hall and the other by Geert Hofstede. Either one can be used to gain deeper insights into a culture. Furthermore, it is important to know the players and to learn their negotiation process. This requires knowing the key individuals who can impact the negotiation; the role each individual plays; and the informal influences, those who carry weight in the negotiation process. Cultural traits that affect negotiations include negotiating goals, negotiating attitude, personal style of the negotiator, communication style, sensitivity to time, emotional makeup, form of the agreement, structure of the agreement, authority to commit, and risk taking.

CHAPTER 3

Selecting Your Negotiating Style

Problem solving is the skilled negotiator's greatest asset.
—Melanie Billings-Yun

Regardless of their past experiences, people have a preference for one approach or the other to negotiations. Over the years, they would have dealt with individuals who showed aggressive behavior, who displayed a cooperative attitude, who settled their differences through an exchange of concessions, and who withdrew from the discussion altogether. A negotiator must know his or her preferred style of negotiation as well as that of the other party. This knowledge allows the negotiator to improve his or her preparation, including selecting the most appropriate negotiation style for the situation. As every negotiation is unique, prior to entering into discussions, a negotiator should have identified the other party's style and adjusted his or hers in order to optimize mutual benefits.

Style Differences Among Negotiators

Each negotiator applies a specific negotiating style. This depends on his or her cultural background, his or her professional responsibilities, and the context in which the discussions are taking place, as well as whether he or she is seeking a onetime deal or repeat business over the long term. Five distinct negotiation styles can be identified. These styles are influenced by two major forces—namely, relationship-oriented outcomes and substantive- or task-oriented outcomes. In most negotiations, there is a trade-off between these two orientations. Cultural characteristics play a significant role in determining the relative impact of these two orientations.[1] In cultures where establishing and maintaining relationships is essential to carrying out business, the predominant negotiating style is more accommodation oriented. In competitive cultures, where only the final outcome is considered important, the negotiation style is more task oriented, relying on competitive and conflicting tactics.[2]

In terms of style, negotiations are grouped into five categories: dodgers, dreamers, hagglers, competitors, and creative problem solvers.

Dodgers

Generally, dodgers do not like facing situations where decisions must be made and risks assumed. In a negotiation, the dodger tries to postpone making decisions or, more likely, tries to find reasons for not getting involved at all. In other words, the dodger is a reluctant party who does not enjoy negotiating and who withdraws from the discussions or simply refuses to participate. These situations are not frequent, although they may be more common in certain cultures whereby an unwillingness to negotiate is seen as a lack of interest. In other situations, by the time the two sides meet, one party may no longer be interested in pursuing the negotiation due to a better offer received from a competitor; the party, therefore, adopts a dodging attitude. At times, executives doing business across cultural boundaries are likely to face dodgers and should decide early on whether to continue the discussions, ask for a recess, or deal only with negotiators who have decision-making responsibilities.

Dreamers

Dreamers approach negotiations with one major goal in mind; that is, to preserve the relationship even if it means giving up unnecessary concessions while reducing their own expectations. At times, they pretend to agree with the other party to maintain the relationship and goodwill, when in reality they have divergent views. In more traditional cultures, relationship plays a dominant role in negotiations. Without a relationship or without a trusted third party making an introduction, negotiations are unlikely to take place. In a competitive culture, dreamers are at a disadvantage, as their behavior is often interpreted as a sign of weakness. For example, face saving in Asian cultures is part and parcel of negotiations. Failing to take into consideration the role of relationship and face saving (or giving face) can result in negotiations that turn into deadlocks or that simply lead to breakdowns.

Dreamers are willing to accept lower outcomes on substantive issues for the sake of the relationship. Such negotiations often make sense to executives seeking entry into new markets by adopting an accommodating attitude in the hope of getting the business going. However, it is difficult to obtain a favorable agreement if concessions are given without obtaining similar ones in return.

Hagglers

Hagglers view negotiations as a give-and-take game. They are willing to lower their expectations provided they can obtain some benefits from the other party. Persuasion, partial exchange of information, and manipulation dominate the discussion. A short-term outlook and quick movements characterized with back-and-forth concessions prevail. Hagglers are flexible in their approach and seek instant compromises. As a result, hagglers fail to reach optimum outcomes, neglect details, and sometimes overlook long-term opportunities.

In their search for quick solutions, hagglers fail to identify the underlying needs of the other party. Hagglers build superficial relationships and are satisfied with splitting the difference to reach a final agreement.

This style is more suitable for one-time deals in domestic market situations. In international negotiations, where long-term relationships and trust are essential ingredients to successful implementation, haggling is not considered an effective approach that satisfies the interests of both parties.

Competitors

Competitors enjoy conflicts, feel comfortable with aggressive behavior, and employ hardball tactics. They enjoy struggling to meet their objectives, even at the cost of alienating the other side. Satisfying their own interests is their primary goal. Competitors use whatever power they have to win and fully exploit the other party's weaknesses. They are extremely persuasive in their discussions and persist in controlling the discussions. In this type of interaction, limited information is exchanged. Generally, such situations lead to win-lose agreements, where the competitor wins most of the benefits by obtaining the majority of concessions while giving few, if any, concessions in return. Frequently, these negotiations result in a breakdown when the weaker party decides to walk away. After all, no deal is better than accepting a bad deal.

Negotiators relying on competitive strategies and tactics are found everywhere, with a greater concentration in task-oriented cultures. In these cultures, only tangible results are considered worth negotiating for. Short-term benefits override long-term gains, and relationships are often considered marginal.[3] As a consequence, these negotiated agreements are unsustainable, often calling for renegotiations when the weaker party can no longer honor its commitments.

Creative Problem Solvers

Problem solvers display creativity in finding mutually satisfying agreements. They take time to identify the underlying needs of the other party in order to explore how they can best meet their mutual interests jointly. In their search for a joint solution, they take into consideration the relationship as well as the substantive issues, since both are equally important to them. Problem solvers ask plenty of questions, share information openly, and suggest options and alternatives. During the discussions, they emphasize common needs and frequently summarize what has been agreed to so far.[4] They tend to have long-term vision, sometimes at the cost of short-term benefits.

During the discussions, creative problem solvers exchange relevant information and ask plenty of questions in a cooperative and constructive environment. This style of negotiation requires more time to prepare and calls for face-to-face discussions. By exploring alternatives and developing multiple options, problem solvers are able to create optimum outcomes where both parties are winners, referred to as the win-win approach.[5] This negotiating style is more conducive to international business deals, where implementation over the long run determines whether an agreement is profitable.

Figure 3.1 summarizes the strengths and weaknesses of each style.

Appropriate Negotiating Style

Of the five styles, creative problem solving is regarded as superior because it attempts to satisfy the needs of both parties. Creative problem solvers realize that a mutually agreeable outcome is the best insurance against the threat of competition or possible backlash from a dissatisfied party. This approach requires a negotiator to prepare thoroughly to identify his or her specific needs as well as the interests of the other party, to develop options, and to plan what concessions to make and what concessions to ask for. It also requires having an open and flexible mind, asking plenty of questions, and listening actively to fully understand the other party. In these discussions, useful information is exchanged, enabling each side to explore the full range of opportunities available to them. In the end, problem solvers place themselves in a position to improve on their expected results by enlarging the zone of agreement.[6] In other words, negotiators applying the problem-solving approach are most likely to achieve superior results (also known as the Pareto frontier, where there are no possible superior outcomes) in which each party gains without giving up more or taking more from the other side.

Figure 3.2 shows how each style fits into the overall field of negotiation and how the creative problem-solving approach allows the negotiators to enter into optimum outcomes and maximizing joint gains.

Determining the Negotiation style

Most people rely on one or more styles depending on the situation they are in, although they probably have a predisposition for one specific negotiation style. A negotiator often adjusts the style as he or she interacts with the other party. If you are meeting a party who relies on competitive or aggressive tactics, you need to respond with appropriate tactics of your own to protect your interests.[7] Equally, you need to project an image of self-confidence to the other party in order to send a message that such

	STRENGTH	WEAKNESS	BEST FOR
Dodger	• Shows indifference • Will assess risk first • Has low needs	• Cannot make decisions • Dislikes negotiating • Fails to prepare • Is not comfortable with people • Is mainly inactive	• Avoiding entry into bad deals • Testing the market when issues are not important • Avoiding no-win situations
Dreamer	• Seeks relationships • Shows concerns for others • Values friendship	• Wants to be well liked • Concedes easily • Preserves relationships at own expense • Gives away too much	• Seeking entry into new markets • Dealing in relationship-oriented markets
Haggler	• Makes quick decisions • Likes making deals • Has no strong positions • Is easy to deal with • Is open to counterproposals	• Is win-lose oriented • Accepts lower outcomes • Is satisfied with quick results • Is short-term oriented • Gives in easily	• Issues that are not considered important • Quick decisions • Breaking deadlocks • Restarting discussions
Competitor	• Is a risk taker • Cares for own needs • Controls discussions • Is persuasive/persistent • Enjoys pressure	• Is not interested in the other party • Is mostly short-term oriented • Is unwilling to shift positions • Is a poor listener • Leads to frequent breakdowns	• Quick decisions • Competitive markets • When similar styles are used
Creative Problem Solver	• Shares information • Creates values • Is win-win oriented • Seeks win-win deals • Develops options • Has good listening skills • Asks a lot of questions	• Is a slow decision maker • Overlooks details • Can be unrealistic at times • Takes time • Requires through preparation	• Long-term deals • Repeat business • Complex negotiations • Important deals

Figure 3.1 Strengths and weaknesses of different negotiation styles

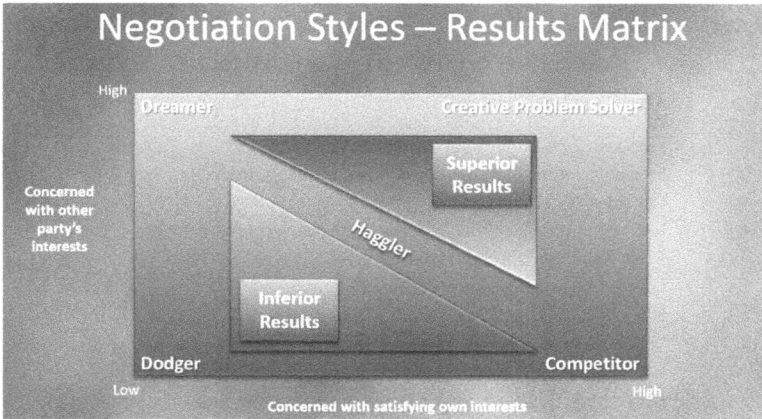

Figure 3.2 Maximizing joint gains

tactics are not conducive to satisfying both of your respective needs. In other words, despite having a tendency to use a certain style, you must modify it in light of the other party's behavior.

You can determine your preferred negotiating style by following the procedure discussed here. First, rate each of the 35 statements in Figure 3.3, Personal Assessment Inventory, on a five-point scale with 1 (strongly disagree), 2 (disagree), 3 (have no specific view), 4 (agree), or 5 (strongly agree).

Whenever possible, try to avoid using a rating of 3, as this rating will not reflect your true preferences. Further, bear in mind that there are no right or wrong answers. Just make sure your rating describes your preferred style when handling a negotiating situation.

Next, enter your ratings to all the 35 statements in Figure 3.4. Each column indicates where you should enter the ratings for the statements. For example, enter your responses to statements 1, 6, 11, 16, 21, 26, and 31 in the dodger column.

The highest total score identifies your dominant style. In most negotiations, you are likely to use a mix of styles ranging from cooperation to competition. Your prevailing style is influenced by the importance you give to the relationship, the style of the other party, the degree of competition in the target market, and your wish to seek a one-time opportunity or repeat orders over the long term.

Rate each statement with a rating ranging from 1 (strongly disagree) to 5 (strongly agree) that best reflects your behavior when negotiating. Your rating

1. (_) I am not comfortable negotiating.
2. (_) I push the other party toward my own positions/interests.
3. (_) I avoid provoking people.
4. (_) I try to learn the real needs of the other party before making a concession.
5. (_) I enjoy making offers and counteroffers.
6. (_) I don't like making difficult decisions.
7. (_) Before negotiating, I know what results to expect and how to obtain them.
8. (_) When negotiating, I like to make quick decisions to speed up the discussions.
9. (_) I am willing to lower my expectations to save the relationship.
10. (_) I encourage the other party to work with me in finding an acceptable solution.
11. (_) I avoid getting involved in difficult situations.
12. (_) I make sure I have power over the other party and use it to my advantage.
13. (_) To advance the negotiations, I like to split the difference.
14. (_) When negotiating, I make sure the other party feels comfortable.
15. (_) I have no problem sharing information with the other party.
16. (_) I don't negotiate when I have little chance of winning.
17. (_) If necessary, I use threats to reach my goals.
18. (_) I like to compromise to expedite the negotiations.
19. (_) I make sure the other party explains his or her real needs.
20. (_) I like to explore innovative approaches with the other party to achieve maximum outcomes.
21. (_) I avoid taking risks.
22. (_) To get what I want, I ask for more than what I am willing to settle for.
23. (_) I look for a fair deal.
24. (_) To me, personal relationships are vital to constructive discussions.
25. (_) I frequently summarize issues we both agreed to.
26. (_) I dislike dealing with difficult negotiators.
27. (_) I try to create doubts in the mind of the other party.
28. (_) To me, negotiating is a game of give and take.
29. (_) I do not like to embarrass other people.
30. (_) When I negotiate, I consider the long-term outlook.
31. (_) I avoid getting involved in controversies.
32. (_) I do not give away information, but I try to obtain as much information as possible from the other party.
33. (_) I look for a middle-of-the-road solution to close negotiations.
34. (_) I avoid getting involved in nonessential details.
35. (_) I enjoy meeting people.

Figure 3.3 Personal assessment inventory

After completing the inventory, add your responses according to the following table:				
The Dodger	**The Dreamer**	**The Haggler**	**The Competitor**	**The Creative Problem Solver**
S R	S R	S R	S R	S R
1 ()	3 ()	5 ()	2 ()	4 ()
6 ()	9 ()	8 ()	7 ()	10 ()
11 ()	14 ()	13 ()	12 ()	15 ()
16 ()	19 ()	18 ()	17 (5)	20 ()
21 ()	24 ()	23 ()	22 ()	25 ()
26 ()	29 ()	28 ()	27 ()	30 ()
31 ()	35 ()	33 ()	32 ()	34 ()
Total	Total	Total	Total	Total

Legend: **S**: Statement
        R: Rating
For example, if you gave statement 17 in the inventory a score of 5, place 5 in The Competitor column next to 17.

Figure 3.4 Interpreting your scores

Any ratings near the top (35) mean that you tend to rely too much on that style in handling negotiations. If you have low ratings for dodger and dreamer and high ratings for the others, you have a good base for negotiations. A high rating for competitor is good, but that style can backfire in some cultures. Ideally, a high rating for creative problem solver is considered the key ingredient for win-win solutions. You can repeat the exercise whenever you want to learn the style of the other party.

Summary

A negotiator should know his or her negotiation style as well as the style of his or her counterpart. The negotiator can then adjust his or her style to match the style of the other party, ensuring smooth negotiations.

The five different negotiation styles are dodgers, dreamers, hagglers, competitors, and creative problem solvers. Among these, the creative problem solver is considered the best style because it satisfies the needs of both parties. Generally, negotiators have two preferred styles: either creative problem solving and competing or creative problem solving and dreaming.

A negotiator can determine his or her negotiation style by following the procedure discussed in the chapter. The same procedure can be utilized to figure out the negotiation style of the other party. Each style is influenced by one of two forces: task orientation or relationship orientation.

PART 3

Negotiation Process

CHAPTER 4

Prenegotiations Planning

By failing to prepare, you are preparing to fail.
—Benjamin Franklin

It is widely recognized that systematic planning and preparation are critical elements of successful business negotiations. Experienced executives devote substantial time to these functions before sitting down at the negotiating table. As a general rule, the more complex the transaction to be negotiated, the longer the planning period. The preparatory phase is lengthier for international transactions than for domestic ones because of the difficulty of gathering all necessary preliminary information.

The most common business negotiation mistakes, shown in Figure 4.1, reflect insufficient preparation. A majority of these errors can be eliminated or greatly reduced when adequate attention is given to doing the background work.

Key Factors

Preparing for negotiations is time-consuming, demanding, and often complex. A golden rule of negotiations is this: *Do not negotiate if you are unprepared*. In the prenegotiation phase, the factors listed here are considered critical and failing to prepare them may result in a less-than-satisfactory outcome. Here is the sequential procedure that a negotiator may follow for prenegotiation planning:

- Unclear objectives
- Inadequate knowledge of the other party's goals
- Insufficient attention to the other party's concerns
- Lack of understanding of the other party's decision-making process
- Nonexistence of a strategy for trading concessions
- Too few alternatives and options prepared beforehand
- Failure to take into account the competition factor
- Unskillful use of negotiation power
- Hasty calculations and decision making
- A poor sense of timing for closing the negotiations
- Poor listening habits
- Aiming too low
- Failure to create added value
- Insufficient time
- Overemphasis on the importance of price

Figure 4.1 Most common negotiation errors

- Define the issues
- Know one's position
- Know the other party's position
- Know the competition
- Know the negotiations limits
- Develop strategies and tactics
- Plan the negotiation meeting

Defining the Issues

The first step in prenegotiation planning is to identify the issues to be discussed. Usually, a negotiation involves one or two major issues (e.g., price, commission, duration of agreement) and a number of minor issues. For example, in the appointment of a distributor in a foreign market, the major issues would be the commission on sales, duration of the agreement, and exclusivity. Other issues could include promotional support provided by the agent, sales training, information flow, and product adaptation. In any negotiation, a complete list of issues can be developed through (a) analysis of the situation at hand, (b) prior experience on a similar situation, (c) research conducted on the situation, and (d) consultation with experts.

After listing all of the issues, the negotiator should prioritize them.[1] He or she must determine which issues are most important. Once negotiations begin, parties can easily become overwhelmed with an abundance of information, arguments, offers, counteroffers, trade-offs, and concessions. When a party is not clear in advance about what it wants, it can lose perspective and agree to suboptimal solutions. A party must decide what is most important, what is second most important, and what is least important, or group the issues into three categories of high, medium, or low importance. A negotiator should set priorities for both tangible and intangible issues. In addition, the negotiator needs to determine whether the issues are connected or separate. When the issues are separate, they can easily be added later or put aside for the time being. When they are linked to each other, settlement on one involves the others as well. For example, making concessions on one issue is inevitably tied to other issues. After prioritizing the list of issues, a negotiator should touch base with the other party to determine his or her list of issues. The two lists are combined to arrive at a final list of issues that form the agenda. In other words, before the negotiation starts, both sides should firmly agree on the issues they are deliberating.[2] There should be no disagreement about the issues to be negotiated.

Each party can develop and prioritize his or her issues and share them with each other. At a prenegotiation meeting or through phone/fax/e-mail communication, the two lists can be combined to develop a common list of issues. This combined list is often called a bargaining list.

Knowing One's position

After issue development, the next major step in preparing for business negotiation is to determine one's goals, a clear understanding of what one is planning to achieve, and an understanding of one's strengths and weaknesses.

Goals

Goals are usually tangibles such as price, rate return, specific terms, contract language, and fixed package. But they can also be intangible, such as maintaining a certain precedent, defending a principle, or getting an agreement regardless of cost. An intangible goal of an automobile parts manufacturer might be to acquire recognition as a reliable supplier of quality products to major car producers.

Negotiators should clearly define their goals. This requires stating all of the goals they wish to achieve in the negotiation, prioritizing the goals, identifying potential multigoal packages, and evaluating the possible trade-offs among them.

Goals and issues are closely related, and they evolve together, impacting each other. What a negotiator wants to achieve through a negotiation can dramatically impact the issues he or she raises at the negotiation. Likewise, how a negotiator sees an issue has an effect in communicating what he or she wants to achieve from an upcoming negotiation. Goals and issues are interactive; the existence of one quickly produces evidence of the other.

It is important to understand the four aspects of how goals affect negotiation.[3]

- *Wishes are not goals*: Wishes may be related to interests or needs that motivate goals themselves. A wish is a fantasy, a hope that something might happen. A goal, however, is a specific, realistic target that a person can plan to realize.
- *One party's goals are permanently linked to the other party's goals*: The linkage between the two parties' goals defines the issue to be resolved. An exporter's goal is to give the distributor a low commission on sales, while the distributor's goal is to settle for the highest commission. Thus, the issue is the rate of commission. Goals that are not linked to each other often lead to conflict.
- *Goals have boundaries*: Goals have boundaries, set by the ability of the other party to meet them. Thus, if a negotiator's goals exceed the boundary, he or she must either change the goals or end the negotiation. Stated differently, goals must be realistic, i.e., reasonably attainable.
- *Effective goals must be concrete and measurable*: The less concrete and measurable a person's goals are, the more difficulty the person will have communicating what he or she wants from the other party, understanding what the other party wants, and determining whether an outcome meets the goals of both parties.

Strengths and Weaknesses

Knowing one's negotiating position also implies an understanding of the company's strengths and weaknesses of the company the negotiator represents. When analyzing strengths, a person should consider those that are real and those that are perceived. For instance, if you are an exporter from a country with an international reputation for producing high-quality goods, you may be perceived as having an advantage over other suppliers. You should identity your firm's strengths so you can bring them to the forefront when you need them during the negotiations.

A negotiator also needs to identify his or her company's weaknesses and take corrective measures to improve the deficiencies when possible. The other party is likely to bring the firm's weak points into the open at a critical moment in the negotiations to obtain maximum concessions. Some weaknesses cannot be eliminated, but others can be reduced or turned into strengths.

Small- and medium-sized exporters often view themselves as being in a weak position with buyers from larger organizations. If you are negotiating on behalf of a small export firm with limited production capacity, you can turn this perceived weakness into a strength by stressing low overhead costs, flexibility in production runs, minimal delays in switching production lines, and a willingness to accept small orders. Too often small- and medium-sized firms fail to recognize that many of their perceived weaknesses can become strengths in different business situations.

Knowing the Other Side's Position

Just as important as knowing what one's company wants from the forthcoming negotiation is understanding what the other party hopes to obtain. This information is not always available, particularly when the discussions are with a new party. A negotiator may need to make assumptions about the other party's goals, strengths and weaknesses, strategy, and so on. Whatever assumptions are made, they should be verified during the negotiations. Usually, a negotiator attempts to obtain the following information about the other party: current resources, including financial stability; interests and needs; goals; reputation and negotiation style; alternatives; authority to negotiate; and strategy and tactics.

Current Resources, Interests, and Needs

A negotiator should gather as much information as possible about the other party's current resources, interests, and needs through research.

What kind of facts and figures makes sense depends on what type of negotiation will be conducted and who the other party is. A negotiator can draw useful clues from the history of the other party and from previous negotiations the party might have conducted. In addition, the negotiator might gather financial data about the other party from published sources, trade associations, and research agencies. Interviewing people who are knowledgeable about the party is another way the negotiator can acquire information. Furthermore, where feasible, a great deal of information can be sought by visiting the other party.[4] Additionally, the negotiator can explore the following ways to learn the perspectives of the other party: (a) by conducting a preliminary interview or discussion in which the negotiator talks about what the other party wants to achieve in the upcoming negotiation; (b) by anticipating the other party's interests; (c) by asking others who have negotiated with the other party; and (d) by reading what the other party says about itself in the media.

Goals

After determining the other party's resources, interests, and needs, the next step for a negotiator is to learn about the party's goals. It is not easy to pinpoint the other party's goals with reference to a particular negotiation. The best way for the negotiator to figure out the other party's goals is to analyze whatever information he or she has gathered about the party, make appropriate assumptions, and estimate the goals. After doing this groundwork, the negotiator can contact the other party directly to share as much information about each other's perspectives as is feasible. Because information about the other party's goals is so important to the strategy formulation of both parties, professional negotiators are willing to exchange related information or initial proposals days (or even weeks) before the negotiation. The negotiator should use the information gleaned directly from the other party to refine his or her goals.

Reputation and Style

A negotiator wants to deal with a dependable party with whom it is a pleasure to do business. Therefore, he or she must seek information about the reputation and style of the other party. There are three different ways to determine that reputation and style: (a) from one's own experience, either in the same or a different context; (b) from the experience of other firms that have negotiated with the other party in the past; and (c) from what others, especially business media, have said about the other party.

While past perspectives of the other party provide insight into how it conducts negotiations, provision must be made for management changes that might have taken place, which can affect the forthcoming negotiations. Furthermore, people do change over time. Thus, what they did in the past might not be relevant in the future.

Alternatives

In the prenegotiation process, a negotiator must work out the alternatives. The alternatives offer a viable recourse to pursue if the negotiation fails. Similarly, the negotiator must probe into the other party's alternatives. When the other party has an equally attractive alternative, it can participate in the negotiation with a great deal of confidence, set high goals, and push hard to realize those goals. On the other hand, when the other party has a weak alternative, it is more dependent on achieving a satisfactory agreement, which might result in the negotiator driving a hard bargain.

Authority

Before beginning to negotiate, a negotiator must learn whether the other party has adequate authority to conclude negotiations with an agreement. If the other party does not have the authority, the negotiator should consider the negotiation as an initial exercise.

A negotiator should be careful not to reveal too much information to someone who does not have the authority to negotiate. The negotiator does not want to give up sensitive information that should have been used only with someone with the authority to negotiate.

A negotiator should plan his or her negotiation strategy, keeping in mind that no final agreement will result. Otherwise, he or she may become frustrated dealing with someone with little or no authority who must check every point with superiors at the head office. The negotiator may, therefore, indicate how far he or she is willing to negotiate with someone without the proper authority.

Strategy and Tactics

A negotiator can find it helpful to gain insights into the other party's intended negotiation strategy and tactics. The other party will not reveal the strategy outright, but the negotiator can infer it from the information he or she has already gathered. Thus, reputation, style, alternatives, authority, and goals of the other party can throw light on his or her strategy.

Knowing the Competition

In addition to the above considerations, it is important to know who the competition will be in a specific transaction. Negotiators often prepare for business discussions without giving much attention to the influence of competition. During business negotiations between two sides, an invisible third party consisting of one or more competitors is often present that can influence the outcome. As shown in Figure 4.2, competitors, although invisible, are key players in such discussions.

For example, how many times has a supplier been asked to improve an offer because he or she is told by the other party that competitors can do better? Unless a negotiator plans for such situations in advance and develops ways to overcome them, he or she may find it difficult to achieve the desired outcome in the negotiations.

A negotiator must conduct research about the competition in order to identify the relative strengths and weaknesses of such third parties for the discussions ahead. A competitor may be able to offer better terms than the negotiator's company, but because the competitor is currently working to full capacity, it may not be in a position to accept additional orders. Such information, if known, can help a negotiator resist requests to improve his or her offer. When gathering information, the negotiator should address such questions as who the competitors are for this transaction, what his or her company's strengths are versus the competition, what his or her company's weaknesses are versus the competition, and how competition can affect his or her company's goals in this negotiation.

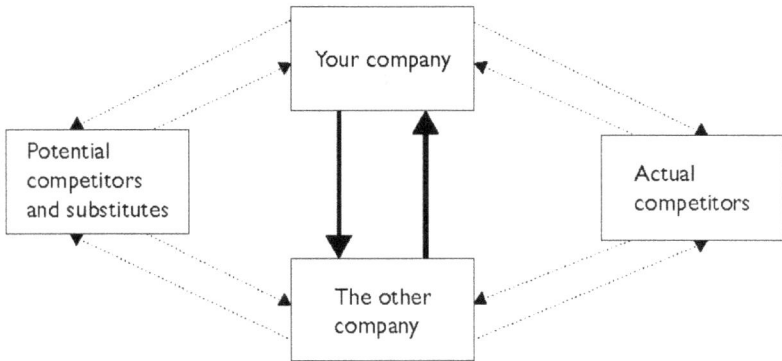

Figure 4.2 Competitors–The third party in negotiations

Essentially, knowledge about competitors includes their size, growth, and profitability; the image and positioning of their brands; objectives and commitments; strengths and weaknesses; current and past strategies; cost structure; exit barriers limiting their ability to withdraw; and organization style and culture. The following procedure can be adopted to gather competitive intelligence[5]:

- Recognize key competitors.
- Analyze the performance record of each competitor (i.e., sales growth, market share, profitability).
- Study how satisfied each competitor appears to be with its performance. (If the results of a product are in line with expectations, the competitor will be satisfied. A satisfied competitor is likely to follow its current strategy, while an unsatisfied competitor is likely to come out with a new strategy.)
- Probe each competitor's marketing strategy (i.e., different moves in the areas of product, price, promotion, and distribution).
- Analyze current and future resources and competencies of each competitor.

Knowing One's Negotiation limits

A crucial part of preparation is setting limits on concessions—the minimum price as a seller and the ceiling price as a buyer. During the prenegotiation phase, each party must decide on the boundaries beyond which there are no longer grounds for negotiation. For example, as a seller, you should know at which point a sale becomes unprofitable, based on a detailed costing of your product and other associated expenses. Similarly, as a buyer, you must determine in advance the maximum price and conditions that are acceptable. The difference between these two points is the zone of possible agreement (ZOPA). Generally, it is within this range that a negotiator and the other party make concessions and counterproposals.

A negotiator's opening position as a supplier should, therefore, be somewhere between the lowest price he or she would accept for his or her goods and the highest price he or she perceives to be acceptable by the other party (the buyer). It is important that the initial offer be realistic, credible, and reasonable in order to encourage the other party to respond. An opening position highly favorable to the negotiator cannot be justified, for example, if it is likely to send a negative message to his or her counterpart, resulting in a lack of trust and possibly more aggressive tactics by the other party.

Target and Reservation Points

A **target point** refers to a negotiator's most preferred point, an ideal settlement. The target point should be based on a realistic appraisal of the situation. For example, an exporter wants to pay as little sales commission to an overseas distributor as possible, but that does not mean the distributor is willing to represent the exporter for a meager commission of 1 percent. Thus, the exporter may set his or her target point for distributor commission at 6 percent, but not 2 percent.

A **reservation point** represents a point at which a negotiator is indifferent between reaching a settlement and walking away from negotiation. The outcome of negotiation depends more on the relationship between parties' reservation points than on their target points. A method of determining one's reservation point is to utilize one's BATNA—**Best Alternative To a Negotiated Agreement.**

BATNA

The term *BATNA*[6] refers to the **Best Alternative To a Negotiated Agreement**. Although it appears simple, BATNA has developed into a strong and useful tool for negotiators. This concept was initially introduced by Fisher and Ury while they were associated with the Harvard Negotiation Project.

BATNA is the standard against which a proposed agreement should be evaluated. It is the only standard that can protect a negotiator from accepting terms that are too unfavorable and from rejecting terms that are in his or her best interest to accept.

In some cases, there is no settlement range because the BATNAs do not overlap. Cases where no settlement range exists can deadlock a negotiation.

Assessment of BATNA requires the following steps:

- *Brainstorm alternatives*: The negotiator should brainstorm to generate alternatives if the overseas distributor refuses to accept 6 percent commission on sales. The alternatives should be realistic and based on reliable information. For example, the negotiator may consider distributing in the overseas market through a home-based company. Another alternative may be to utilize the Internet to participate in the overseas market. A third alternative may be to increase the commission of the distributor.
- *Evaluate each alternative*: The negotiator should evaluate each alternative identified above for its attractiveness or value. If an alternative has an uncertain outcome, such as the amount of sales that can be generated through a home-based company, the negotiator should determine the probability of sales outcome.

Bargaining Zone

The bargaining zone refers to the region between parties' reservation points.[7]

The zone of potential agreement (ZOPA) serves a useful purpose since it determines whether an agreement is feasible and whether it is worthwhile to negotiate. To establish the bargaining zone, a negotiator needs not only his or her reservation point, but also the reservation point of the other party. Needless to say, determining the other party's reservation point is not easy. However, based on the available information, the reservation point must be established, even if it is a mere guess.

The bargaining zone can be positive or negative. In a positive bargaining zone, parties' reservation points overlap. This means it is possible for the parties to reach an agreement. If the parties fail to reach an agreement, the outcome is an impasse and is insufficient since both parties are worse off by not coming to some kind of agreement.

Power

Power plays a distinctive role in negotiations. Power in negotiations can be of different forms: reward, coercive, legitimate, referent, and expert. *Reward power* is attributable to a person's ability to influence the behavior of another person by giving or taking away rewards. Rewards can be tangible (e.g., money) or intangible (e.g., praise and recognition). *Coercive power* is related to a person's ability to influence the behavior of another person through punishment. Punishment can be tangible (e.g., a fine) or intangible (e.g., faint praise). *Legitimate power* refers to a person's authority to demand obedience (e.g., authority of a senior military officer over a lower-ranking officer). *Referent power* is based on a person's respect and admiration of another, which may be related to one's position, money, or status. Finally, *expert power* is attributable to a person's knowledge, skills, or abilities.

With regard to negotiations, no single type of power is more or less effective. However, reward (and punishment) power is less stable since it requires perpetual maintenance. In comparison, status, attraction, and expertise are more intrinsically-based forms of power. The ultimate power of a negotiator is to walk out due to having a better alternative.

Developing Strategies and Tactics

A negotiator should prepare strategies based on his or her company's goals in the forthcoming negotiation, knowledge about the other firm's goals and position, the presence and strength of competition, and other relevant information. A negotiator has several strategies to choose from, ranging from a competitive to a cooperative stance. The approach he or she selects will probably be a mix of both.

Each negotiation is a separate situation requiring specific strategies and appropriate tactics. For example, in some cases, the negotiator who concedes first is considered to be in a weak position, encouraging the other party to press for more concessions; an early concession in other circumstances is sometimes regarded as a sign of cooperation, inviting reciprocity.

The long-term implications of one's actions should be taken into consideration when designing strategies and corresponding tactics. For example, if you have been doing business with the same buyer for some years and are generally satisfied with the business relationship, you are likely to adopt a cooperative strategy in negotiations with that buyer. This means both of you are willing to share information, reciprocate concessions, and seek a mutually beneficial result. In contrast, an inexperienced negotiator is generally more interested in short-term gains and often uses more competitive tactics.

Competitive Versus Cooperative Strategies

Negotiating strategies are broadly categorized as competitive and cooperative.[8] Competitive strategies are followed when the resources, over which negotiations are to be conducted, are finite. Strategies are developed with the objective of seeking the larger share of the resources.

Competitive strategies require making high initial demands and convey the impression of firmness and inflexibility. Under this strategy, the concessions are made grudgingly and in small quantities. A negotiator using a competitive strategy likes to convince the other party that he or she cannot accommodate any more and if an agreement is to be reached, the latter must concede. Competitive negotiators speak forcefully, appearing to be making threats and creating a chaotic scenario that intimidates the other party, thereby putting him or her on the defensive.

Competitive strategies are common in circumstances where the negotiation involves a one-time deal and where a future relationship is meaningless. Further, when there is a lack of trust, negotiating parties tend to resort to competitive strategies. Sometimes a negotiator switches to a competitive strategy when the negotiations are not progressing well or when a deadlock occurs.

Overall, competitive strategies do not make sense since they fail to create harmony between the parties and focus on a one-time deal. The emphasis of this strategic posture is a win-lose situation; emphasis is not about enlarging the size of the outcome.

Cooperative (or collaborative) strategies refer to a win-win situation where negotiators attempt to strike a mutually satisfying deal. Cooperative negotiators are willing to work with each other, sharing information and understanding each other's point of view. The emphasis of cooperative negotiations is on understanding the perspectives of the other party and developing strategies that benefit both. Cooperative strategies lead to creative solutions that enlarge the outcome, whereby both parties get more than what they aspired to initially.

Choice of a Negotiation Strategy

In international business, it is in the interest of both parties in a transaction to consider cooperative strategies that are conducive to the establishment of sound business relationships and in which each side finds it beneficial to contribute to the success of the negotiated deal. A purely cooperative strategy may be impractical, however, when the other side seeks to maximize its own interests, leading to competitive tactics. Therefore, a combination of cooperative and competitive strategies is advisable (with cooperative moves prevailing during most of the discussions and with some competitive moves used to gain a share of the enlarged outcome).

A negotiator must consider alternative competitive strategies in advance, in case the other party interprets a willingness to cooperate as a sign of weakness. Similarly, if the other party becomes unreasonable and switches to more competitive moves to extract extra concessions, the negotiator may need to change his or her negotiating approach.

Other Strategic Aspects of Negotiations

A number of other strategic issues must be determined and analyzed before the negotiations begin. These include setting the initial position, identifying potential concessions, and developing supporting arguments.

Setting the Initial Position. An important issue in any negotiations is to set the initial position. When a negotiator does not know much about the other party, he or she should begin with a more extreme position. Since the final agreements in negotiations are more strongly influenced by initial offers than by subsequent concessions of the other party, particularly when issues under consideration are of uncertain or ambiguous value, it is better to begin with a high position, provided it can be justified. Further, response to an extreme offer gives it some measure of credibility, which can highlight the dimensions of the bargaining zone.

In the context of international business, a negotiator should base his or her decision about initial position in reference to the culture of the other party. In some cultures, negotiators begin with extreme positions, leaving enough room for maneuvering. In Asia, Africa and the Middle East, bargaining is commonly employed in business deals. Therefore, a negotiator must start with a high position in order to become fully involved in the bargaining. In most Western societies, negotiators are less inclined to haggle; therefore, a negotiator should set the initial position close to the terms he or she is willing to accept.

Trading Concessions. A business negotiator must plan in advance which concessions to trade, if necessary; calculate their cost; and decide how and when to trade them. Successful executives consider the timing and the manner in which they trade concessions just as important as the value of the concessions. For instance, a small concession can be presented in such a way that the other party believes it is a major gain. When the other party sees that worthwhile concessions are being traded, he or she becomes more cooperative and reciprocates with better offers too.

The sequences of concessions are important in international business negotiations. For instance, in some cultures, negotiators trade small or no concessions in the early stage of the session and wait until the end to trade major tradeoffs. In other cultures, frequent concessions are presented in the opening phase, with fewer trade-offs offered in the closing period. For this reason, a negotiator must plan in advance a few inexpensive yet high-value concessions for emergency purposes, in case further offers are expected or necessary to close the deal. Last-minute concessions are anticipated by many negotiators when a transaction is nearing completion. In fact, in some countries, this practice is interpreted as a sign of cooperation and a willingness to find a mutually agreeable outcome.

The identification of concessions is, therefore, a critical element in negotiation preparation. In addition to determining which concessions are relevant for the negotiations, a negotiator must also estimate their value, establish their order of importance, determine what is expected in exchange, and plan when and how to offer them.

Developing Supporting Arguments. An important aspect of conducting successful negotiations is the ability to argue in favor of one's position, duly supported by facts and figures, and to refute the points made by the other party through counterarguments. This requires prior preparation through the analysis of collected information from various sources. In this process, seeking answers to the following questions can help:

- What kind of factual information would support and substantiate the argument?
- Whose help might be sought to clarify the facts and elaborate on them?
- What kind of records, databases, and files exist in the public domain that might support the argument?
- Has anybody negotiated before on similar issues? What major arguments were successfully used?
- What arguments might the other party make, and how might he or she support them? How can those arguments that go further in addressing both sides' issues and interests be refuted and advanced?
- How can the facts be presented (e.g., using visual aids, pictures, graphs, charts, and expert testimony) to make them more convincing?

Planning the Negotiation Meeting

A variety of logistical details should be worked out before the negotiations begin so that the meeting runs smoothly. These include planning the agenda, choosing the meeting site, setting the schedule, and deciding the order of formal introductions.

Agenda

The agenda of each meeting of the negotiations should be carefully set to decide what topics will be discussed and in what order. When the other party shares his or her agenda, the negotiator should reconcile the two, making sure critical issues are adequately addressed.

Opinions differ about the order in which the issues should be discussed. Some suggest the issues should be taken up according to the difficulty involved in resolving them. Thus, the parties begin with the easiest issue, followed by the next issue (which may be a little more involved), and so on, with the most complex issue coming up last. This way the parties strengthen their confidence in each other so that by the time a complex issue is examined, they have developed a relationship of harmony and trust. In contrast, many negotiators recommend resolving the most difficult issue first, believing that less important issues will fall in place on their own without the parties needing to expend much effort. According to these negotiators, this method is more efficient than spending time on insignificant issues first.

Further, the parties need to decide whether to tackle one issue at a time or to discuss the issues randomly, jumping from one issue to the next. Culturally speaking, Americans prefer the one-issue-at-a-time approach. In other societies, all of the issues are examined together. The latter approach is preferred particularly by the Japanese. They discuss issues one after the other without settling anything. Toward the end, however, concessions are made to come to mutually agreeable solutions.[9] This disorganized approach is resented by Westerners, particularly North Americans, since they must wait until the end to find out whether an issue has been resolved.[10]

Meeting Site

Many negotiators believe that the site of the meetings has an impact on the outcome. Therefore, a negotiator should choose a site where he or she might have some leverage. Basically, there are three alternatives to site selection: (1) the negotiator's place, (2) the other party's place, or (3) a third place (i.e., neutral territory).[11]

The home place gives the negotiator a territorial advantage. Psychologically the negotiator is more comfortable in familiar surroundings, which boosts his or her confidence in dealing with the visiting party. Further, negotiating at home obviates the need for travel and, thus, saves money. The negotiator is closer to his or her support system; i.e., home, family, and colleagues. Any information needed becomes readily available. In addition, playing host to the other party enables the negotiator to enhance the relationship and potentially obligates the other party to be more reasonable.

On the other hand, the home site can put the other party at a disadvantage. He or she is away from home, is probably jet-lagged, and runs the risk of culture shock. All of this is beneficial to the home-based negotiator.

Choosing the other party's place as the site has merits and demerits as well. A negotiator can see the actual facilities of the other party. Simply being told the party has a large factory may not mean much since the concept of size varies from nation to nation. The negotiator can also meet all of the people involved and has the opportunity to assess their connections in the business community and government. Of course, the negotiator must travel to the other party's site, incurring expenses; suffer from jet lag; and must negotiate in an unfamiliar environment.

The third alternative is to choose a neutral place. For example, Geneva could be a central site for parties from the United States and Singapore. However, if the other party has been there before and speaks French, the negotiator is no longer negotiating in a neutral place. Negotiators often alternate sites. The first meeting may be held at the negotiator's place, while the next meeting is scheduled at the other party's place. This ensures that neither party has a territorial advantage.

A survey of U.S. professional buyers dealing with foreign suppliers showed that 60.5 percent prefer negotiating in their offices compared to only 6.7 percent in the supplier's premises and 17.5 percent at a neutral site. Of the buyers, 20.9 percent considered the impact of the negotiation site on the outcome significant; 49.8 percent, moderate; and 26.9 percent, slight.[12]

Schedule

A schedule allocates time to different items on the agenda. The schedule must be realistic and flexible. Enough time must be budgeted for all contingencies. Introductions may take more time than planned. Coffee breaks/lunches do not always coincide with the time allocated. Further, it is difficult to anticipate how many questions each side will raise and how long it will take to answer each question.

In many nations, the tempo is slow and people move at ease. They are not under any time pressure. But if a negotiator comes from a country where time is money and every minute counts, he or she would be frustrated. A negotiator should not force his or her own values in developing the schedule.

The party that has traveled a long distance from a different time zone needs time to relax. A negotiator should also value the party's desire to see cultural and historic places. In any event, the schedule must remain flexible so the parties can remain responsive to changing situations.

Introductions

Some societies are very formal; others are not. For example, in the United States and Australia, addressing each other on a first-name basis is readily accepted. But overseas, people are often conscious about their status and title. Therefore, they want to be introduced with their appropriate titles. Further, there is the question of protocol, i.e., who should be addressed first, next, and last. Making a mistake in identifying someone and mispronouncing a person's name are social blunders to avoid. It is important that attention be devoted to all of these minute details.

Summary

In any negotiations, the actual interface between the two parties is only one phase of the negotiation process, representing the tip of the iceberg. The most crucial element is the planning and preparatory phase. Yet negotiators, particularly those who are new to the game, often neglect it. Experienced executives know that one can be overprepared, but not underprepared. Each party has its own strengths and weaknesses, but the party that is more committed and works harder for its goals achieves the best results. Being prepared is probably the best investment a business executive can make before entering into international negotiations.

Prenegotiation planning requires defining the issues, knowing one's position, knowing the other side's position, knowing the competition, knowing one's negotiation limits, developing strategies and tactics, and planning the negotiation meeting. Among these factors, one stands out and that is knowing one's negotiation limits. This factor deals with determining BATNA, i.e., the best alternative to a negotiated agreement. BATNA is the standard against which any negotiated agreement is evaluated.

CHAPTER 5

Initiating Global Business Negotiations

Making the First Move

Openings are opportunities

—Michael Wheeler

The way a person opens business negotiations influences the entire process, from the initial offer to the final agreement. For first-time negotiations, especially between different cultures, these opening moments are even more critical.

Doing business in the global arena is a long-term prospect, where personal relationships are essential. Skilled negotiators create a favorable atmosphere that has a positive impact on the tone, style, and progress of negotiations, as well as on the final agreement.

Once made, first impressions are difficult to change, particularly if they are negative. People tend to have quicker, stronger, and longer-lasting reactions to bad impressions than to positive ones. Thus, extra care is needed when formulating opening statements. For fruitful negotiations, the opening offer should (a) stress mutual benefits, (b) be clear and positive, (c) imply flexibility, (d) create interest, (e) demonstrate confidence, and (f) promote goodwill.

Making the First Offer

If a negotiator wishes to take the initiative and set the tone of the discussions, he or she should make the first offer. The negotiator gains a tactical advantage by submitting his or her position first by establishing a reference or anchor point.

A person's anchor point can influence the other party's response. When the other party knows the negotiator's *position*, he or she either rejects the offer or requests a counteroffer. The other party may also revise its acceptance limits in light of the opening offer.

At this point, the negotiator should not make unnecessary concessions; he or she should seek clarification instead. This approach assumes that the initial offer was based on recent market information, was credible, and was presented with conviction. In other words, when a negotiator is highly confident of the other party's reservation point, making the first offer is to the negotiator's advantage. The ideal first offer should barely exceed the other party's reservation point. The other party will consider such an offer to be serious because it is within the bargaining zone. If the other party accepts the offer, the negotiator can keep a big share of the bargaining surplus.

In most international business deals, sellers are expected to make the first offer since buyers consider themselves in a position of power. In some markets, buyers dictate and control the discussions from the beginning of the negotiations to the final agreement. If a negotiator is not familiar with the market in which he or she is trying to do business, making an offer without adequate information or a clear understanding of what the other side wants places him or her in a risky position. For example, having the first offer immediately accepted means the negotiator underestimated the market; he or she experienced the winner's curse. If the negotiator must make the first offer, he or she can avoid the winner's curse by making the offer so low or so high (depending on his or her role as buyer or a seller) that it is virtually impossible for the other party to accept. But the danger is that a ridiculous offer can create an unfavorable impression and may jeopardize the relationship. Thus, as a rule, a negotiator should not make the first offer if the other party has more information.

Opening High/Low

As the negotiations begin, a negotiator faces a dilemma about whether the opening offer should be high or low. If the negotiator makes a high offer, he or she may lose the business. Alternatively, a low offer might mean giving up profits, since an offer seen as modest by the other party probably could have been higher. If a negotiator has accurate knowledge about the reservation point of the other party, the offer could be within the bargaining zone, suggesting a cooperative stance. Unfortunately, in most cases, negotiators possess limited information about the perspectives of their counterparts; thus, the perplexing question of high or low remains unresolved.

Empirical work on the subject shows that negotiators who make extreme opening offers achieve higher settlements than those who make low or modest opening offers.[1] An initial high price is suggested for three reasons. First, it allows the negotiator to gather and exchange information without making early concessions. Second, it communicates to the other party that the negotiation process is going to be time-consuming—and that the other party must be prepared to grant more concessions than it initially intended. Third, it allows the negotiator to continue discussions, despite the rejection of a high initial offer.

An extreme opening presents two problems. One, it might be summarily rejected by the other party, and two, it shows an attitude of toughness, which is not conducive to a long-term relationship.

Any objections to a high offer should be dealt with through questions and answers, not through concessions. The negotiator should determine which parts of the proposal are acceptable and which areas are problematic. Based on this knowledge, the negotiator can justify his or her initial offer or eventually make a counterproposal. Proposals and counteroffers should be handled step by step, with repeated questioning, as shown in Figure 5.1. This allows the negotiator to gather and exchange information without making early concessions.

Starting high is common in markets where business executives rate their superior negotiating skills by how many concessions they obtain. For example, a high initial offer is expected in many countries in Latin America, Africa, and the Middle East. In highly competitive markets, frequently found in Southeast Asia, North America, and Northern Europe, opening offers are slightly above the bottom line.

The main mistake to avoid with the high-offer strategy is to present an offer considered so high by the other party that it results in a deadlock.

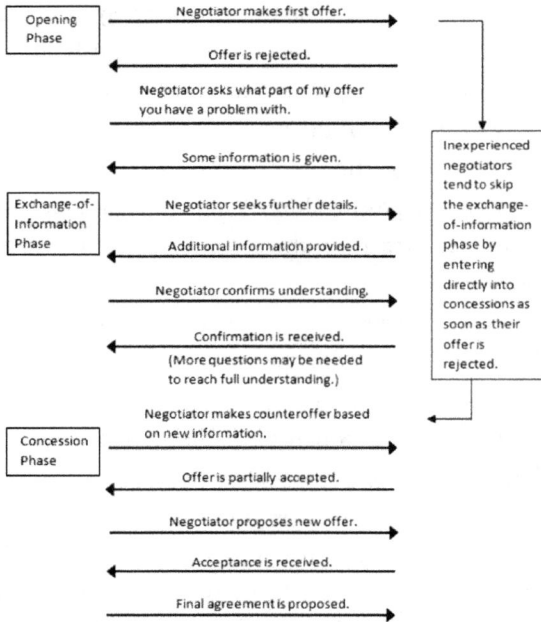

Figure 5.1 Negotiate successfully through repeated questioning

Another common pitfall is to start with a high offer and not be prepared to justify it. To overcome the lack of justification, negotiators wrongly begin to make concessions immediately, without asking for reciprocity.

Skilled negotiators sometimes make a low initial offer near the bottom line, not so much to get the business, but to be invited to the negotiation. They intend to improve their offer on the basis of new information gathered during the discussions. In some industries and markets, a product is sold at a going price and at predetermined conditions, leaving the negotiator with little choice in setting an opening offer.

In such a situation, your offer must be more or less in line with that of the competition. An advantage of having an opening offer close to competition is that it allows the negotiator to remain in contention for the business. To increase his or her chances of being retained, the negotiator's proposal must address the specific needs of the other party and demonstrate how the offer best meets the party's requirements.

When a negotiator enters a new market or wants to get a foot in the door with a new customer, he or she should open with a proposal that is close to, or at times below, the bottom line. In such cases, the negotiator must explain that the offer is valid for a limited time only. For example, an exporter may be faced with extra production capacity during the last quarter of the year. In this situation, the exporter could propose a limited business deal at a one-time price preferential in order to utilize the extra capacity and thus recover the fixed costs and part of the variable costs.

At times, a negotiator may wish to make a low offer in order to secure business with well-known global firms. This strategy is common among small- and medium-sized firms seeking business deals from world-class companies. Advantages of being associated with large international firms often override the need for immediate profits. However, such a negotiation strategy places the negotiator in a weak position from the beginning and often results in unprofitable agreements. To avoid being caught in this situation, the negotiator should shift the discussions away from the initial offer to the needs of the other party. The negotiator should take charge of the discussion through questions and make sure he or she has a clear understanding of the real needs of the other party. Once the negotiator knows exactly what the other party's requirements are, he or she can propose additional features such as better quality, faster delivery, individual versus bulk packaging, short and flexible production runs, and other intangibles to improve profit margins. By managing successfully even with a low-offer strategy, he or she can obtain a profitable agreement. Professional buyers are known to seek the best-quality products or services from the most reputable firms at the lowest possible price. In the end, these same buyers often end up paying a premium price to avoid the risk of getting inconsistent quality or receiving late deliveries.

There are times when entrepreneurs from small- or mid-sized firms propose very low offers in the hope of receiving large orders at higher prices in the future. Too often, promises for future business opportunities remain just that—promises. Negotiating deals at low prices in the hope of recovering lost profits from future orders is a dangerous strategy. Wise negotiators avoid such a strategy because of the high risks involved. The moment they raise the price (with or without justification), the buyer is likely to shift business away, to a competitor.

Overcoming Objections

The question of overcoming objections arises after the first offer has been made and rejected. Figure 5.2 provides a summary of the most common objections in the opening phase of face-to-face discussions and appropriate responses. A negotiator should not resort to concessions right away. Experienced negotiators expect objections. They turn objections into opportunities, without taking a defensive attitude and getting into concessions.

Objections are generally meant to put the negotiator on the defensive. By handling the objections strategically, the negotiator can successfully overcome the objections and be in a favorable position to steer the negotiation toward his or her goals. Chapter 6 explores trading concessions in depth.

Influencing Negotiation

Influence refers to tactics negotiators use to utilize their power with the intention of seeking a favorable outcome of negotiations for themselves. Cialdini has identified six different categories of influence: reciprocity, consistency, social proof, liking, authority, and scarcity.[2]

Either party to the negotiation can use influence to its advantage. A negotiator should attempt to influence the outcome of negotiation in a way that is favorable to him or her. At the same time, the negotiator should be sensitive to the use of influence by the other party.

Reciprocity

The principle of reciprocity means that if someone does a person a favor, that person must return the favor, since he or she feels obligated to do so. In negotiation, reciprocity is often used by one party to seek concessions from the other. A negotiator feels indebted to the other party to make concessions because the party did something for the negotiator in the past. The other party will tactfully remind the negotiator that he or she owes the party the concessions.

Basically, there is nothing irrational or illogical about reciprocity in negotiation. However, a negotiator should be careful not to yield too much ground in the name of reciprocity. In other words, the negotiator does not

Your offer is too expensive.
- Ask what is meant by "too expensive."
- Find out what is considered acceptable and on what basis.
- Respond by providing justification.
- Avoid lowering your price until you learn more about what the other party is looking for.
- Find out if the objection is due to your price offer or if it reflects other factors.
- Ask yourself: If I'm too expensive, why is the other party negotiating with me?

We don't have that kind of budget.
- Find out how large the budget is and for what time frame.
- Explore whether your offer can fit within the overall budget by checking whether the other party can combine several budget lines.
- Propose deferred payment schedules.
- Confirm the order and postpone deliveries until a new budget allocation is confirmed.
- Split the order into smaller units or mini orders to meet current budget limitations.

That's not what we are looking for.
- Ask what they are looking for and insist on specifics.
- Find out which aspects of your offer they like best.
- Keep asking questions until you have a clear understanding of the other party's real needs.
- Repackage your offer in light of the new information received.

Your offer is not competitive.
- Ask what is meant by "not competitive."
- Find out if your competitors' offers are comparable to yours.
- Look for weaknesses in the other offers and stress your strengths.
- Reformulate your offer by avoiding direct comparison with the competition. Stress the unique features of your products/services.

Figure 5.2 Reasons for rejection of the first offer

Source: Claude Cellich, "Business Negotiations: Making the First Offer," *International Trade FORUM*, 2/2000, p. 16.

want to be victimized or exploited by the other party. The negotiator must weigh what the other party did for him or her and what he or she might do for the party to repay the favor. Nothing should be conceded beyond that. A situation to avoid is to give away concessions now with the promise of receiving concessions in future deals. Unfortunately, concessions received in the past are easily forgotten, and the future deal never materializes.

Consistency

Psychologically, people like to be consistent in their behavior since inconsistency is a sign of irrationality.[3]

Following the consistency principle, a negotiator should not agree to terms he or she cannot and/or does not want to follow through. For example, an exporter is negotiating with an overseas distributor about commission on sales. The distributor accepts the exporter's terms on the condition that the exporter make adaptations to the product to be shipped. The exporter agrees to such product adaptation, probably without thinking about what it might entail, and the negotiations are successfully completed. Now, to be consistent, the exporter must comply with the product adaptation even if it costs him more than he had anticipated. It is the principle of consistency that makes him follow through with the agreed-upon adaptation.

Social Proof

People often justify their behavior based on what others have done or might do under similar circumstances. In business negotiation, the other party may ask for concessions using the principle of social proof. For example, an overseas distributor may influence the exporter to pay for the transportation costs of defective products that are returned, citing the example of other foreign companies the distributor represents. The distributor convinces the exporter using the behavior of other companies as proof that it is the exporter's responsibility to absorb the transportation costs of returns. If the exporter's information shows that statement to be untrue, the only way he can counter the social proof advanced by the other party is to demand evidence. If the exporter's knowledge of the industry practice shows that the transportation costs of returns are absorbed by the distributor, the exporter should obtain some proof to support it. He can then submit his own social proof and discount the distributor's argument.

Liking

Generally speaking, people are more agreeable with those they like. A negotiator is more likely to make concessions to those of the other party he or she likes. Thus, the other party in negotiations can take steps to make the negotiator like him or her, which leads the negotiator to making the concessions the party desires.

A negotiator can use the liking principle to his or her advantage in negotiation by making the other party like him or her. This can be achieved in various tangible and intangible ways. For example, the negotiator can present the other side with a gift or talk positively about the other party's country; for example, "You have a wonderful country with a long history and a rich culture." Once the negotiator has created an atmosphere in which the other party likes him or her, the negotiator will find it easier to seek concessions in negotiation. Savvy negotiators go a long way in making themselves likable, humorous, knowledgeable, and friendly so the other party like them.[4] By the time negotiation begins, the other party believes he or she is dealing with an accomplished friend. This influences the other party's behavior favorably.

Authority

Behaviorally speaking, people accept the opinions, views, and directions of those they consider an authority on the subject. When people are sick, they accept the advice of a doctor because they consider the doctor an authority on health matters. Similarly, in negotiation, the other party will accept a negotiator's offer without much questioning if the negotiator is considered an authority.

It is important, therefore, that people assigned to negotiate on one's behalf are capable, are knowledgeable about the details of the situation, and can present themselves as authoritative. A weak person lacking the necessary authority might give in too soon, providing more concessions to the other party than necessary.

Authority has another connotation in negotiations. It has to do with the authority of the negotiators to finalize the agreement on behalf of his or her organization. If the negotiator does not have the authority to make a deal, he or she will be considered by the other party as a go-between, and the other party will be less willing to strike a deal. For example, if the other party is seeking concessions and the negotiator has no authority to make concessions, the other party might as well end the negotiations. In the other party's eyes, the negotiator has no credibility. Whoever is responsible for handling negotiations must be equipped with adequate authority.

Scarcity

It is human nature to want things that are rare, are hard to get, or are in great demand. This tendency applies to negotiations as well. In accordance with the principle of scarcity, a negotiator should make different attributes of an offer seem rare and scarce, which would result in the other party wanting them. A negotiator may be willing to include those attributes in his or her first offer but should hold them back, emphasizing that such attributes cannot be provided.

Since the negotiator makes the attributes seem scarce, the other party wants them at all costs. The negotiator then makes them available, grudgingly, as negotiations advance. Such concessions will be valued highly by the other party, and the negotiator might obtain additional concessions in return.

Common Concerns

Frequently, negotiators face many questions to which there are no easy answers. While the negotiators must address these questions on their own based on the environment in which they are placed, the basic guidelines are examined here.[5]

Sharing Information about Reservation Price

The previous chapter discussed the term *zone of potential agreement*, which is the final price agreed upon between the reservation points of the two parties. Each party seeks as much portion of the zone of potential agreement as it can. And the parties negotiate for that. If one party reveals its reservation point, that strengthens the bargaining position of the other party. Thus, it is not a good idea to share information about one's reservation point with the counterpart.

Some negotiators believe the task becomes easier when both the parties trust each other and reveal their reservation points. Thus, they can negotiate to share the surplus in a rational fashion. However, the problem in negotiations is not a matter of trust, but strategy. The strategy calls for maximizing the surplus. Therefore, trusting the other party will only cause conflict.

Lying about Reservation Point

Lying about one's reservation point is dysfunctional for several reasons. First, it shortens the zone of potential agreement, which renders the making of concessions difficult. The negotiations may end in impasse. Further, lying can impact the negotiator's reputation negatively in the marketplace. People often talk about their negotiation endeavors, and a lying negotiator would be mentioned as an undependable party. Remember, good news travels fast, but bad news travels faster.

Catching the Liar

A negotiator should make sure the other party is not lying. Three strategies can be used to catch a lie in negotiation. First, test the consistency in the other party's statements. Negotiations involve asking each other a variety of questions. One should watch for any inconsistencies in the answers the other party supplies. Of course, questions should be adequately designed so that inconsistencies show up if an opponent is lying. Second, enrich the mode of communication by adopting a multichannel strategy. For example, if a person suspects the other party is lying and the person has been negotiating by phone, written correspondence, or e-mail, he or she should ask the other party for a face-to-face meeting. It becomes difficult for liars to monitor themselves when communicating through different channels. Signs of lying are often revealed through nonverbal communication, such as gestures and eye contact. Third, ask the other party to support what he or she said by providing tangible proof or evidence.

Determining the Reservation Point of the Other Party

As a negotiator should not reveal his or her reservation point for the reasons examined previously, it would be counterproductive for the negotiator to ask the other party for his or her reservation point. The other party might lose respect and withdraw from the negotiation. Frankly, it is unethical for a negotiator to probe into the other party's reservation point while not wanting to reveal his or her own.

Choosing between Tough and Soft Negotiation Stance

A tough negotiator is inflexible, demands much, yields few concessions, and holds out. Tough negotiators are stubborn and do not hesitate to walk away from negotiations that might be highly rewarding. A soft negotiator, on the other hand, reveals his or her reservation point, makes too many generous concessions, and attempts to make the other party feel good.

Neither of the two approaches mentioned above—tough or soft—works well from the perspective of global negotiation. The best approach for successful negotiations is strategic creativity. This approach suggests the use of strategies to seek the larger proportion of the zone of potential agreement through sharing information, making select concessions, and creating a lasting relationship.

Playing a Fair Game

Conceptually, it is appealing if both parties play a fair game. The negotiations are finalized quickly, and both parties end up as winners. Unfortunately, in practice, this ideal approach may not work. First, what is fair and what is not fair is difficult to define. The concept of fairness is vague, and different people define it differently. Thus, even though, in their estimation, both parties are playing a fair game, they may be far apart from each other. Further, while parties desire a fair outcome, their ideas about how to achieve fairness can vary. Thus, negotiations cannot be conducted on the basis of fairness alone.

Making the Final Offer

A negotiator should not rush into making a final offer, an irrevocable commitment, until he or she is ready. Once the negotiator reaches the point at which he or she is comfortable walking away from the negotiations, only then should he or she take the stance of final offer. This happens when his or her BATNA represents a more attractive option.

Buyer and Seller's Point of View

Figure 5.3 provides insights into key points that a buyer or seller should consider in negotiating an agreement.

BUYER	SELLER
The negotiating goal should be kept in mind	Investigate the buyer's goals
Be ready to say "no" and ask for a new offer	Find out what are the objections to the offer
Refer to better offers from competition	Create added value/stress scarcity
Seek concessions	Propose both tangible and nontangible benefits
Insist on a better offer	Change the price and propose a new package/counteroffer
Check if the latest proposal satisfy the original goal/needs	Ensure the deal is doable, profitable, and sustainable

Figure 5.3 Key points to consider

Summary

For every negotiation, a negotiator's initial offer should stand on its own merit within the prevailing context surrounding the discussions. Entering the negotiation under false pretenses or unfounded premises can prove costly or result in a deadlock. A negotiator must make the first offer competitive in the eyes of the other party and be ready to defend it with valid arguments.

The worst-case scenario is to make concessions immediately following objections to an initial offer. Unskilled or unprepared negotiators frequently face this dilemma in their business dealings. Asking questions, listening actively, and being patient go a long way in conquering this tendency. A negotiator should anticipate the typical objections he or she is likely to face, prepare appropriate replies in advance, and formulate information-seeking questions before meeting the other party.

One's knowledge of the market, a clear assessment of the competition, and an understanding of the other party's real needs should help in this crucial initial phase. As the opening offer shapes the outcome of the negotiation, a negotiator's ability to make a good impression from the outset is critical. He or she may not get a second chance to make a good first impression.

Although it is better to place an initial offer slightly higher in order to reach a better outcome, a negotiator may lower it if he or she is doing business in highly competitive markets. In more traditional and less competitive markets, offers should be on the higher side with plenty of built-in concessions available to the other party.

An initial offer should be presented with confidence and conviction, yet imply flexibility. The issue is not to have an offer accepted or rejected or to be the first to make an offer, but to be in a position to start strong and maintain control of the discussions. Only through a series of high-yield questions can a negotiator learn what the other partly really requires, enabling the negotiator to reformulate the offer to meet the party's specific needs.

The initial phase of the negotiation should be regarded as an opportunity to create an atmosphere of trust, leading to an exchange of strategic information. It is not the time to begin making concessions. Some executives from certain corporations consider this initial phase a waste of time and begin trading away concessions immediately. Successful negotiators know better. They invest their time by finding out the real needs of the other party and by determining how they can best satisfy those needs in an acceptable package. In other words, a negotiator's first offer should reflect the best-case scenario, supported by first-class justification.

CHAPTER 6

Trading Concessions

The art of negotiating consists of knowing how, why, where, to whom, and when to make concessions.

—Gerald Nierenberg and Henry Calero

Trading concessions are an essential element of the negotiation process. Concessions are made possible when the parties involved have different interests, priorities, and goals. In fact, they play an even greater role in cultures where negotiating is a part of everyday life. In these cultures, negotiators expect to trade concessions back and forth taking whatever time necessary to reach an agreement. As a part and parcel of any concession, it is crucial for negotiators to prepare in advance the type of concessions they are willing to trade and concessions they want in return. Reciprocity is a must. Furthermore, after offering a concession, it is important to immediately receive a concession in return as its value loses over time. Trading concessions is the exchange of offers and counteroffers preferably of equal or greater value. Ideally, it is best to trade low-value concessions for higher priority issues.

The best tactic to trade concessions is to phrase them into conditional or hypothetical questions. For example, a negotiator wishing to make a concession could say, "If I expedite delivery by one week, will your firm absorb the extra costs?" or, "What if my firm agrees to modify the product to meet your specifications, will you agree to extend the contract from one year to three years?" These types of questions invite the other party to enter into exchanging concessions. In case of nonacceptance, both parties can continue negotiating by identifying the reasons for the objection before trading further concessions. For concessions to be traded successfully, negotiators create value by stressing the benefits of their concessions and how it meets the other party's interests.

Develop A Concession Strategy

Trading concessions demands a thorough preparation. During the planning stage each negotiator develops a list of potential concessions to be traded, their respective priorities, and which issues are negotiable and which ones are not negotiable. These eventual concessions are then ranked by key issues in terms of importance from high to low or classified into three categories: must have, good to have, and trade-offs. The more comprehensive the list of potential concessions, the greater the chance of exchanging concessions that satisfy the needs of both parties. In addition, negotiators identify which concessions are wanted in return and how important these concessions are to the other party.

When negotiating in a relationship-oriented culture, it is advisable to plan more concessions than in a deal-oriented culture as haggling is considered a significant part of negotiations. In any culture, it is best to keep in reserve a few concessions that can include both tangible and nontangible benefits in case of last minute objections. Negotiators adopting a competitive strategy tend to demand major concessions at the start of the discussions at the expense of the other party. This approach fails to optimize the benefits each side can obtain due to a lack of sharing vital information. To overcome this type of behavior, negotiators have to resist giving away concessions by asking information gathering questions until each party fully understands their respective interests. The development of a clear-cut concession strategy requires two steps: concession identification, and information exchange.

Concession Identification

Concession identification involves:

(a) identifying the concessions to be traded (tangible and nontangible);
(b) estimating the value of concessions and ranking them by priority;
(c) establishing which concessions are non-negotiable;
(d) understanding which concessions are wanted from the other party;
(e) ranking potential concessions according to musts, good to have, and trade-offs;
(f) preparing a few minor concessions to give away if needed to start or restart reciprocity;

(g) developing valid arguments or demonstrating benefits for every concession to enhance its value; and

(h) keeping a few potential concessions in reserve to overcome last minute objections.

To optimize concession trading, it is critical to exchange low-value
items for high-value ones. For this to happen, both sides must be willing to share information by adopting cooperative strategies leading to a
problem solving situation. By sharing information, each negotiator is in a
position to identify the underlying needs of the other party, its goals, the
importance given to different issues, and what is non-negotiable. When
a party states that certain items are non-negotiable, the other negotiator
needs to find out whether these items are really non-negotiable and why
or whether it is a ploy to extract further concessions. Once the negotiator understands what the other side is really looking for, its constraints
and concerns, concessions can start to be traded. Generally, this problem
solving approach requires that one or both parties think outside the box
(expand the pie) thereby creating additional value and options. Besides
identifying potential concessions, each party should evaluate their respective value.

Concessions should be classified into hard (measurable) and soft
value benefits (difficult to measure). For example, hard items include
price, cost, delivery dates, penalties, financial terms, quality standards,
and so forth. Soft value concessions are subject to different interpretation due to the perception given by the negotiators. For instance, soft
value items include extended warranty, free training, longer contracts,
samples, flexible payment terms, trust, reputation, satisfaction, referrals,
maintaining the business relationship, and the prestige to be associated
with the firm among others. Soft and hard value items are also known as
tangible and nontangible concessions. In a relationship-oriented culture,
nontangible benefits are highly appreciated and play a significant role in
reaching agreements. To improve the chances of concluding a deal in a
global context, negotiators stress both tangible and nontangible benefits.
Concessions considered soft are very useful in breaking a deadlock, getting the negotiations back on track, or influencing the other party to
conclude. The main advantage of these soft concessions is that despite

being appreciated highly, their cost is low. After all, no amount of money can buy trust, respect, or reputation.

By considering both soft and hard concessions, negotiators can shift the discussion away from price issues, particularly in the initial phase. Price is an important and sensitive issue in most negotiations, but too often dominates the discussions at the expense of other key elements. For instance in business to business negotiations, when concluding a deal, professional buyers give priority to nonprice issues by allocating greater weights to financial stability of the firm, its management, performance record, ability to deliver on time, capacity to meet quality standards, cost of production, flexibility to cope with change, and more recently, whether management has adopted corporate social responsibility standards. In addition to considering nonprice issues, executives negotiating international business deals take a long-term outlook and adopt an implementation mindset to ensure that the agreement will be doable, profitable and sustainable.

Information Exchange

In any negotiation, major concessions are traded after an exchange of relevant information has taken place. It is only after each party understands the underlying needs, priorities, and concerns of the other side that important concessions are traded. In the initial stage of the discussions, however, minor concessions are exchanged to encourage negotiators to share information and create a problem solving environment. Generally, the most important concessions are made toward the end of the negotiations due to approaching deadlines, nearing the bottom line, or willing to conclude. By applying the 80/20 principle, 80 percent of all major concessions are traded during the 20 percent remaining time allocated to the negotiations.[1] This point is particularly relevant when negotiators from monochronic cultures (where time is considered a rare commodity and not to be wasted) are trading concessions in polychronic environments.

To avoid giving away unnecessary concessions, it is wise to manage the available time efficiently by concentrating on key issues. Whenever possible, negotiators can request additional time, set up another meeting, or postpone the discussions for the time being to avoid making quick decisions under time constraints.

In relationship-oriented cultures, late concessions are highly appreciated by negotiators as it shows how successful they are. In deal-oriented cultures, late concessions are expected especially by professional buyers as it demonstrates their superior negotiating skills, thereby enhancing their career prospects. Too often negotiators concentrate their efforts on the cost of a single item while overlooking the total cost of the overall transaction.

By applying cooperative negotiation strategies, purchasing managers and suppliers can reduce the total cost of a transaction by redesigning a product, changing product specifications, and reducing service or maintenance costs. Generally, this applies to more complex business deals, although it can be useful in everyday negotiations as well. The following example illustrates how two firms were able to overcome a price reduction request by adopting cooperation strategies, exchanging information, and adopting a long-term outlook.[2]

This example shows that through cooperation, information sharing, relying on a creative problem solving approach and an implementation mindset, both parties obtained greater outcomes by expanding the number of issues under discussions.

A construction firm purchasing plasterboards for office buildings asked its long-term supplier to reduce its price due to rising competition from foreign firms. The current price of the plasterboards was between $3.80 and $4.15 per board. The construction firm wanted a price reduction to $3.40. After reviewing its cost structure, the supplier requested a meeting with the representatives of the construction firm to discuss the problem as it was unable to meet this price reduction.

Both firms wanted to continue working together, but due to increasing competition from foreign suppliers, the cost of the plasterboards had to be reduced. The supplier suggested to look at the total cost of the boards from the time the boards left its manufacturing plant to their final installation at the construction site. At the moment, the total cost to the construction firm came to $22.50. In other words, the cost of the boards represented only 16.9 percent of the total cost. This finding is in line with the 80/20 principle whereby 80 percent of the cost of any product is made up of 20 percent of the parts. The additional costs consisted of packing, transporting, handling, and installing the boards at the site.

(continued)

A review of each stage of the process revealed that 40 percent of the boards were damaged during installation, required two workers to install them, and incurred high transport costs. In view of these findings, the supplier developed a smaller board (half the size of the current one) which was easier to pack, transport, and required only one worker to install it. In addition, it would reduce the number of boards being damaged and the time taken to install. The construction firm found this suggestion attractive due to substantial savings. The total costs of the new boards came to $16.25 resulting in a saving of $6.25.

Flexibility in Negotiating

After gathering enough information, the negotiator is ready to make a counteroffer. The counteroffer may mean holding on to the original position or making some concessions. Holding on to the original offer implies a position of firmness, which does not go far and might lead to a breakdown of the negotiations because the negotiator appears to capture most of the bargaining range. The other party may adopt a similar posture and reciprocate with firmness. The parties may become disappointed or disillusioned and withdraw completely.[3]

The other alternative is to adopt a flexible position and establishing a cooperative rather than a combative relationship.[4] This shows there is room for maneuvering and the negotiations continue.

Concessions are an essential part of negotiations. Studies have shown that parties feel better about an agreement if it involves a progression of concessions. Concession making shows an acknowledgment of the need of the other party and an attempt to reach the position where that need is at least partially met.[5] Three aspects of flexibility in negotiation are reciprocity, size, and pattern.

Reciprocity

An important aspect of concession making is reciprocity. If a negotiator makes a concession, he or she expects the other party to yield the same. As a matter of fact, sometimes a negotiator seeks reciprocity by making his or her concessions conditional. For example, I will do A and B for you if you do X and Y for me.[6]

Size

The size of concession is also important. In the initial stages, a higher-level concession is feasible, but as a negotiator gets closer to his or her reservation point, he or she tends to make the concession smaller. Suppose a supplier is setting the price of her product with the agent and makes the first offer $100 below the other party's target price. A concession of $10 would reduce the bargaining by 10 percent. When negotiations reach within $10 of the other party's target price, a concession of $1 gives up 10 percent of the remaining bargaining range. This example shows how the other party might interpret the meaning of concession size.

Concesssion Patterns

Negotiators have a wide choice of patterns to select from when exchanging concessions. The choice of any one pattern depends on several factors including the existing relationship between the parties, their preferred negotiating style, the degree of competition, cultural factors, whether it's one time transaction or repeat business, and so forth. Negotiators can choose up to eight different types of patterns when planning the exchange of concessions. An example describing each pattern consisting of trading $1,000 in concessions over five rounds of negotiations is given Figure 6.1.

		Patterns							
		One	Two	Three	Four	Five	Six	Seven	Eight
Concession Rounds	1		$200	$400	$50	$1,000	$300	$25	$150
	2		$200	$300	$100		$100	$50	$150
	3		$200	$150	$150		$200	$125	$350
	4		$200	$100	$300		$250	$450	$250
	5	$1,000	$200	$50	$400		$150	$350	$200

Figure 6.1 An example in choosing a pattern

Pattern One

Negotiators adopting pattern one refuse to make any concessions until the last minute, when a large concession is made. Generally, this approach is likely to lead to a breakdown as the other party will probably walk away from the negotiation. Besides, the other party is not in a position to make counteroffers due to the lack of progress during the first four rounds. Finally, making one large concession towards the deadline may encourage the other party to ask for more concessions. It is best to avoid this pattern by promoting the exchange of information from the beginning to allow each side to start trading minor concessions.

Pattern Two

This pattern is easily recognizable as each concession is of equal value. A variant of this pattern consists of reducing each successive concession by a certain percentage. For example, the first concession is reduced by 10 percent, then by 8 percent in the second round, 6 percent in the third round, and so on. After a few rounds, the other party recognizes the pattern and will keep asking for more concessions knowing in advance what to expect. Less experienced negotiators may resort to this pattern, but because it is predictable it is not recommended.

Pattern Three

By making each concession smaller than the previous one, negotiators using this pattern give a clear signal to the other party that the bottom line is getting near. When trading concessions, negotiators should ensure not only that each concession is of lesser value, but also that the other party has to work harder and harder to obtain additional concessions. This pattern is by far the most effective as long as negotiators plan carefully the concessions to be traded.

Pattern Four

In this pattern, negotiators keep increasing the value of each concession. It does not take long before the other party realizes what is taking place.

This pattern invites the other side to keep asking for more and more concessions. Although some negotiators may like to use this pattern due to their weak bargaining position, pressure from competition, or wanting to reach the deal at all cost, this pattern should be avoided.

Pattern Five

Negotiators make only one major concession at the beginning of the discussions and then refuse to make any more concessions for the remainder of the negotiation. This pattern is likely to discourage the other party to keep negotiating as there is no reciprocity, eventually leading to an end of the discussions. Negotiators are better off avoiding this pattern as it is not conducive to a win-win outcome. In special situations, this pattern may be used by negotiators under time pressure hoping to reduce the discussions to one round of negotiation, or when one party considers itself in a powerful position thereby imposing its own conditions at the outset without any further discussions.

Pattern Six

Negotiators using pattern six are doing so to either confuse the other party or have no clear concession strategy in mind. It can be an effective strategy; however the inconvenience outweighs its benefits. For instance, the other party will not know how to reciprocate and may be reluctant to exchange information or make concessions until a clear pattern emerges. Negotiators can adopt this pattern when they are not sure of what they want or are testing the other party's intentions. This pattern may reflect changing interests, new information becoming available during the discussions, unexpected competition, and so on. In some circumstances, this pattern can lead to a mutually beneficial outcome.

Pattern Seven

Negotiators applying this pattern start by making a few minor concessions to build momentum as well as encouraging reciprocity. The major concessions are then traded during the middle of the discussions followed by smaller concessions toward the end signaling, the time to bring the negotiations to a close. This pattern is consistent with 80/20 principle, where 80 percent of the concessions are made in the 20 percent of the time left for the negotiations.[7] Generally, this pattern together with pattern three are most effective when planning concessions strategy.

Pattern Eight

There are times when negotiators find themselves trading concessions beyond the bottom line. In these situations, negotiators get carried away by the dynamics of the discussions or need to save face, satisfy their egos or wanting to get the contract even at a loss. By keeping a log of the concessions traded, negotiators can have an overview of the status of their position and assess how close they are to the bottom line. There are instances where executives accept deals below their bottom line in the hope of recovering the loss in future business, or where they have not evaluated their BATNA correctly. Generally, this pattern can lead to renegotiations, one time only transactions, difficulties in the implementation phase, loss of credibility, and so on. In view of the negative consequences of accepting offers below the bottom line, wise negotiators take time out to review all the concessions traded before making a final offer.

In large scale negotiations where discussions cover a wide range of issues, it is critical to keep records of the offers, counteroffers, and concessions exchanged. In view of the difficulties of keeping track of the discussions, this task should be assigned to a team member. A log listing which concessions have been made, by whom, under what circumstances, how much time it took from the last concession, and what are their values are most useful in monitoring progress. It also indicates which party has been more active, who has made more concessions, whether these concessions are of less, equal, or greater value and which remaining issues need to be addressed. This log needs to be reviewed frequently (after a break, or at the end of the day) in order to reorient the negotiation if necessary by changing strategies and/or tactics. A simplified log for less complex negotiations is equally useful as it allows both parties to assess their relative progress of the discussions. Finally, a review of the concessions traded and obtained can be helpful in detecting a pattern as well as assessing how close each side is approaching their respective bottom line.

An analysis of the recorded information provides an overview of what has been accomplished to date and answers the following questions:

- Who made more concessions?
- Are they of equal or greater value?
- How much time it took to start exchanging concessions?
- Is there a pattern in the concessions being made?
- How much more ground is needed to conclude?
- What concessions are left before closing?
- What remaining key issues need to be discussed before the deadline?
- Is the bottom line being reached?

Best Practices In Making Concessions

As the exchange of concessions is at the heart of negotiations, it is vital for negotiators to be aware of the typical mistakes to avoid, objections to overcome, and techniques to neutralize threats. A list of best practices concerning the exchange of concessions has been developed and grouped into dos' and don'ts as given below.

DOs
<ul><li>Plan concessions in advance.</li><li>Concentrate on the other party's underlying interests.</li><li>Provide sufficient margins, particularly in cultures that are extremely demanding.</li><li>Set aside a few concessions in reserve to be used when concluding the deal.</li><li>Trade small concessions early on to encourage the other party to start sharing information and promote reciprocity.</li></ul><ul><li>Insist on obtaining immediate reciprocity after making a concession (future promises lose value over time).</li><li>Determine the real value of the concessions and what the other party is willing to pay for.</li><li>Remember that 80 percent of the concessions are traded in the 20 percent remaining time.</li><li>Have the party work hard in obtaining concessions in order to be appreciated as well as to encourage the other party to reciprocate generously.</li><li>Provide justification or demonstrate benefits for each concession to enhance its value.</li><li>Set aside small concessions of lesser value to be traded near the deadline.</li><li>Keep a few nontangible concessions, including symbolic ones, to break a deadlock or to conclude.</li></ul>

(continued)

- Observe the other party's body language to detect hidden motives.
- Take into consideration that negotiators from different cultures concede differently.

- Pay attention to how you concede, as it is just as important as what you concede.
- Trade concessions in fewer and fewer amounts, taking more and more time and effort.
- Manage time efficiently by concentrating on key issues.
- Know the competition in order to resist giving away unnecessary concessions.
- Be aware of false concessions.
- Build trust, otherwise reciprocity is not adhered to.

DON'Ts

- Confuse cost and value.
- Accept concessions too easily.
- Be the first to make concessions on key issues.
- Offer a large concession early in the discussions as it encourages the other party to ask for more.
- Give away important concessions under time pressure.

- Show too much enthusiasm when accepting concessions (winner's curse).
- Accept future promises in exchange of valuable concessions.
- Assume that the other party values concessions the same way you do.
- Suppose that the other party has similar priorities, needs, goals and motivation.
- Trade concessions without first creating value.

- Make concessions that affect the bottom line negatively.
- Claim value before creating value.
- Be arrogant when refusing a concession.
- Adopt a concession strategy that can be easily detected by the other party.
- Make quick decisions under time pressure.
- Give away information to the other party without reciprocity.
- Negotiate against yourself.
- Rush into concessions to satisfy the other party.

Summary

Concessions are valuable in closing negotiations. But concessions should not be made without prior homework. Rushing into making concessions without preparation does not create goodwill. Rather it will suggest weakness on your part. A good negotiator clearly identifies the concessions that can be made and exchanges information with the other party to understand their needs, priorities, and concerns before trading the concessions.

It is desirable to adopt a flexible position in trading concessions since this leads to a cooperative relationship. Three essential aspects of flexibility are reciprocity, size of concession, and pattern of offering the concession. The ultimate objective of trading concessions is to create a win-win situation which opens the door to future business.

CHAPTER 7

Price Negotiations

As I hurtled through space, there was only one thought on my mind—
that every part of the capsule was supplied by the lowest bidder.

—John Glenn

Firms entering new markets, particularly small- and medium-sized firms, often face problems in initial negotiations with importers, agents, and buyers in the target markets. These difficulties generally center on pricing questions, particularly the fact that their prices may be too high. Although price is only one of many issues that must be discussed during business negotiations, too frequently it tends to influence the entire negotiation process. New exporters may be inclined to compromise on price at the beginning of the discussions, thereby bypassing other negotiating strengths they may have, such as the product's benefits, the firm's business experience, and the firm's commitment to providing quality products.

As pricing is often the most sensitive issue in business negotiations, it should be postponed until all of the other aspects of the transaction have been discussed and agreed upon.[1] Decisions involving a long-term commitment to place export orders are, in any case, rarely made on the basis of price alone, but rather on the total export package. This is particularly so in markets where consumers are highly conscious of quality, style, and brand names, where marketing channels are well structured, and where introduction of the product in the market is time-consuming and expensive.

By presenting a more comprehensive negotiating package in a well-planned and organized manner, exporters should be able to improve the effectiveness of their negotiation discussions and, in the long term, the profitability of their export operations.

Pricing Factors

As a prelude to undertaking the negotiation, a negotiator should analyze his or her flexibility in negotiating on price. This requires examining the factors that influence the pricing decision.[2] The factors to consider in international pricing exceed those in strictly domestic marketing not only in number, but also in ambiguity and risk. Domestic price is affected by such considerations as pricing objectives, cost, competition, customers, and regulations. Internationally, these considerations apply at home and in the host country. Further, multiple currencies, trade barriers, and longer distribution channels make the international pricing decision more difficult. Each of these considerations includes a number of components that vary in importance and interaction in different countries.

Pricing Objectives

Pricing objectives should be closely aligned to the marketing objectives. Essentially, objectives can be defined in terms of profit or volume. The profit objective takes the shape of a percentage markup on cost or price, or a target return on investment. The volume objective is usually specified as a desired percentage of growth in sales or as a percentage of the market share to be achieved.

Cost Analysis

Cost is one important factor in price determination. Of all the many cost concepts, fixed and variable costs are most relevant to setting prices. Fixed costs are those that do not vary with the scale of operations, such as number of units manufactured. Salaries of staff, office rent, and other office and factory overhead expenses are examples of fixed costs. On the other hand, variable costs, such as costs of material and labor used in the manufacture of a product, bear a direct relationship to the level of operations.

It is important to measure costs accurately in order to develop a cost/ volume relationship and to allocate various costs as fixed or variable. Measurement of costs is far from easy. Some fixed, short-run costs are not necessarily fixed in the long run; therefore, the distinction between variable and fixed costs matters only in the short run. For example, in the short run, the salaries of salespeople would be considered fixed. However, in the long run, the sales staff could be increased or cut, making sales salaries a variable instead of a fixed expense.

Moreover, some costs that initially appear fixed are viewed as variable when properly evaluated. A company manufacturing different products can keep a complete record of a sales manager's time spent on each product and, thus, may treat this salary as variable. However, the cost of that record keeping far exceeds the benefits derived from making the salary a variable cost. Also, no matter how well a company maintains its records, some variable costs cannot be allocated to a particular product.

The impact of costs on pricing strategy can be studied by considering the following three relationships: (1) the ratio of fixed costs to variable costs, (2) the economies of scale available to a firm, and (3) the cost structure of a firm with regard to competitors. If the fixed costs of a company in comparison with variable costs form the higher proportion of its total costs, adding sales volume will be a great help in increasing earnings. Such an industry would be termed *volume-sensitive*. In some industries, variable costs constitute the higher proportion of total costs. Such industries are *price-sensitive*, because even a small increase in price adds a lot to earnings.

If substantial economies of scale are obtainable through a company's operations, market share should be expanded. In considering prices, the expected decline in costs should be duly taken into account; that is, prices may be lowered to gain higher market share in the long run. The concept of obtaining lower costs through economies of scale is often referred to as the *experience effect*, which means that all costs go down as accumulated experience increases. Thus, if a company acquires a higher market share, its costs will decline, enabling it to reduce prices. If a manufacturer is a low-cost producer, maintaining prices at competitive levels will result in additional profits. The additional profits can be used to promote the product aggressively and increase the overall scope of the business. If, however, the costs of a manufacturer are high compared to its competitors, prices cannot be lowered in order to increase market share. In a price-war situation, the high-cost producer is bound to lose.

Competition

The nature of competition in each country is another factor to consider in setting prices. The competition in an industry can be analyzed with reference to such factors as the number of firms in the industry, product differentiation, and ease of entry. Competition from domestic suppliers as well as other exporters should be analyzed.

Competitive information needed for pricing strategy includes published competitive price lists and advertising, competitive reaction to price moves in the past, timing of competitors' price changes and initiating factors, information about competitors' special campaigns, competitive product line comparison, assumptions about competitors' pricing/marketing objectives, competitors' reported financial performance, estimates of competitors' costs (fixed and variable), expected pricing retaliation, analysis of competitors' capacity to retaliate, financial viability of engaging in a price war, strategic posture of competitors, and overall competitive aggressiveness.

In an industry with only one firm, there is no competitive activity. The firm is free to set any price, subject to constraints imposed by law. Conversely, in an industry comprising a large number of active firms, competition is fierce. Fierce competition limits the discretion of a firm in setting price. Where there are a few firms manufacturing an undifferentiated product (such as in the steel industry), often only the industry leader has the discretion to change prices. Other industry members tend to follow the leader in setting price.

A firm with a large market share is in a position to initiate price changes without worrying about competitors' reactions. Presumably, a competitor with a large market share has the lowest costs. The firm can, therefore, keep its prices low—thus discouraging other members of the industry from adding capacity—and further its cost advantage in a growing market.

When a firm operates in an industry that has opportunities for product differentiation, it can exert some control over pricing even if the firm is small and competitors are many. This latitude concerning price occurs when customers perceive one brand to be different from competing brands. Whether the difference is real or imaginary, customers do not object to paying a higher price for preferred brands. To establish product differentiation of a brand in the minds of consumers, companies spend heavily for promotion. Product differentiation, however, offers an opportunity to control prices only within a certain range.

Customer Perspective

Customer *demand* for a product is another key factor in price determination. Demand is based on a variety of considerations, price being just one. These considerations include the ability of customers to buy, their willingness to buy, the place of the product in the customer's lifestyle (whether a status symbol or an often-used product), prices of substitute products, the potential market for the product (whether the market has an unfulfilled demand or is saturated), the nature of nonprice competition, consumer behavior in general, and consumer behavior in segments in the market. All of these factors are interdependent, and it may not be easy to understand their relationships accurately.

Demand analysis involves predicting the relationship between price level and demand, simultaneously considering the effects of other variables on demand. The relationship between price level and demand is called *elasticity of demand*, or *sensitivity of price*, and it refers to the number of units of a product that would be demanded at different prices. Price sensitivity should be considered at two different levels: the industry and the firm.

Industry demand for a product is elastic if demand can be substantially increased by lowering prices. When lowering price has little effect on demand, it is considered inelastic. Environmental factors, which vary from country to country, have a direct influence on demand elasticity. For example, in developed countries when gasoline prices are high, the average consumer seeks to conserve gasoline. When gasoline prices go down, people are willing to use gas more freely; thus, the demand for gasoline in developed countries can be considered somewhat elastic. In a developing country such as Bangladesh, where only a few rich people own cars, no matter how much gasoline prices change, total demand is not greatly affected, making demand inelastic.

When the total demand of an industry is highly elastic, the industry leader may take the initiative to lower prices. The loss in revenues from a decrease in price will presumably be more than compensated for by the additional demand generated, thus enlarging the total market. Such a strategy is highly attractive in an industry where economies of scale are possible. Where demand is inelastic and there are no conceivable substitutes, prices may be increased, at least in the short run. In the long run, however, the government may impose controls or substitutes may develop.

An *individual firm's demand* is derived from the total industry demand. An individual firm seeks to find out how much market share it can command in the market by changing its own prices. In the case of undifferentiated, standardized products, lower prices should help a firm increase its market share as long as competitors do not retaliate by matching the firm's price. Similarly, when business is sought through bidding, lower prices should help. In the case of differentiated products, however, market share can actually be improved by maintaining higher prices (within a certain range).

Products can be differentiated in various real and imagined ways. For example, a manufacturer in a foreign market who provides adequate warranties and after-sale service might maintain higher prices and still increase market share. Brand name, an image of sophistication, and the impression of high quality are other factors that can help differentiate a product and hence afford a company an opportunity to increase prices and not lose market share. In brief, a firm's best opportunity lies in differentiating its product. A differentiated product offers more opportunity for increased earnings through premium prices.

Government and Pricing

Government rules and regulations pertaining to pricing should be taken into account when setting prices. Legal requirements of the host government and the home government must be satisfied. A host country's laws concerning price setting can range from broad guidelines to detailed procedures for arriving at prices that amount to virtual control over prices.

Although international pricing decisions depend on various factors (such as pricing objective, cost competition, customer demand, and government requirements), in practice, total costs are the most important factor. Competitors' pricing policies rank as the next important factor, followed by the company's out-of-pocket costs, the company's return-on-investment policy, and the customer's ability to pay.

Aspects Of International Price Setting

The impact of such factors as differences in costs, demand conditions, competition, and government laws on international pricing is factored in by following a particular pricing orientation.[3]

Pricing Orientation

Companies mainly follow two different types of pricing orientation: the cost approach and the market approach. The *cost approach* involves computing all relevant costs and adding a desired profit markup to arrive at the price. The cost approach is popular because it is simple to comprehend and use, and it leads to fairly stable prices. It has two drawbacks though. First, definition and computation of cost can become troublesome. Should all (both fixed and variable) costs be included or only variable costs? Second, this approach brings an element of inflexibility into the pricing decision because of the emphasis on cost.

A conservative attitude favors using full costs as the basis of pricing. On the other hand, incremental-cost pricing would allow for seeking business otherwise lost. It means as long as variable costs are met, any additional business should be sought without any concern for fixed costs. Once fixed costs are recovered, they should not enter into the equation for pricing later orders.

The profit markup applied to the cost to compute final price can simply be a markup percentage based on industry practice. Alternatively, the profit markup can represent a desired percentage return on investment.

$$\text{Percentage markup cost} = \frac{\text{Total invested capital}}{\text{Standard cost of annual normal production}} \times \text{Percentage desired return on investment}$$

This method is an improvement over the pure cost-plus-profit method because markup is derived more scientifically. Nonetheless, the determination of *rate of return* poses a problem.

Under the *market approach*, pricing starts in a reverse fashion. First, an estimate is made of the acceptable price in the target country segment. An analysis should be performed to determine if this price meets the company's profit objective. If not, the alternatives are to give up the business or to increase the price. Additional adjustments in price may be required to cope with competitors, the host country government, an expected cost increase, and other eventualities. The final price is based on the market rather than estimated production costs.

Essentially, the cost and market approaches consider common factors in determining the final price. The difference between the two approaches involves the core concern in setting prices. The market approach focuses on pricing from the viewpoint of the customer. Unfortunately, in many countries, it may not be easy to develop an adequate price-demand relationship; therefore, implementation of the market approach can occur in a vacuum. It is this kind of uncertainty that forces companies to opt for the cost approach.

Export Pricing

Export pricing is affected by three factors:

1. The price destination (that is, who will pay the price—the final consumer, independent distributor, a wholly owned subsidiary, a joint venture organization, or someone else)
2. The nature of the product (that is, whether the product is a raw or semiprocessed material, components, or finished or largely finished products, or whether it is services or intangible property—patents, trademarks, formulas, and the like)
3. The currency used for billing (that is, the currency of the purchaser's country, the currency of the seller's home country, or a leading international currency)

The price destination is an important consideration since different destinations present different opportunities and problems. For example, pricing to sell to a government may require special procedures and concessions not necessary in pricing to other customers. A little extra margin might be called for. On the other hand, independent distributors with whom the company has a contractual marketing arrangement deserve a price break. Wholesalers and jobbers who shop around have an entirely different relationship with the exporter as compared to independent distributors.

As products, raw materials and commodities give a company very little leeway for maneuvering. Usually, a prevalent world price must be charged, particularly when the supply is plentiful. However, if the supply is short, a company may be able to demand a higher price.

Escalation of Export Prices

The retail price of exports is usually much higher than the domestic retail price for the same product. This escalation in foreign price can be explained by costs such as transportation, customs duty, and distributor margins— all associated with exports. The geographic distance the goods must travel results in additional transportation costs. Imported goods must also bear taxes in the form of customs duty imposed by the host government. In addition, completion of the export transaction can require passage of the goods through many more channels than in a domestic sale. Each channel member must be paid a margin for the service it provides, which naturally increases cost. Also, a variety of government requirements, domestic and foreign, must be fulfilled, resulting in further costs.

Export Price Quotation

An export price can be quoted to the overseas buyer in any one of several ways. Every alternative implies mutual commitment by the exporter and importer, and specifies the terms of trade. The price alters according to the degree of responsibility the exporter undertakes, which varies with each alternative.

There are five principal ways of quoting export prices: ex-factory; free alongside ship (FAS); free on board (FOB); cost, insurance, and freight (CIF); and delivered duty-paid. The *ex-factory* price represents the simplest arrangement. The importer is presumed to have bought the goods at the exporter's factory. All costs and risks from thereon become the buyer's problem.

The ex-factory arrangement limits the exporter's risk. However, an importer may find an ex-factory deal highly demanding. From another country, a company could have difficulty arranging transportation and taking care of the various formalities associated with foreign trade. Only large companies or specialized trading firms can smoothly handle ex-factory purchases in another country.

The *FAS* contract requires the exporter to be responsible for the goods until they are placed alongside the ship. All charges incurred up to that point must be borne by the seller. The exporter's side of the contract is completed upon receiving a receipt indicating safe delivery of goods and getting the goods through customs. Delivery and transfer of title take place at the side of the ship. The FAS price is slightly higher than the ex-factory price because the exporter undertakes to transport the goods to the point of shipment and becomes liable for the risk associated with the goods for a longer period.

The *FOB* price includes the actual placement of goods aboard the ship. The FOB price may be the FOB inland carrier or FOB foreign carrier. If it is an FOB inland carrier, the FOB price will be slightly less than the FAS price. However, if it is an FOB foreign carrier, the price will include the FAS price plus the cost of transportation to the importer's country.

Under a *CIF* price quotation, the ownership of the goods passes to the importer as soon as they are loaded aboard the ship, but the exporter is liable for payment of freight and insurance charges up to the port of destination.

Finally, the *delivered duty-paid* alternative imposes on the exporter the complete responsibility for delivering the goods at a particular place in the importer's country. Thus, the exporter makes arrangements for the receipt of the goods at the foreign port, pays necessary taxes/duties and handling, and provides for further inland transportation in the importer's country. Needless to say, the price of delivered duty-paid goods is much higher than goods exported under the CIF contract.

Planning for Price Negotiation

To achieve a favorable outcome from a negotiation, an exporter should draw up a plan of action beforehand, which addresses a few key issues. Experienced negotiators know that as much as 80 percent of the time they devote to negotiations should go to such preparations. The preliminary work should be aimed at obtaining relevant information about the target market and the buyers of the product. Preparation should also include developing counterproposals in case objections are raised on any of the exporter's opening negotiating points.[4] So, the preparations should involve formulating the negotiating strategy and tactics.

Knowing what a buyer wants or needs requires advance research. In addition to customers' preferences, an exporter should assess the competition from domestic and foreign suppliers and be familiar with the prices they quote. The exporter should also examine the distribution channels used for the product and the promotional tools and messages required. Such information will be valuable when negotiating with buyers. The more the exporter knows about the target market and the buyers for the products concerned, the better able he or she is to conduct the negotiations and match an offer to the buyer's needs.[5] On the other hand, making counterproposals requires that the buyer know detailed information about the costs of the exporter's production operations, freight insurance, packaging, and other related expenses. An exporter should carry out a realistic assessment of the quantities his or her company can supply and schedule for supplying them. Every effort should be made to emphasize the export firm's size, financial situation, production capacity, technical expertise, organizational strength, and export commitment with compatible buyers.

As part of the preparations for negotiations, the negotiator should list the potential price objections the buyer may have toward the offer along with possible responses. Some of the most common price objections, together with suggested actions, are listed in Figure 7.1. Sellers should adapt this list to their own product, the particular competitive situation, and specific market requirements.

Into Negotiations

The preliminary groundwork should provide a negotiator with enough information to initiate the price negotiation. He or she should know the needs and requirements of the other party. If the subject of price is raised at the outset, the negotiator should avoid making any commitments or concessions at this point. The proceeding talks should include the following substantive topics.

Objectives Importer's Reaction to the Price Offer	Exporter's Possible Response
1. The initial price quoted is too high; a substantial drop is expected.	Ask the buyer what is meant by "too high"; ask on what basis the drop is called for; stress product quality and benefits before discussing price.
2. Lower offers have been received from other exporters.	Ask for more details about such offers; find out how serious such offers are; convince the buyer that your firm has a better offer.
3. A counteroffer is required; a price discount is expected.	Avoid making a better offer without asking for something in return, but without risking loss of interest; when asking for something in return, make a specific suggestion, such as, "If I give you a 5 percent price discount, would you arrange for surface transport, including storage costs?"
4. "The price of $.... is my last offer."	Avoid accepting such an offer immediately; find out the quantities involved; determine whether there will be repeat orders; ascertain who will pay for storage, publicity, after-sales service, and so on.
5. The product is acceptable, but the price is too high.	Agree to discuss details of the costing; promote product benefits, reliability as a regular supplier, timely delivery, unique designs, and so on.
6. The initial price quoted is acceptable.	Find out why the importer is so interested in the offer; recalculate the costing; check the competition; contact other potential buyers to get more details about market conditions; review the pricing strategy; accept a trial order only.

Figure 7.1   Handling potential price objections

Source: Claude Cellich, "Negotiating Strategies: The Question of Price," *International Trade FORUM*, April–June 1991, p. 12.

Emphasize the Firm's Attributes

A negotiator should promote the strength of his or her firm as a reliable commercial partner who is committed to a long-term business relationship. The other party should be convinced that the negotiator is capable of supplying the type of goods needed on acceptable terms. This can be accomplished by stressing the following aspects of a firm's operations:

- Management capability
- Production capacity and processes, quality control system
- Technical cooperation, if any, with other foreign firms
- Export structure for handling orders
- Export experience, including types of companies dealt with
- Financial standing and references from banking institutions
- Membership in leading trade and industry associations, including chambers of commerce
- ISO certification

Highlight the Product's Attributes

Once the other party is convinced he or she is dealing with a reliable firm, negotiations can be directed toward the product and its benefits. The attributes of a product tend to be seen differently by different customers. Therefore, a negotiator must determine whether his or her product fits the need of the other party.

In some cases, meeting the buyer's requirements is a simple process. For example, during sales negotiations, a Thai exporter of cutlery was told by a U.S. importer that the price was too high, although the quality and finish of the items met market requirements. In the discussions, the exporter learned that the importer was interested in bulk purchases rather than prepackaged sets of 12 in expensive teak cases, as consumers in the United States purchase cutlery either as individual pieces or in sets of eight. The exporter then made a counterproposal for sales in bulk at a much lower price based on savings in packaging, transportation, and import duties. The offer was accepted by the importer, and both parties benefited from the transaction. This example illustrates that knowing what product characteristics the importer is looking for can be used to advantage by the exporter.

An exporter may not have a unique product, but by stressing the product attributes and other marketing factors in the negotiation, he or she can offer a unique package that meets the need of the importer.

Maintain Flexibility

In the negotiation process, the buyer may request modifications in the product and its presentation. The exporter should show a willingness to meet such a request if possible. The exporter should analyze whether the product adaptation would allow him or her to run a profitable export business. For example, in one case, negotiation on the export of teak coffee tables was deadlocked because of the high price of the tables. During the discussions, the exporter realized that the buyer was interested primarily in the fine finish of the tabletop. Therefore, the exporter made a counterproposal to supply the coffee table at a lower price, using the same teak top but with table legs and joineries made of less expensive wood. The importer accepted the offer, and the exporter was able to develop a profitable export business.

Offer a Price Package

After covering all of the nonprice issues, the exporter can shift the discussion in the final phase of the talks to financial matters that have a bearing on the price quotation. This is the time to come to an agreement on issues such as credit terms, payment schedules, currencies of payment, insurance, commission rates, warehousing costs, after-sales servicing responsibilities, costs of replacing damaged goods, and so on. Agreement reached on these points constitutes the price package. Any change in the buyer's requirements after this agreement should be reflected in a new price package. For example, if the buyer likes the product but considers the final price to be too high, the exporter can make a counterproposal by, for example, cutting the price, but asking the buyer to assume the costs of transportation, to accept bulk packaging, and to make advanced payment.

Differentiate the Product

In some cases, price is an all-important factor in sales negotiation. The most obvious situation is when firms are operating in highly competitive markets with homogeneous products. Bypassing the pricing issue at the outset of negotiations is difficult when buyers are interested only in the best possible price, regardless of the source of supply. In such a situation, the negotiator should consider differentiating the product from those of the competition in order to shift the negotiations to other factors, such as product style, quality, and delivery.

Guidelines for Price Negotiations

An importer may reject an exporter's price at the outset simply to get the upper hand from the beginning of the negotiation, thereby hoping to obtain maximum concessions on other matters. The importer may also object to the initial price quoted to test the seriousness of the offer, to find out how far the exporter is willing to lower the price, to seek a specific lower price because the product brand is unknown in the market, or to demonstrate a lack of interest in the transaction as the product does not meet market requirements.

If the importer does not accept the price, the exporter should react positively by initiating discussions on nonprice questions, instead of immediately offering price concessions or taking a defensive attitude. Widening the issues and exploring the real reasons behind the objections to the price quoted will put the talks on a more equal and constructive footing. Only by knowing the causes of disagreement can an exporter make a reasonable counteroffer. This counteroffer need not be based merely on pricing; it can also involve related subjects.

To meet price objections, some suppliers artificially inflate their initial price quotations. This enables them to give price concessions in the opening of the negotiation without taking any financial risk. The danger of this approach is that it immediately directs the discussion to pricing issues at the expense of other important components of the marketing mix. Generally, such initial price concessions are followed by more demands from the buyer that can further reduce the profitability of the export transaction. For instance, the buyer may press for concessions on the following:

- Quantity discounts
- Discounts for repeat orders
- Improved packaging and labeling (for the same price)
- Tighter delivery deadlines, which may increase production and transportation costs
- Free promotional materials in the language of the import market
- Free after-sales servicing
- Supply of free parts to replace those damaged from normal wear and tear

- Free training of staff in the maintenance and use of the equipment
- Market exclusivity
- A long-term agency agreement
- Higher commission rates
- Better credit and payment terms

To avoid being confronted by such costly demands, an exporter should from the outset try to determine the buyer's real interest in the product. This can be ascertained by asking appropriate questions but must also be based on research and other preparations completed before the negotiations. Only then can a suitable counterproposal be presented.

Summary

Prices determine the total revenue and, to a large extent, the profitability of a business. When making pricing decisions, the following factors deserve consideration: pricing objective, cost, competition, customer, and government regulations. In price negotiations, these factors must be examined in reference to one's own country and the other party's country. Each factor is made up of a number of components that vary in each nation, both in importance and in interaction.

Price negotiations follow either a cost approach or a market approach. The cost approach involves computing all relevant costs and adding a profit markup to determine the price. The market approach examines price setting from the customer's viewpoint. Export price negotiation is affected by three additional considerations: the price destination, the nature of the product, and the currency used in completing the transaction. Price escalation is an important consideration in export retail pricing. The retail price of exports usually is much higher than the domestic retail price for the same goods. This difference can be explained by the added costs associated with exports, such as transportation, customs duty, and distributor margin.

Satisfactory price negotiations require a negotiator to draw up a plan of action ahead of time with regard to buyer wants, willingness, and/ or ability to pay, and objections likely to be raised on initially quoted price. The negotiator must prepare responses to the objections and decide whether he or she is willing to make a counterproposal on pricing.

While negotiating price objections likely to be raised on initially quoted price, the negotiator should emphasize his or her firm's attributes, highlight his or her product's attributes, maintain flexibility, offer a price package, and attempt to differentiate his or her products from those of the competition. In most negotiations, price is important; however, often at the time of closing, factors such as reliability, reputation, and financial stability are also taken into consideration.

CHAPTER 8

Closing Business Negotiations

In closing, timing is everything.

—Anonymous

Bringing business negotiations to a close requires special skills and techniques. As no two negotiations are alike, no single approach to closing is better than another. Negotiators must use their own judgment in selecting the most appropriate method to close the negotiations.

Methods Of Closing Negotiations

A wide range of methods exists for closing the negotiations.[1] Choice of the appropriate method depends on the existing relationship between the parties, the objectives of the negotiation, the cultural environment, the negotiating styles of the participants, the state of the discussions, and the goal of whether the talks concern new business opportunities or the extension of existing contracts. The following are common methods of closing.

Alternative

Also known as the "either-or" technique, in this approach, one party makes a final offer consisting of a choice for the other side. For example, one party is willing to lower his or her commission rate if the other agrees to deliver the goods to the warehouse at its own cost.

Assumption

With this method, the negotiator assumes the other side is ready to agree and to proceed with detailed discussions of delivery dates, payment schedules, and so on. Sellers use this method frequently to rush buyers into agreement. It is a useful approach when the initiating party has more than one option to offer the other side.

Concession

This method is characterized by the negotiator keeping a few concessions in reserve until the end of the talks to encourage the other party to come to an agreement. It is particularly effective in situations in which concessions are expected as a sign of goodwill before final agreement is given. These last-minute concessions should not be overly generous; they should, however, be significant enough to encourage the other party to finalize the discussions.

Incremental

Another approach is for the negotiator to propose agreement on a particular issue and then proceed to settle other issues until accord is reached on all pending matters. This method is used when the negotiation process follows an orderly sequence of settling one issue after another.

Linkage

Another approach is linking a requested concession to another concession in return. Linkage is usually most effective when both sides have already agreed on the outstanding issues and need to settle remaining ones prior to reaching consensus.

Prompting

Prompting is used to obtain immediate agreement by making a final offer with special benefits if the offer is accepted immediately. The purpose of prompting is to overcome all objections by offering special incentives such as free installation and maintenance, no price increase for next year's deliveries, and free training if the other party agrees to conclude the transaction on the spot.

Summarizing

This method requires one negotiator to summarize all of the issues being discussed, to emphasize the concessions made, and to highlight the benefits the other party gains by agreeing to the proposal. As the discussions near the deadline and consensus is reached on all outstanding issues, one party summarizes the points and asks the other party to approve them. The summaries should be short and should accurately reflect what has been discussed. This approach can be applied in any cultural environment or business situation.

Splitting the Difference

A useful closing method is "splitting the difference," in which both parties are close to agreement and the remaining difference is minimal. At this point, it may be preferable to split the difference rather than continue endless discussion on minor issues that may be secondary to overall negotiation objectives and possibly jeopardize the relationship.[2] Splitting the difference supposes that both sides started with realistic offers; otherwise, this method would give an unfair advantage to the party with an extremely low offer (from the buyer) or a very high offer (from the seller). This is a common method that can expedite closure, but negotiators must ensure that it does not result in an unbalanced agreement.

Trial

Trial is a method used to test how close the other side is to agreement. In a trial offer, one party makes a proposal, giving the other party an opportunity to express reservations. Objections to the trial offer indicate the areas requiring further discussion. By making a trial offer, the initiating party is not committing itself, and the other party is not obligated to accept. Generally, a trial offer results in a constructive discussion on remaining issues while maintaining a fruitful dialogue between the parties until a consensus is reached.[3] This technique is useful to determine what remaining matters need to be clarified.

Ultimatum/or Else

Another method is to force the other party to make a decision on the last offer. If the other party fails to respond or accept the offer, the initiating party walks away from the negotiation. The "or else" method, also known as an ultimatum, is generally not recommended for negotiations in which trust and goodwill are required to execute the agreement.

Choosing A Closing Method

The closing method should be selected during the prenegotiation phase. Once chosen, it must be carefully understood to ensure its mastery. The method selected should fit the environment in which the discussions take place and should match the overall objectives of the negotiations. With experience, negotiators can shift from one method to another or combine one or more as part of their negotiation strategy.[4]

Overall, experienced negotiators prefer either the concession, the summarizing, or splitting the difference method, although the other methods (assumption, prompting, linkage, and trial closings) are effective in certain types of negotiations and cultures.

Time To Close

As nearly every negotiation is different, the time to bring the discussion to a close varies greatly from one situation to another. Timing is also influenced by the cultural background of the negotiators, the complexity of the deal, the existing relationships, and the degree of trust between the parties. For example, when two companies have been doing business for years and are discussing repeat orders, they are likely to arrive at a settlement rather rapidly. Discussions concerning the setting up of a joint venture, however, may take months or years to finalize.

When making a final offer, a negotiator must ensure that the other party has the authority to decide; otherwise, the party may need additional time to discuss the offer within his or her organization. In some countries, where decisions are made by consensus, closing is time-consuming, as negotiators are required to consult other members of the organization for approval. These additional discussions can result in delays as well as further demands for last-minute concessions. To counter such demands, the initiating party must clearly state when making the final offer that any further changes requested will call for a review of all issues on which agreement has been reached.[5]

Clues

A few clues can help experienced negotiators detect when it is time to close the talks. The most obvious one is when the concessions by one party become less important and less frequent, and are given more reluctantly. Generally, this is a sign that no further compromises are possible. Any concessions beyond that point may lead to a breakdown of the negotiations.

In nearly all negotiations, a time comes when both parties have met most of their objectives and are ready to concede on some lesser issues to reach agreement. Up to this point, both sides exchange views to determine their respective needs, validate their assumptions, and estimate the negotiating range and type of concessions required. Most concessions are traded toward the end of the discussions, particularly as the deadline approaches. As much as 80 percent of all concessions are exchanged in the closing phase of the discussions. By this stage, the parties have become familiar with each other's interests, tend to take a creative problem-solving attitude, and usually consider making concessions to reach agreement.

Another clue that it is time to close the discussions is when one party decides he or she has reached a maximum outcome and makes a final offer. This final offer must be made with conviction and must be followed by a request for a firm commitment from the other party. It is sometimes difficult to determine whether the party making the final offer is trustworthy or is simply employing a closing tactic to arrive at a settlement in his or her favor.

Again, a great deal depends on the relationship and trust between the two parties, as well as the cultural environment in which the negotiation is taking place. In some countries, a final offer is considered final, while in others, it conveys a willingness to reach agreement. When making a final offer, the party initiating the proposal must be willing to terminate negotiations if the other side refuses to accept. To avoid breaking the negotiation process, however, the party making the final offer can introduce a deadline for the other side to consider the "final" offer. This gives the receiving side more time to reexamine the proposal and/or to obtain additional facts to make the continuation of the negotiation possible.

In some countries, such as France, negotiators begin the discussions with general principles followed by more specific issues.[6] The party shifting to specific issues is usually expressing its interest in bringing the discussions to a close. In the United States, however, negotiators begin to compromise on specific issues one by one until all outstanding matters have been agreed to. These different approaches illustrate the influence cultural background has on business negotiations and the need for executives to be flexible in concluding international negotiations.

It is widely accepted that negotiators, before agreeing to a final offer, ask for last-minute concessions. Such requests are expected and are part of the negotiating process. To be prepared to respond to last-minute requests, negotiators should keep a few concessions in reserve to maintain the momentum and to encourage the other party to close. These concessions should be valued and appreciated by the requesting party, yet not be too costly to provide. For this reason, negotiators should identify the real needs of the other party and the likely concessions they must make before closing, and build them into the overall package.

Before applying any of the closing methods, the negotiators should ask themselves the following questions:

- Does the agreement meet our goals?
- Will we be able to fulfill the agreement?
- Do we intend to commit the resources required to implement the agreement?
- Do we consider the other party capable of meeting its commitment to the agreement?
- Will top management/stakeholders commit to this agreement?

Only when each question is answered with a "yes" can both parties be ready to bring the discussions to a close.

Deadline

The most obvious sign that it is time to close discussions is when the deadline approaches. Both parties should agree to the deadline in advance, at the initial stage of the negotiation, or when setting the agenda. A deadline arbitrarily set by one party in the course of the discussions can lead to undue pressure on the other side to close.

Deadlines should, however, be flexible. They can be renegotiated to allow the discussions to proceed until agreement is reached. In particular, when negotiators enter into complex discussions in different cultural environments, they should allow for the possibility of extra time when planning the discussions.

Final Points

When a deal is about to be concluded, negotiators need to ask themselves certain questions in order to avoid unpleasant experiences in the implementation phase. In most cases, agreements that run into problems do not suddenly become difficult to implement. Instead, it is generally minor issues that are unattended to or left to degenerate over time that lead to major crises.[7] To ensure smooth implementation, negotiators should ask themselves the following questions:

- Have all the essential issues been discussed?
- Is the agreed-upon proposal workable by both parties?
- Does the agreement clearly specify what is to be done by both sides, including payment terms, delivery schedules, product specifications, and so on?
- Have the major barriers to implementing the deal been identified and the means to overcome them agreed to?
- In case of potential disputes during implementation, what mechanisms have been instituted to resolve them?
- If either of the parties needs to renegotiate the terms, what procedures should be followed?

The executives engaged in the discussions should remain involved in the implementation phase whenever possible. Each party should monitor

Dos:

- Anticipate last-minute demand when planning your negotiating strategy and tactics.
- Agree to an agenda that reflects your objectives and set realistic deadlines.
- Listen to the other party's objections and ask why he or she is not agreeing.
- Emphasize the benefits to be gained by the other party's acceptance of your proposal.
- Look for a change in the pattern, size, and frequency of the other party's concessions.
- Overcome objections by giving clear explanations.
- Take notes throughout the discussions, including your concessions and the ones made by the other party.
- Make your "final" offer credible and with conviction.
- Examine the draft agreement and clarify any points that you do not understand before signing.

Don'ts:

- View the closing as a separate step in the negotiations.
- Be in a hurry to close.
- Make large concessions at the last minute.
- Rush into costly concessions because of deadlines.
- Push your advantage to the point of forcing the other side to leave the negotiations.
- Lose sight of your long-term objectives when getting blocked on minor issues.
- Become too emotional when closing. (You need to think as clearly as possible during the closing.)
- Discuss the deal with the other party once you have agreed. (You run the risk of reopening negotiations.)

Remember:

- Flexibility is the heart of closing a deal.
- Experienced negotiators plan their closing tactics during their preparations for the negotiation.
- Successful negotiators follow their preset goals and concentrate their efforts on essential issues.
- Successful negotiators encourage the other party to close when the time is appropriate because many negotiators are afraid of closing or do not know how and when to close.
- The best time to close is when both sides have achieved their expected goals.
- Successful negotiators close only when the deal is good, not only for themselves but for the other party as well.
- The notion of closing varies in different parts of the world because of cultural factors requiring different closing methods.
- Closing is not done in a hurry.
- Overcoming objections is a part of getting approval of proposals.
- Successful closers seek consensus.
- Buyers often say "no" one more time before saying "yes."
- Nothing is agreed to until everything is agreed to.
- Not all negotiations lead to the closing of a deal. Sometimes no deal is better than a bad deal.

Figure 8.1 Closing a negotiation: Some dos and don'ts

Source: Claude Cellich, "Closing Your Business Negotiations," *International Trade* FORUM, 1/1997, p. 16.

the execution of the contract through the agreed procedures by periodic visits and ongoing communications. By maintaining regular contact, keeping accurate records of all transactions, and paying attention to minor details, the parties can help ensure a smooth business relationship. Figure 8.1 lists some dos and don'ts and points to remember about closing.

Summary

Many negotiators do not know how to bring business talks to a successful close. They should be thoroughly prepared, including knowing when and how to apply appropriate methods and how to respond to the other party's use of closing tactics. By mastering closing techniques, negotiators can achieve agreements that both parties can implement smoothly throughout the life of the agreed-upon transaction. When closing a deal, negotiators should remember that negotiations based on trust and fair play may lead to repeat business and referrals. As it is expensive and time-consuming to find new business partners, negotiators should retain existing ones by agreeing to terms and conditions with which both sides feel comfortable.

CHAPTER 9

Undertaking Renegotiations

Contract is an agreement that is binding on the weaker party.
—Frederick Sawyer

Today's business executives are finding it more and more difficult to negotiate "static" agreements that withstand the pressure of change. As a result, renegotiations are a growing trend in international business. Every day, companies operating in the global arena sign agreements expected to be mutually beneficial and long-lasting. Despite good intentions and iron-clad contracts, unexpected difficulties do arise once contracts are under way, making renegotiations essential.

Too often, at the time of closure, parties assume that the negotiations are over and that both sides can look forward to a successful outcome. In reality, negotiations are only the beginning. A negotiation is not complete until the agreement is fully implemented. With so many unexpected changes occurring in the global marketplace, smooth implementation is the exception rather than the rule.

Although the main purpose of entering into a business deal is to make a profit, frequently contracts turn out to be unprofitable. The parties may also have different interpretations about their respective responsibilities. Thus, continuous monitoring of an agreement is important. And when difficulties arise, parties should not hesitate to undertake renegotiations.

Reasons for Renegotiation

Anecdotal evidence shows that renegotiations are more prevalent in international business than in domestic deals. This is because international business negotiation involves situations not present in domestic settings. When one party believes the deal has become overly burdensome or unreasonable due to changes beyond his or her control, the party considers renegotiation as a distinct possibility over outright rejection. The situations that can lead to renegotiations are examined below.[1]

Dimensions of International Business Environment

International business deals are susceptible to political and economic changes, which are different from those that result when business is conducted at home. Politically, a country may face internal strife, such as civil war, a coup, or a radical shift in policy. On the economic front, currency devaluation or a natural calamity can create conditions not conducive to fulfilling a negotiated deal.

Mechanisms for Settling Disputes

If the other party to the negotiation does not have effective access to the legal system in the negotiator's country, the negotiator may believe he or she has little to lose by not implementing a burdensome deal. Under such circumstances, renegotiation is a satisfactory solution in order to keep the deal alive.

Involvement of Government

In developing countries in particular, international business often entails dealing with government departments or with a public sector corporation, a company that is owned and operated by a government. Governments may refuse to abide by a contract, which they, at a later date, consider burdensome. They may force renegotiation for the sake of the welfare of their people or in the name of their national sovereignty.

Cultural Differences between Nations

Doing business with diverse cultures requires extra care in ensuring full understanding of an agreement's content. For instance, in countries where contracts are lengthy and detailed, little or no flexibility is allowed. In such cases, all possible events that could affect the deal over the period of the contract are identified and appropriate clauses are included in the agreement. To avoid deviations, penalties for noncompliance are built in to ensure strict adherence.

Some cultures are more likely to consider the contract as the beginning of a business relationship. In these cultures, the possibility of reopening the discussions is rather high. Because interpretations can vary due to different cultural views of the negotiation process, negotiators doing business with a different culture seriously consider the follow-up phase and eventual post-negotiation discussions.

Reducing the Need to Renegotiate

In today's dynamic global market, it is difficult to avoid renegotiating business agreements. Negotiators can, however, reduce the frequency and extent of renegotiations by clarifying all major issues, introducing penalties for noncompliance, insisting on regular meetings to monitor implementation, and explaining the negative impact problems can have on future business opportunities. Doing this should alert both parties to their responsibilities and risks.

Conducting business in different parts of the world requires alternative negotiating approaches. In some cultures, negotiations do not end with the signing of an agreement, but continue throughout the duration of the relationship. So that business can take place in these environments, the contract should include built-in early warning signals to detect the presence of problems. Instead of insisting on a detailed, lengthy contract leaving nothing to chance, a shorter agreement acknowledging the possibility of eventual amendments may be more appropriate. Penalties or similar deterrents should be included, however, to avoid potential abuses in critical areas of the agreement.

For instance, when a manufacturer requests an order of spare parts that is larger than the supplier expects, the supplier should consider it a warning signal. Perhaps the equipment is not being used properly or maintenance is inadequate. In this example, the supplier can review clauses concerning warranty, responsibility for repairs, supplying of spare parts, and other matters relating to equipment breakdown. The manufacturer can offer to train operators on proper use of the equipment, adapt the operations manual to local conditions, translate the manual into the language of the user, or agree to participate in the maintenance of the equipment during the initial installation phase. By taking these

> If you can safely answer "yes" to most of the questions below, you are close to entering into an agreement that is unlikely to require much renegotiation. For those questions where the answer is "no," however, you need to conduct additional discussions. When you can answer all the questions with a "yes," you can be fairly certain that renegotiation may not be needed.
> - Does the agreement fit the overall long-term business strategies of both parties?
> - Will both parties benefit from the agreement? (Is it a win-win business deal?)
> - Are you convinced the other party is fully committed to implementing the agreement?
> - Will management support you unconditionally in executing the contract?
> - Are you sure the other party has the capacity (managerial, technical, and financial) to fulfill its obligations?
> - Have all major potential problems been identified, discussed, and resolved?
> - Do you consider the agreement fully enforceable?
> - Are the penalties for noncompliance sufficient to ensure full adherence to the contractual terms?
> - Has a feedback mechanism been put in place to monitor execution of the agreement?

Figure 9.1   Reducing the need to renegotiate

Source: Claude Cellich, "Contract Renegotiations," *International Trade FORUM*, 2/1999, p. 13.

additional precautions, both parties can look forward to the execution of the contract with minimum difficulty.

A question most experienced international negotiators ask themselves at the time of closing is, "What does the contract mean to the other party?" In other words, is it the beginning or end of negotiations? Another key question to be raised toward closing is, "How much is the other party committed to the agreement?" Answers to these and other questions can alert the negotiator to potential problems likely to arise during the life of the contract. Such probing at "closing" should help reduce the need for renegotiation. A more thorough examination is presented in Figure 9.1.

Prevent Renegotiation

Renegotiation can be prevented (or at least minimized) if both parties anticipate the problem ahead of time and make due provision. Another underlying principle relative to renegotiation is this: If costs to the other party of rejecting an agreement are less than fulfilling, the risk of repudiation and renegotiation goes up. Thus, as a matter of strategy, to give stability to an agreement, a negotiator should make sure that sufficient benefits accrue to the other party in order to keep the deal alive. To implement this strategy, a negotiator should follow these steps:

- *Lock the other party in.* This is accomplished by including detailed provisions and guarantees for proper implementation. The agreement should have built-in mechanisms to reduce the likelihood of rejection and renegotiation. These mechanisms either raise the cost to the other party for not fulfilling his or her obligations under the contract or provide compensation for the negotiator for having lost the benefit of the agreement he or she made. The two popular mechanisms for this purpose are performance bond and linkage. Under the performance bond, the other party or some reliable third party (multinational bank, investment house) allocates money or property that is turned over to the negotiator if the other party fails to perform. The linkage mechanism involves increasing the costs of noncompliance to the party that fails to implement the deal. An example of linkage is the formation of an alliance of several banks to finance a project in a developing country. The developing country may find it difficult to go against the entire alliance group by noncompliance of the agreement. The country will find the cost of losing its credibility detrimental to future development plans.

- *Balance the deal.* A successful deal is one that benefits both the parties. Thus, a negotiator should make sure the deal leads to a win-win agreement. If the agreement is mutually beneficial, neither party will consider noncompliance. A balanced deal allocates risks according to the strengths of the parties and not merely on the basis of bargaining power. In addition, unexpected windfalls or losses should be shared by both parties.

- *Control the renegotiation.* This amounts to specifying a clause in the agreement for periodically undertaking intradeal renegotiation on issues that are susceptible to change. In other words, a negotiator should have a provision in the negotiated deal for opening up the deal and undertaking negotiations at defined intervals. It is better to recognize the possibility of renegotiation at the outset and specify a procedure for conducting it. An intradeal negotiation is examined later in this chapter.

Before the contract begins

- Consider negotiations as a dynamic process, requiring constant monitoring of the agreement.
- Build extra costs into the contract to cover future expenses related to renegotiations.
- Make the implementation phase an integral part of the overall negotiation strategy.
- Encourage a healthy relationship between the parties, as it is the best guarantee for a lasting agreement.

During the contract

- Prepare for the possibility of renegotiations—maintain records of all transactions, from initial discussions to the actual execution of the agreement.
- Remember that agreements mean different things to different cultures, requiring flexibility, understanding, and patience.
- Do not blame the other party of any wrongdoing until you know all the facts.
- Do not wait for minor problems to develop into major ones before considering renegotiations.

If renegotiations appear inevitable

- Before beginning renegotiations, consult everyone involved in the original negotiation as well as those responsible for implementation.
- Be sure you clearly understand the factors that trigger the reopening of negotiations.
- Foster constructive discussions between concerned parties, which is preferable to legal recourse.
- Keep long-term business objectives in mind when renegotiating.
- Encourage steps that ensure that all parties are satisfied, even if it means renegotiations. Higher profits come from satisfied parties through repeat business and referrals.
- Do not criticize the other party since you need its cooperation in resolving the issues.

Figure 9.2 Renegotiation: Key points to remember

Source: Adapted from: Claude Cellich, "Contract Renegotiations," *International Trade FORUM*, 2/1999, p. 15.

Build in Renegotiation Costs

Experienced international business executives include potential renegotiation costs in their final offer. Renegotiations can be costly in time and money, and there are ways to build additional costs into the original offer to absorb such future expenses.

One possibility is to separate implementation into several stages, with payment made after successful execution of each stage. This type of agreement is appropriate for lengthy and complex contracts, such as initiating a joint venture. The most effective preparation requires access to accurate information of all past transactions. This helps parties eliminate time-blaming each other for deviating from the agreed-upon terms.

The introduction of penalties for noncompliance is another way to discourage the other party from deviating from the initial agreement. One party giving excessive attention to penalties, however, may indicate his or her lack of confidence in the other party, which could lead to mistrust and resentment. This is hardly the basis for developing a stable business relationship in an ever-changing competitive environment. The key points for dealing with renegotiations are summarized in Figure 9.2.

Overcoming Fear to Reopen Negotiations

More often than not, companies underestimate potential problems that call for renegotiating specific terms contained in an agreement. When something goes wrong, it is only natural that parties get together to resolve the problem. Surprisingly, the party who is the source of the problem is generally reluctant to seek changes or revisions. Often the people in charge of implementation are afraid to address the issue for fear of rejection.

When a business deal is developed in a spirit of cooperation, one party may consider it inappropriate to ask the other party for special conditions, which may be interpreted as taking advantage of the relationship. Fear of receiving a negative answer can lead to missed opportunities for improving the business relationship and fulfilling the agreed-upon terms.

In some cultures, fear of embarrassment is so great that indirect "signals" are sent to indicate the need for revisions. For instance, a sudden lack of communication, vague answers, or an inability to contact the other party, including periods of prolonged silence, may suggest a problem.

As soon as one party sees a problem (for example, products of inferior quality or inability to meet delivery dates), it should take the initiative to contact the other party. It is desirable to take corrective action from the outset by recognizing the problem and suggesting ways of resolving it. Sometimes, lack of international business experience or insufficient knowledge of stringent market specifications means suppliers are not fully aware of what is required to produce top-quality products.

Strict adherence to delivery is another sensitive issue, especially with firms relying on just-in-time inventory. Concerns with delivery are likely to increase in the years ahead as more and more enterprises outsource some of their production and/or services. To minimize problems, executives must maintain open communication lines, make contact early, and be willing to discuss problems openly should they arise.

A real-life example is the case of an Australian furniture importer, who received a large shipment from China in December that exceeded the contract agreement.[2] This unexpected shipment resulted in extra storage costs, handling charges, and other indirect expenses. Instead of lodging a complaint or sending back the extra goods, the importer contacted the supplier immediately. It turned out that this huge shipment was initiated by the export manager since this would have given him a large Christmas bonus. After hearing the views of the supplier, the importer explained the economic hardship caused by this shipment and requested compensation on future orders. By doing so, the importer did not antagonize or criticize the other party, but tried to find a workable solution while expressing a commitment to continue the business relationship over the long term.

Types of Renegotiation

It is unrealistic to assume stability of a contract in a rapidly changing global setting. Although negotiators attempt to anticipate the future and make provisions in the contract for eventualities that may arise later on, it is virtually impossible to foresee every possibility. Therefore, business executives negotiating international contracts realize that ongoing discussions and consultations are necessary ingredients for successful outcomes. Thus, renegotiations are unavoidable.

Four different types of renegotiations are used: preemptive, intradeal, extradeal, and postdeal. Each type is relevant under particular circumstances, raises different problems, and demands varying solutions. In any renegotiation, open communications and continuous monitoring are critical to success. Flexibility, commitment, and recognition that renegotiation may be necessary should be part and parcel of a negotiator's strategy.

Preemptive Negotiation

After a deal has been struck but before it has been implemented, unforeseen events may take place that make it difficult to fulfill the negotiated agreement. Shrewd negotiators control the situation by resorting to pre-emptive negotiation, that is, renegotiation before the disturbing event happens. Preemptive negotiation requires (a) searching for potential problems, (b) creating a mechanism to manage voluntary change, and (c) establishing a mechanism to settle differences and disputes that threaten relations between the two parties.[3]

From a business standpoint, the problems fall mainly into three categories: late performance, defective performance, and nonperformance.

- *Late performance:* Meeting a deadline is the accepted norm in modern-day commerce—goods must be delivered on the appointed day, defects must be corrected promptly, and payments must be made on time. But if a company cannot meet a deadline because of unexpected events at its end (for example, a labor strike) or in the external environment (for example, unavailability of a component), the firm must renegotiate with the other party for late performance.
- *Defective Performance:* Suppose you negotiated to custom-design furniture and deliver it to an overseas buyer. Subsequently, you ordered components and parts to complete the order. As the product was readied to be shipped, you found problems with one of the components. This forces you to renegotiate with the part supplier to correct the defect, give you a price break on the product with the defective component, or to undertake to supply a new product at a later date.
- *Nonperformance:* A furniture factory is not able to fulfill an agreement because of a fire at its warehouse. This requires renegotiation with the other party to invalidate the agreement. The renegotiation may nullify the deal, with no compensation due to the other party, or the firm may become liable for damages due to nonperformance.

Intradeal Renegotiation

The most common type of renegotiation occurs within the life of the contract due to the failure of one party to fulfill its obligations. In such cases, known as intradeal, one party seeks relief from its commitments. Another example of intradeal negotiation is when one party wishes to withdraw from the agreement due to its inability to meet the commitments. This type of renegotiation is often found in small- and medium-sized firms entering foreign markets for the first time. Their limited capacity to meet high-quality standards, to produce large quantities, and to meet strict delivery dates forces them to renegotiate the contract or to request cancellation.

Intradeal renegotiations run smoother when the initial agreement contains a clause that permits them. Acceptance at the outset that specific clauses may need to be renegotiated due to unforeseen events goes a long way toward reducing tensions and misunderstandings. In such cases, renegotiation is regarded as a legitimate activity in which both parties can engage in good faith.

The opportunity to renegotiate also arises when both parties establish specific dates or time frames to review an agreement. For example, when a long-term agreement is put in place, both parties may decide to meet at specified times on a regular basis to review the deal based on the experience gained so far. These meetings also identify issues that arise from changing market conditions.

Intradeal renegotiations are used particularly in countries where an agreement is considered to be more of a relationship than just a business deal. Inclusion of intradeal provisions formalizes their way of doing business—during times of change, parties to a negotiation should meet to decide how to cope with the change.

While periodic renegotiation is worthwhile, where deals extend over a length of time, it does have its downside. First, periodic renegotiation increases uncertainty of the terms agreed upon. Second, it raises suspicion that one of the parties might demand renegotiation using changed circumstances as the excuse to gain better terms for itself. Finally, it questions the validity of the agreement since it is open to renegotiation.

Postdeal Renegotiation

Renegotiations can also take place after an agreement expires. There are instances when one or both parties may decide to wait for the expiration of the contract before reentering into new negotiations. Postdeal negotiations may reflect a change in existing business strategies or may indicate that one party is no longer convinced of the benefits in continuing the business relationship.

In a way, the postdeal renegotiation is similar in process to the initial negotiation although there are some crucial differences. First, the two parties have a shared experience of knowing each other. Each party understands the other's goals, methods, intentions, and reliability, which become a significant input in renegotiation. Second, many concerns relative to risks and opportunities of the deal have been examined and need not be revisited in renegotiation. Third, parties have made investments in money, time, and commitment and are eager to continue the relationship if the result has been mutually satisfying.

Extradeal Renegotiation

This type of renegotiation amounts to dropping the existing agreement and inviting the other party to renegotiate. Generally, there is no provision in the agreement to resort to renegotiation, but if one party claims it is unable to implement the agreement, it may suggest renegotiations. The other party finds accepting renegotiation to be emotionally disturbing because its hopes of expected benefits are shattered. Furthermore, extradeal renegotiations often begin with a feeling of pessimism. In circumstances where renegotiation is the only viable option, parties reluctantly participate as unwilling partners. The environment surrounding extradeal renegotiation is marked with bad feelings and mistrust.

Both parties to the negotiation feel offended. One party thinks the other should appreciate its difficulties and, thus, fully cooperate in renegotiating the deal. The other party feels deprived of the profits expected from the agreement and believes it is being asked to give up something to which it had legal and moral right.

The extradeal renegotiation has a variety of implications for both parties. The party seeking renegotiation may lose credibility in the business community. On the contracts it renegotiates, the other party may demand stricter terms or penalties for noncompliance. The party yielding to renegotiation may gain the reputation of being weak and susceptible to pressure. This can encourage other parties on other agreements to demand renegotiation and better terms. The ripple effect of renegotiation can weaken the yielding party with regard to future deals with other parties.

Approaches To Renegotiation

The following approaches are available for conducting renegotiation.[4]

- *Clarify ambiguities in the existing agreement.* This approach entails appending clarification to ambiguities in the existing agreement rather than creating a new agreement. It accepts the validity of the current agreement, but changes are made in it to accommodate an emerging situation. For example, assume an exporter has negotiated to pay for air transportation of goods to a foreign destination. After a few months, there is a worldwide energy crisis, with the price of crude oil doubling every two weeks. The exporter finds that transportation costs have wiped out her profits, and she cannot afford to continue in business unless the importer agrees to renegotiation to relieve her from excessive air transportation costs. An amendment to the main contract is added with the importer absorbing part of the extra cost of air freight. This nominal change is agreed upon without questioning the validity of the original contract.
- *Reinterpret key terms.* Sometimes terms in an agreement lead to different interpretations based on the background of the parties involved. Under this approach, renegotiation amounts to redefining these terms such that both parties attach the same meaning to them.
- *Waiver from one or more requirements of the agreement.* As a part of renegotiation, the burdened party is relieved from fulfilling some aspect of the agreement.
- *Rewrite the agreement.* If all else fails, the parties may be forced into invalidating the existing agreement and renegotiating a new deal.

Summary

With intense competition, greater outsourcing, and the increase of electronic commerce, renegotiating business contracts is likely to become the norm rather than the rule. Instead of looking at the implementation stage as a separate entity, successful business executives consider the follow-up phases to be an integral part of negotiating strategies.

Renegotiation of business deals may be necessary and can prove to be more profitable in the long term even if renegotiation offers some temporary disadvantages. Global managers know that relying on a contract alone is unlikely to resolve pending issues. Personal relationships and mutual trust are essential in order to build a solid foundation for repeat business in a highly competitive global environment, particularly when doing business in relationship-oriented cultures. Both parties should keep in mind the long-term benefits of a business relationship when renegotiating existing agreements.

Experienced negotiators keep negotiating even after reaching agreement. In the end, satisfying and retaining current customers—by working together in solving problems through renegotiations—is less expensive and less time-consuming than seeking new partners or entering into costly litigation procedures. Skilled executives know that it is not the agreement alone that keeps a business going, but the strength of the relationship.

PART 4
Negotiation Tools

CHAPTER 10

Communication Skills for Effective Negotiations

He who knows does not speak. He who speaks does not know.
—Lao Tzu

With a growing number of countries becoming actively engaged in world trade resulting in intensified contacts between exporters and importers from different cultures, and with increased competition in both domestic and international markets, business executives are faced with a demanding environment for their commercial negotiations. In particular, those in small-and medium-size firms entering the global market for the first time need to master negotiating skills in a multicultural setting. Communication techniques are an important part of these skills. Negotiating is first and foremost about communications. It is a dialogue in which each person explains his or her position and listens to what the other person is saying. During this exchange of views, proposals are made and concessions are explored. The end result is intended to create added value for both parties.

In negotiations, communication occurs at two levels: the logical level (for example, a specific price offer) and the pragmatic level (for example, semantics, syntax, and style). The meaning of the communication received by the other party is a combination of logical and pragmatic messages. What matters is not simply what is said and how it is said, but also the inferred information intended, conveyed, or perceived. Thus, extreme care must be taken to control pragmatic messages. Many times negotiators are not aware of the potential of pragmatic miscommunication, and often, they end up sending a wrong message—even with the best of intentions.

Communication between two negotiators tends to be more difficult and complex when it involves people from diverse cultures than when it involves people with similar backgrounds.[1] For example, negotiators from a traditional culture often attach more importance to the way in which a proposal is made than to what is being said. In such discussions, what is not said may be just as important as what is said. In the opening minutes of the discussions, a negotiator has the opportunity to set the climate of the talks by making a short, clear statement of what is expected. Establishing credibility from the outset is essential if the negotiation is to progress smoothly. The first impression tends to influence the rest of the discussions.

Negotiators discussing in a language other than their mother tongue should rely to a great extent on visual aids, printed materials, samples, and references to facts and figures. The old saying "A picture is worth a thousand words" is appropriate in this context. Furthermore, these negotiators should use simple, clear language with frequent questioning to ensure that the other person is following the discussions. Idioms, colloquialisms, and words with multiple meanings should be avoided. Similarly, certain words or phrases that can irritate the other party should be omitted. For example, phrases such as "To tell the truth," "I'll be honest with you," "I'll do my best," and "It's none of my business but . . ." convey a sense of distrust and make the other person more apprehensive and possibly less cooperative. Likewise, a negotiator should avoid stating or accepting from the other party the reply "No problem" when discussing a specific point. The negotiator should explain what he or she means or seeks clarification about what the other party means.

In addition, one cannot assume that a message has been received and understood in the same way as the person speaking meant it to be. A typical example is when someone answers with a yes or no. In some cultures, *yes* means "Yes, I understood the question," or "Yes, I will consider it," or "Yes, I heard you." In certain cultural environments, the word *no* is uncommon and is replaced by a number of expressions to convey the message in an ambiguous indirect or neutral manner.

In cultures in which conflict avoidance is predominant, the negotiator is unlikely to receive straightforward refusals to proposals, but will get vague responses instead. An inexperienced or unprepared negotiator may interpret these messages as relatively positive, or may be led to believe that the other party is not ready to negotiate or is not in a position to make decisions. Vague replies should be followed by more discussion until it becomes clear what the problem is.

Cross-Cultural Communication-Related Problems

Communication with someone from a different culture can lead to two problems: perceptual bias and errors in processing information.[2]

Perceptual Bias

Perception is the process of attaching meaning to a message by the person who receives the communication. The receiver's own needs, desires, motivations, and personal experience create certain predispositions about the other party, which lead to perceptual bias, such as stereotyping, halo effects, selective perception, and projection.

Stereotyping: Stereotyping refers to assigning attributes to another party based on his or her membership in a particular society or group. Generally, the individual is assigned to a group based on very little perceptual information; then other characteristics of the person are derived or assumed. For example, at the first meeting, you see the negotiator, who happens to be in her fifties; you immediately think of her as "old" and perceive her to be conservative, risk-averse, and not likely to accept new ways of doing things. Cultural differences between negotiators significantly enhance stereotyping.

Halo Effect: The halo effect is the generalization made about numerous attributes of a person based on the knowledge of one attribute. For example, due to the halo effect, a negotiator may be judged as friendly, knowledgeable, and honest simply because he greets you with a smile in your language, following your custom. In reality, there may be no relationship between smiling and honesty, knowledge, and friendliness. Halo effects can be positive or negative. A good attribute leads to a positive halo effect and vice versa.

Halo effects are common in negotiations because people tend to form quick impressions of one another based on limited information such as appearance, group membership, and initial statements. Thus, matters such as clothing, greeting, posture, tone of voice, eye contact, and so on, assume great significance.

Selective Perception: In terms of negotiations, selective perception means choosing certain information that supports one's earlier beliefs and leaving out other information from consideration. For example, based on initial impression, you judge another person as friendly and sensitive to your culture. Later in the day, the person relates a joke that is not in good taste in your culture. According to selective perception, you tend to ignore the joke and remember only the information that reinforces your prior belief that the person has due regard for your cultural values.

Projection: Projection means using one's own attributes to describe the characteristics of another person. Projection occurs because people have a need to project their own self -concept. One person believes that honestly sharing the facts will enhance the process of negotiation. And that person assumes the other person has the same tendencies.

Errors in Processing Information

Negotiations involve sharing information. A person must correctly process the information received from the other party. Often, however, negotiators make systematic errors in processing the information. Such errors or cognitive biases can impede performance. Examples of such errors include the following:

- An irrational escalation of commitment (maintaining commitment to a chosen course of action even if it appears irrational)
- The mythical belief that issues under negotiation are a fixed pie (assuming the negotiation to be a zero-sum game of a win-lose exchange)
- The process of anchoring and adjusting in decision making (the effect of a faulty anchor or standard against which subsequent adjustments are made)
- Issue and problem framing (negotiators' perceptions of risk and behavior are determined by the manner in which a negotiation issue is framed)

- Availability of information (the information made available may be presented badly, leading to bias)
- Winner's curse (the feeling of discomfort generated by a quick settlement of the issue)
- Negotiator's overconfidence (leading him or her to accept less or give up more)
- The law of small numbers (drawing conclusions based on limited experience)
- Self-serving biases (justifying one's errors to unavoidable circumstances)
- The tendency to ignore others' cognitions (ignoring the perceptions and thoughts of the other party)
- The process of reactive devaluation (attaching little value to the concessions made by the other party)

Improving Communication in Negotiation

Communication is the core of negotiation. If communication is disrupted or distorted, negotiation fails. Parties have difficulty coming to an agreement if the communication process breaks down. This is true even when the goals of both parties are compatible. There are, however, techniques for improving the communication in negotiation. These include listening, asking questions, reversing roles, and ensuring clear understanding.

Listening

A major weakness of inexperienced negotiators in any cultural context is their inability to listen carefully to what the other person is saying. Their main concern is usually to present their case and then to counter objections made by the other party. This approach can only lead to a monologue, rather than a real discussion.

The perception that good negotiators talk a lot and dominate the discussions to achieve optimum results is false. In reality, skilled negotiators spend more time listening and asking questions to ensure that they fully understand the other side than they do talking. The ability to listen effectively is fundamental to the success of any business negotiation.

Good listeners do more than listen; they think, analyze, and assess what the other party is saying. They hear everything that is being said, not only what is important to them. By listening attentively, a negotiator can obtain valuable information about the other party and eventually gain more negotiating power. Effective listening contributes to identifying alternatives and options not considered during the preparatory phase. For example, by taking care to listen to an importer's needs and concerns, an exporter can adapt his or her offer and make counterproposals to meet the exporter's requirements.

Good listening habits include observing body language. Studies on the effectiveness of communication reveal that words account for only 7 percent of the message being received versus the voice accounting for 38 percent, and body language for 55 percent.[3] For example, movements such as nodding one's head, inspecting a sample, taking notes, and moving the chair forward indicate interest in what is being said.

An experienced negotiator spends more than 50 percent of the time listening; the remaining time is used for talking and asking questions. By developing good listening skills and asking relevant questions, both parties can move closer to a negotiated agreement.

Three forms of listening can be distinguished: passive listening, acknowledgment, and active listening.[4]

- *Passive listening* amounts to receiving a message without providing any feedback. It tends to show one's complete lack of interest in what the other person is saying.
- *Acknowledgment* involves some interest in the information delivered. The acknowledgment occurs through nodding one's head, maintaining eye contact, or interjecting responses (such as "I see," "interesting," "sure," "go on," and "please continue.") Such acknowledgment encourages the other party to continue sending messages.
- *Active listening* means being thoroughly involved in the messages received and carefully analyzing and attaching meaning to the information contained in the messages. Active listening is characterized by placing greater emphasis on listening than on speaking, responding to personal rather than

abstract points (i.e., feelings, beliefs, and positions rather than abstract ideas), following the other party rather than leading him or her into areas to explore, clarifying what the other party says without diverting attention away from what one thinks or feels, and responding to the feelings the other party expresses.

An experienced negotiator engages in active listening. This encourages the other party to speak more fully about his or her feelings, views, and priorities. In this process, the other party is likely to state his or her position, which often leads to successful negotiation.

Asking Questions

In international business negotiations, one of the most important skills is the ability to ask good questions. By asking relevant questions, negotiators can obtain valuable information from the other party as well as test various assumptions they made when preparing for the discussions. During the preparatory phase, negotiators collect information, but not all data and facts may be available; negotiators need to supplement this information during the discussions. A negotiator should not ask questions to show his or her knowledge of the subject or to impress the other party. Such an attitude can easily lead to a monologue. Instead, questions should be used to obtain information from the other party, to exchange concessions, and to move toward agreement. Therefore, they should be used selectively and they should be timely.

Good questions must be prepared in advance. For example, in the initial phase of the business discussions, exporters present their offers. The importers are most likely to want more details about the product specifications, after-sales service, payment conditions, delivery schedules, quantity requirements, price discounts, and so on. Information about such details is best obtained by asking relevant questions.

Broadly, questions can be classified as open-ended questions, and probing or conditional questions. *Open questions* allow respondents to talk freely about their needs. In such situations, listening to the answers is extremely important as the essential elements must be sorted out, notes need to be taken of the key points, and critical information must be used to phrase succeeding questions. Open-ended questions are useful for clarifying specific points, for seeking details, for obtaining missing information, as well as for validating assumptions. For example, if a buyer refers to a product as being of inferior quality, the seller should ask what standards the buyer is applying, insisting on specifics.

A typical question an exporter is likely to hear after stating price is, "Can you do better than that?" This type of question should be answered with another question instead of a concession. For example, the exporter should reply by asking for clarification, such as, "What is meant by *better*?" or "Better than what?" At that stage, the importer may say that a competitor is offering better terms. Again, the exporter should ask for more details about the conditions and terms.

Before asking a question, particularly in the early phase of the discussions, a negotiator should ask permission to do so. If the other party agrees, he or she is most likely to be more cooperative in replying to the question. Another benefit when the answer is yes is that the discussions begin with a positive answer, which is conducive to a productive atmosphere.

After a series of questions that give both the parties a good idea of what each other wants, the discussions enter into an exchange of proposals and counterproposals. This requires shifting from open questions to *conditional questions*. These are probing questions that seek specific information for repackaging of the proposal. Some of the most useful questions are, "What . . . if" and "if . . . then." For example, the exporter can say, "What if we agree to a two-year contract? Would you give us exclusive distribution rights in your territory?" This question permits one party to make a proposal subject to the acceptance of one or more conditions. The other party can accept the offer, make a counterproposal, or reject the offer. No harm is done in case of rejection. The other negotiator can continue making further conditional offers until common ground is reached.

An example of such conditional questions from the viewpoint of exporters and importers is provided in Figure 10.1. These questions illustrate how one party can make conditional offers while asking reciprocity through concessions. The other party can counter the offers with his or

For the exporter or supplier

- What do you think of our proposal?
- Why don't you give us a trial order to see for yourself our capacity to produce to your specifications?
- If you waive the penalty clause, would you be ready to accept . . . ?
- If we maintain last year's prices, would you place an order by . . . ?
- If we guarantee weekly shipping, would you agree to . . . ?
- Yes, I understand what you are saying. However, would you be ready to consider . . . ?
- Yes, we could meet your additional requirements. But would you be willing to meet the extra costs?

For the importer or buyer

- Can you provide us with the necessary additional information so we can reconsider your offer?
- Can you tell me more about your company's manufacturing process?
- If we give you assistance in this technical aspect, would you agree to . . . ?
- If we modify our specifications, will you consider . . . ?
- What is your exact production capacity?
- What are your quality assurance procedures?
- If we agree to a long-term contract, would you be ready to . . . ?
- What is your price for a larger order?

Figure 10.1   Example of useful questions when negotiating

Source: *Adapted from* Claude Cellich, "Communication Skills for Negotiation," *International Trade FORUM*, 3/1997, p. 25.

her own conditions. The conditional offer allows the negotiating process to move forward until common ground is identified and agreement is in sight.

The use of "what if" is most appropriate when objecting to an offer. By responding with a conditional counterproposal, instead of rejecting it outright with a "no," a negotiator gives the other party the opportunity to provide more details about his or her offer. This exchange of offers and counterproposals eventually leads to the areas important to each side.

A negotiator should prepare a list of key questions in advance since this enhances the effectiveness of the negotiation. The questions should be well thought-out. They should generally be asked to obtain additional information currently unavailable and to test assumptions made when the negotiator was developing negotiating strategies and tactics. These questions should include finding out what is and is not negotiable, what is important to the other party, how badly the other party needs the transaction, and what the other party's minimum and maximum limits are. To gain this information, a negotiator should complete a thorough analysis of his or her strengths and weaknesses along with those of the competition.

Reversing Roles

The role reversal technique implies the negotiator putting himself or herself in the shoes of the other party and, then, contemplating various aspects of the negotiation. This gives the negotiator the opportunity to better understand the position of the other party. For example, another party may insist on certain terms you find unreasonable. But self-reversal role-playing allows you to appreciate the other party's position of asking for the terms. Subsequently, you can come up with a solution acceptable to both of you, that is., modifying your position while responding to the needs of the other party. This way your respective positions become compatible, leading to the agreement.

Ensuring Clear Understanding

Techniques that can help provide clear understanding in negotiations include *restating, rephrasing, reframing,* and *summarizing.* Restatement of the other person's comments encourages clear communication between the parties. Repeating the main issues in different ways by rephrasing them is helpful during the discussions. For example, a negotiator can rephrase what he or she just heard by saying, "If I understand you correctly, what you are really saying is . . ." The negotiator expresses in his or her own words the understanding of the point just made. This technique acknowledges the other person's point of view as well as indicates what was heard.

Reframing is also a useful tool for getting discussions back to the main issues. By reframing, a negotiator recasts what the other party said in a way that redirects attention of the discussions to the core theme that needs to be addressed.

Summarizing is considered a useful tool for bringing negotiations to a close. It consists of one person presenting in his or her own words the points agreed to and asking the other side to approve them. Precise note taking throughout the discussion can serve as the basis for summarizing. If the summaries are accurate, both parties can concentrate on the remaining issues or proceed toward finalizing the agreement. The person presenting the summaries must be careful to be factual.

Nonverbal Communication

Nonverbal communication refers to meaning given to behavior beyond words. It includes body language, facial expressions, physical appearance, space, time, and touch. In the context of cross-cultural negotiations, even when people do not speak a word, through nonverbal communication such as appearance, facial expression, and use of time, they send certain messages to the party. The other party receives the messages and attaches meanings to them. Unfortunately, the meanings a person attaches to nonverbal communication vary from culture to culture. Thus, without intending to do so, a negotiator's nonverbal communication can send a wrong message to the other party, inadvertently harming the negotiations. Therefore, a negotiator must be aware of his or her nonverbal cues to avoid transmitting false or unilateral messages to the other party. After all, 60 percent to 70 percent of meaning in social interactions is interpreted from nonverbal cues.[5]

Figure 10.2 lists the different types of nonverbal behavior. All of these behaviors have an impact on negotiations, as illustrated below.

Body Language

Body movements vary from culture to culture. Consider the following conversation in a hotel lobby with a Japanese businessperson asking the North American about the hotel.

The American responds with a well-known "A-OK" ring gesture. To the Japanese, this means "money," and he concludes that the hotel is expensive. The Tunisian onlooker thinks that the American is telling the Japanese that he is a worthless rogue and is going to kill him. But the

1. Body Language: gestures, body movement, facial movement, and eye contact
2. Vocalics (also called paralanguage): tone, volume, and sounds that are not words
3. Touching
4. Use of Space
5. Use of Time
6. Physical Appearance: body shape and size, clothing, jewelry
7. Artifacts: objects associated with a person, such as office size, office furniture, a personal library, and books.

Figure 10.2   Different types of nonverbal behavior

Frenchman, overhearing the question, thinks the hotel is cheap because the ring gesture in France means "zero."[6]

Aspects of body language vary depending on where people are negotiating. Consider the case of eye contact. In the United States, maintaining eye contact is important because this shows a person is interested in what is being said. In Japan, however, anything more than brief eye contact is considered rude, amounting to invasion of privacy of the other party.

Vocalics

In the United States, people often raise their voice when they get upset. In China, on the other hand, people maintain prolonged silence when they are unhappy, rather than speaking in a loud tone. A wise negotiator should try to behave normally without using this aspect of vocalics to his or her advantage. For example, if a negotiator is not accustomed to pounding on the table to emphasize a point, the negotiator should not do so simply because he or she heard this would strengthen his or her argument in the context of the other party's culture. The best advice to follow is to be yourself.

Touching

In some cultures, people rarely touch each other. In other cultures, touching is common. For example, physical closeness between men is not commonplace in the United States. But men holding hands and hugging each other are gestures of friendship in some societies. In Latin America, a warm embrace, called *abrazo*, is common among well-acquainted businessmen, but is not found in other parts of the world.

What should a negotiator do when touching practices vary worldwide? The best thing to do is to avoid touching at all. This way he or she avoids doing the wrong thing. Just shaking hands is the safest way to avoid the touching dilemma.

Use of Space

In negotiations, space refers to the distance at which people feel comfortable when interacting with another person. In some parts of the world, such as Latin America, Italy, France, and the Middle East, people maintain short distances. The Americans, Germans, Chinese, and Japanese feel comfortable with more space. In addition, such factors as age, status, and gender of the opposite party affect the comfort distance.[7]

When a person with a preference for more space interacts with a person who likes less space, the latter often keeps coming closer to the first person to reduce the distance. The first person then begins to move back to maintain his or her comfort distance. Such a situation becomes very embarrassing for the parties involved.

What should be done when two negotiators have different perspectives on distance? The rule of thumb is to let the host set the distance limit, with the guest adapting to the cultural traits of the host.

Time

Different cultures have varying attitudes about time. In the United States, time is a precious commodity. The U.S. attitude toward time is common among Anglo-Saxons. In many societies, time is a boundless resource. It need not be distributed into time slots. People in such societies are relaxed about schedules and deadlines. If something cannot be accomplished today, it can always be accomplished tomorrow.

In negotiations, the time attitude becomes relevant with regard to three areas: keeping appointments, pursuing the meeting agenda, and devoting time to unrelated items. People who attach more importance to time like to start the meeting on time, like to discuss each item one at a time rather than moving from one issue to the other without any order, and prefer to avoid "wasting" time on unrelated matters. One type of attitude toward time is no better than the other. Both parties should adapt to the needs of the other through mutual respect and understanding.

Physical Appearance

There is a suitable business attire in each society. A person appears properly dressed following the professional perspectives of his or her society. A negotiator can expect the other party to dress according to his or her culture. No adaptation is necessary. A negotiator respects the way the other party appears and the other party respects the way the negotiator presents himself or herself. Not all people are alike. They dress differently and have different customs with regard to physical appearance.

Artifacts

In the United States, a large corner office on the top floor communicates status. Status symbols are common in other cultures too. A guest should abstain from criticizing the host about his or her artifacts. An executive may make positive comments about something with which he or she is familiar, but should otherwise ignore bothersome artifacts. For example, if an executive finds a picture on an office wall to be in bad taste, he or she should just ignore it instead of characterizing the other party based on the picture.

Summary

To negotiate, a person must communicate. In negotiations, communication occurs at a logical level (for example, a specific price offer) and a pragmatic level (for example, semantics, syntax, and style). Communication between negotiators is more complex when the negotiators belong to different cultures even if the discussion takes place in the same language.

Cross-cultural communication leads to two problems: perceptual bias (i.e., attaching meaning to a message received by a person) and errors in processing information (e.g., maintaining an irrational escalation of commitment, considering negotiation to be a zero-sum game, using faulty standards, among others). These problems can be overcome by using the following techniques: listening, questioning, reversing roles, and incurring clear understanding. Three types of listening are passive listening, acknowledgment, and active listening. A good negotiator should engage in active listening. By asking relevant questions, negotiators can obtain valuable information. Two types of questions are open-ended questions and probing or conditional questions. In the context of negotiations, both types of questions make sense depending on the type of information sought. Reversing roles means putting oneself in the position of the other party and examining various aspects of the negotiations. This helps the negotiator understand the position of his or her counterpart. To seek clear understanding in communications, the parties should employ restating, rephrasing, reframing, and summarizing.

Nonverbal communication is equally important in cross-cultural negotiations. Even when a person does not speak a word, his or her appearance; facial expressions; and use of time, space, and touch send certain messages to the other party. Nonverbal communication takes place through body language, vocalics, touching, use of space and time, physical appearance, and artifacts. A person should control his or her behavior related to these matters in order to send the right message to the other party.

CHAPTER 11

Demystifying the Secrets of Power Negotiations

Let us never negotiate out of fear. But let us never fear to negotiate.
—John F. Kennedy

Chapter 2 passingly mentioned various forms of power and how power impacts negotiations. This chapter further explores the subject of power. The chapter is divided into two sections. The first section discusses the sources of personal negotiating power. The second section is devoted to using power effectively.

Sources of Power

Negotiation power has a lot to do with perception. Although power can be real or perceived, what is important is how others see the negotiator. If the other party thinks the negotiator has power, he or she can negotiate from a position of strength. It is commonly believed that executives having personal charisma or representing larger firms have negotiation power. This view is based on the assumption that, due to their status or because they come from bigger companies, executives have the power to achieve their goals, often at the expense of the other party. This, however, may not be true. Generally, the party who comes to the negotiation thoroughly prepared is the one likely to optimize the outcome. Successful negotiators develop their power based on superior preparation and excellent communication skills instead of a reliance on positional or visible power.

Although skilled negotiators rely on both positional and personal power, they tend to give more attention to personal power when preparing for discussions, interacting with the other party, and reaching agreement.[1] Personal negotiating power comes from a variety of sources, discussed below. The core of power is:

- information and expertise—presenting information to prove one's viewpoint or pushing one's viewpoint based on special skills, knowledge, or experience;
- control over resources—influencing the other party through the control of factors of production; and
- location in the organization—leveraging one's position in the organization to gain concurrence from the other party.

Knowing Various Aspects of the Business is Power

Knowing the company business and industry well and showing expertise about the issues being discussed projects an image of power. Because doing business on a global scale is becoming more complex, mastering all of the various aspects provides negotiating power. If there are areas about which an executive does not have much knowledge, he or she can call on staff members to join in the discussions or have them provide a briefing in advance about key issues. The Internet and mobile phones allow executives to reach company experts without incurring the costs of traveling. In case an executive does not have in-house expertise in a specific area, he or she can hire a consultant for the duration of the negotiations. What is important is to have this expertise readily available during the discussions. Displaying expertise at the right time enhances an executive's reputation and gains the executive respect in the eyes of the other party while advancing his or her own goals. The more expertise you demonstrate tactfully, the more power the other party is likely to give you.[2] However, overdoing it can become counterproductive.

Knowing the Other Party is Power

Knowing the other party well increases one's negotiating power. The more an executive knows about the other party's interests, motivation, and negotiating style and what is important to him or her, the greater the negotiating power.

Effective negotiators put themselves in the other person's shoes when preparing their own strategies. If an executive has been dealing with the same party for some time, he or she probably has a fairly good idea of what to expect. Even in such cases, however, it is wise to consider the changes that have taken since the last negotiations. For example, if a new competitor has entered the market and is making headway in the market or if new safety standards are being introduced that could affect product demand, the negotiator should revise his or her strategy.

When negotiating with a new party for the first time, the task is more demanding, time-consuming, and risky. In view of the difficulties of getting reliable information, a negotiator may need to make certain assumptions during the preparatory phase. However, these assumptions should be examined during the initial discussions. The best way to test assumptions is to turn them into questions to be raised when meeting the other party. If a negotiator's early assumptions were incorrect, he or she should ask for a recess to readjust the negotiating plan.

Knowing the other party assumes the negotiator has a clear understanding of his or her negotiating style, whether it is task- or relationship-oriented. On the basis of preparation, the negotiator should be able to predict to some extent the negotiating style likely to be used by the other party. For example, if the other party is relationship-oriented, a negotiator can look forward to accommodating strategies and nonthreatening moves. Of course, the likelihood is that the other party relies on a combination of both approaches. If a negotiator's style differs significantly from that of the other party, the negotiator needs to find out how to best meet his or her own objectives by adapting the strategy and developing appropriate tactics. This advance groundwork provides greater negotiation power.

Knowing the Competition is Power

Knowing the competition is key to making preparations. Unless a negotiator has an in-depth understanding of how he or she compares to competitors, including relative strengths and weaknesses, he or she does not have much bargaining power. Having such knowledge allows a negotiator to plan a strategy that will protect his or her interests as well as contribute to optimizing his or her goals.

If a negotiator has only limited knowledge about what the competition is doing, all the other party needs to say is, "We can get a better deal from the competition" to put the negotiator on the defensive. When the negotiator is prepared, he or she can neutralize this threat by justifying his or her position with valid arguments. Otherwise, the negotiator may be forced to make concessions to meet competitive pressures without finding out what the competition is really offering. Even worse is the fact that the negotiator may begin making unnecessary concessions without receiving reciprocity.

As a part of the preparation, a negotiator must find out whether the other party plans to negotiate with him or her only or with competitors too. If the other party plans to negotiate with several parties simultaneously, the negotiator must decide whether to get involved. If a negotiator is confident about the discussions, he or she should devote all resources to preparing thoroughly. Otherwise, the negotiator should withdraw from the discussions. To avoid being compared to competitors, the negotiator must develop first-rate proposals to differentiate his or her company from them. In fact, negotiators can dominate the negotiations when they know more about competitors than the other party does—and when they know more about competitors than the competitors know about them.

Knowing the competition in the market is crucial for achieving optimum results. Although being well informed is power, knowing how one compares to the competition provides "extra" bargaining power.

Developing Options and Alternatives Extends Power

Going into negotiations with a set of alternatives gives a negotiator bargaining power. Having several firms interested in doing business with his or her company puts the negotiator in a strong negotiating position. Even if you have weak alternatives, it may be sufficient to give you power as long as the other party is not aware of how strong or weak your alternatives are.[3]

Options provide leverage and increase a negotiator's chances of meeting the other party's interests as well as his or her own. When developing options, the negotiator can consider a wide range of possibilities, such as design modifications, packaging alterations, payment terms, faster delivery dates, quality improvements, increase of length of warranty, and performances clauses. The more options and alternatives a negotiator develops, the greater the chances of reaching mutually beneficial outcomes.

Setting the Agenda Is Power

The party setting the agenda automatically gains power. For this reason, experienced negotiators propose to prepare it. By doing so, negotiators make sure their interests are well served. A critical review of the proposed agenda is crucial because it provides useful information: meeting time, place of the meeting, people expected to be in attendance, and the issues to be discussed. Sequence of the issues indicates the relative importance given to them by the initiating party. If a negotiator receives a proposed agenda from the other party for approval or information, he or she should request changes even if the draft is acceptable. By insisting on amendments, the negotiator becomes a real partner in the negotiation, thus gaining valuable bargaining power. Extra care is called for when reviewing the other party's agenda because what is not mentioned is often more important than what is written.

Negotiating in One's Own Environment Is Power

Power means the ability to influence others, and the best place to do so is in one's own environment. That is why successful negotiators propose to have the discussions at their site. Negotiating in a familiar place offers several advantages, particularly when doing business on a global scale. The main benefits are the ability to control the logistics (such as selecting the room, making seating arrangements, and overseeing planned interruptions) and access to staff, experts, and files. In addition, a negotiator does not suffer from jet lag and other discomforts from working in unfamiliar surroundings. It also provides the opportunity to showcase the company facilities.

Unfortunately, negotiating from one's power base is not fully utilized by executives from small and medium enterprises. Because they have limited travel budgets and staff, they should invite their foreign parties to visit them and offer to arrange the negotiations at their own site. Providing services such as booking hotels, facilitating visas, and arranging for cultural and social activities would place them in a dominant position to lead the discussions and control the environment.

When the negotiating parties decide to hold the discussions in a neutral location, the selected site should really be neutral. For example, if the other party has a subsidiary there, the location is not neutral.

Having Time to Negotiate and Setting Deadlines Is Power

Executives who have time to plan and interact with the other party gain valuable negotiation power. This power can be even greater if one party is under time constraints but the other is not. Negotiations do require substantial time for preparation and interface discussions. When a party enters a negotiation under time constraints, he or she may try to skip the early steps of discussions and rush into concessions in order to expedite the process. By doing so, he or she fails to identify the real needs of the other party, including priorities, and fails to build any rapport. On the other hand, the party without time constraints is patient, is comfortable with silence, listens to proposals, accepts concessions, and lets time run out. Consequently, the party with time on hand gains initial information, makes fewer concessions, and eventually takes control of the discussions.

When dealing in different cultures where the notion and value of time differs from that of the negotiator, it becomes crucial to set aside appropriate time to conclude the agreement. Likewise, a complex negotiation or an important business deal calls for the allocation of more time than a routine deal.

A golden rule among effective negotiators is that if you do not have time to negotiate, you should not enter into discussions; otherwise, you will be negotiating against yourself by giving up power to the other party. However, a negotiator can increase negotiating power by setting deadlines according to his or her own time requirements and having them approved by the other party. If, on the other hand, a negotiator does not believe the deadline suggested by the other party meets his or her timing, the negotiator should ask for an extension. If the other party refuses to do so, the negotiator should ask for clarification. If the explanations given are unsatisfactory, the negotiator should insist on rescheduling the negotiations to a date and for a duration that are acceptable to him or her. If the other party refuses to change the timing or is not providing satisfactory answers, the negotiator should reassess his or her strategy or find another party with whom to conduct business. By agreeing to work under tight deadlines to satisfy the other party's time schedule, a negotiator is, in effect, giving away negotiating power to the other side.

Listening Is Power

As negotiation is essentially an exchange of information between two or more parties, the party with superior communication skills gains power. Experience shows that most negotiations fail due to poor communications, particularly due to lack of active and sustainable listening. This is where negotiators can acquire considerable power.[4] Nothing is more important in negotiation than a negotiator letting the other party know he or she is listening. Once the other party realizes that fact, he or she will begin paying attention to what the negotiator has to say. In fact, good listeners send signals to the other party that they are interested in what is being said by asking clarifying questions, paraphrasing, reframing, acknowledging, observing body language, and paying attention to the feeling behind the words. Successful negotiators avoid using negative expressions, as these are likely to lead to breakdowns in the discussions. Only by encouraging understanding and exchanging information can both parties reach the final stage of negotiation.

A good listener also knows the power of silence. At times, the less a person says, the more power he or she receives from others. When asking questions, a negotiator must allow the other party sufficient time to think through the response before replying.

By improving your listening skills, you are putting yourself in an advantageous position to fully explore how best you can reach mutually beneficial outcomes.[5] It is worth remembering that listening brings parties together while arguing pulls them apart. That is why effective negotiators spend most of their time listening attentively to the other party and taking notes while less successful negotiators talk most of the time. When a negotiator smiles while listening, makes the other person feel good, his or her communication power is that much more effective.

Knowing the Bottom Line Is Power

One negotiation power that is often underrated and frequently misunderstood is that of walking away. This is based on one's resistance point or bottom line. In other words, there is a limit beyond which it is no longer worthwhile to continue the negotiations. The bottom line must be based on a thorough calculation of real cost as well as opportunity cost. Knowing his or her bottom line coupled with alternative options to fall back on gives a negotiator greater bargaining power. Unfortunately, this type of power is not fully used by executives from smaller firms because of their inability to take the time to develop their bottom line and alternatives. Not knowing his or her bottom line only places a negotiator in a weak position, which may result in accepting outcomes that prove to be unprofitable in the long run.

Decision Making/ Commitment Power

A type of power that is often neglected is the power to commit. This is a definite advantage when negotiating with larger organizations. With increasing global competition, greater reliance on suppliers, and just-in-time management, negotiators having the power to commit in the closing moments may well walk away with the deal. In contrast, negotiators from larger firms, besides being overconfident when dealing with smaller companies, may have limited authority, needing to seek prior approval from senior management. Not being outguessed by superiors or by committees gives negotiators from smaller firms an advantage because as more people get involved in decision making (whether directly or indirectly), the more delays can be expected. These delays not only slow down the process, but also lead to reopening of the negotiations with the introduction of new proposals, requests for more concessions, or involvement of new players.

Having the power to commit in the closing phase of a negotiation is critical. The party that is able to decide and commit on the spot gains power. Executives negotiating in cultures where quick decisions are associated with successful management performance are likely to find themselves in a dominant position when they have the power to commit.

Summary

Most types of power are within the range of any negotiator. Entering the negotiation with confidence because of preparation enables a negotiator to achieve superior outcomes. Moreover, when a negotiator is well prepared, the other party is respectful and gives the negotiator additional negotiation leverage. As successful negotiating is, to a large extent, the result of excellent preparations, it is desirable to be overprepared rather than underprepared and overconfident.

CHAPTER 12

Managing Negotiating Teams

Teams improve the overall quality of negotiations by finding creative solutions that work for both sides.

—S. Brodt

International negotiations are complex in nature, requiring the input of multifunctional and multicultural teams. Managing such teams can be even more difficult as team members have different interests, priorities, and values. Despite such difficulties, negotiating teams tend to reach more integrative agreements than individual negotiators due to the greater exchange of interests, priorities, and solutions.[1] Generally, teams are expected to negotiate more effectively than individual negotiators. There are several benefits of using teams instead of individuals for negotiations. Some of the advantages that teams have over individuals are listed below.

- Teams have a greater expertise in handling specific/technical issues.
- Teams generate more options/alternatives.
- Teams increase the exchange of information.
- Teams reach higher levels of commitment.
- Teams are better placed to influence/persuade the other party.

Although negotiating teams are considered more effective, there are times their advantage can be affected negatively. Some of the most likely problems facing teams include the following:

- Lack of coordination among the team members
- Poor selection of team members

- Insufficient time for preparation
- Conflict with personal agendas
- Team leader not respected by the members

For negotiations calling for a large number of experts, it is advisable to divide them into groups, subgroups, or task forces to tackle specific/technical issues.

However, there are problems with teams that if not solved can lead to poor outcomes. To remove any personal conflict of interests as well as getting everyone on board and committed to the task ahead, it is essential to carry out internal negotiations during the preparatory phase. The more the team members have in common, the easier it is to build a unified team. For example, in a multifunctional team, the production specialist is primarily interested in the manufacturing process; the financial expert is concerned about costs, payment terms and/or return on investment; the marketing representative wants to discuss promotion campaigns; the purchasing manager is focused on getting the lowest price; the legal adviser wants to discuss contract clauses; the chief negotiator wants to obtain a deal that meets the organization's objectives. It is up to the team leader to bring all these conflicting interests into a cohesive strategy before meeting the other party as a divided team is not in a position to negotiate successfully. Moreover, discipline and cohesion are one of the most critical aspects of managing negotiating teams. In other words, the chief negotiator can be compared to an orchestra conductor. Both have to plan in advance the input of each team member according to a set of guidelines and observe their given role in order to have a unified team.

Team Preparation

Internal negotiations are held during preparations and are often more demanding, stressful, and time consuming than external ones because the people selected to take part in the negotiation may have personal agendas, may have conflicting interests, or may simply be against the negotiations. In fact, one of the biggest challenges facing teams comes from internal conflicts or undisciplined behavior of its members. These preparatory meetings are well worth the investment in time, money, and staff as they ensure management participation in the planning and assessment of the risks involved as well as in evaluating individual performances. If the team consists of members having common goals, it is best suited for regular negotiations, whereas team members having different backgrounds and experiences are more suitable for specialized negotiations. In addition, these internal meetings provide excellent opportunities for reconsidering the team composition if necessary and for carrying out rehearsals. Although rehearsals and role plays are time consuming, they allow the chief negotiator to resolve internal conflicts and identify the best role for each member. Furthermore, these meetings are ideal for explaining the negotiation strategy, tactics, priorities, and when each member is expected to contribute and when not to.

Once the team strategy is agreed, the team leader assigns specific roles and tasks to each member to capitalize on individual competencies. In other words, each member should be made responsible for his or her assigned role. Moreover, team members tend to be more willing to commit if they are included not only in the planning and preparation stages but also in the development of the strategy and in the decision making process. The team leader has to decide when a team member should intervene and when he or she should remain silent. This is particularly relevant in the case of experts as they tend to give more detailed information than is required. For the team leader, it is no easy task to control the individual interests of the group, particularly when a member steps out of line. Too often, individuals wanting to impress their colleagues or to increase their role may negotiate more aggressively with the other party and tend to undervalue their concessions. For instance, during the middle of the discussions, the production engineer agrees to expedite delivery to meet the other party's requirements without considering the extra costs involved. In such a situation, the chief negotiator must discreetly intervene to retake control of the discussions. Moreover, the team must not display any disagreements among themselves at the negotiating table as this will give the other party an opportunity to exploit this internal weakness.

Maintaining discipline among the team is necessary to avoid a breakdown in the strategy.[2] The opposite can also occur when the team leader either ignores or fails to consult his staff when tackling key issues. For

example, in the middle of discussions between negotiators from traditional cultures, one team leader was asked what will be the final price for
an order of 80,000 metallic door handles. Without hesitation, he stated a
price of $2.49 per unit when in fact the reservation price was $2.94. The
offer was immediately accepted. Although the team members realized the
mistake they did not want to intervene to avoid embarrassing their leader
in front of the other party as negotiators having authority do not appreciate having their judgment questioned. By transposing two numbers,
the firm lost $36,000 on the order due to the leader's impatience and
failure to rely on the team expertise. In negotiation, once a concession or
a promise is made, it is not possible to take it back without jeopardizing
one's credibility.[3]

Team Makeup

How the team leader and team members are selected is crucial and must
be carried out with great care. In any negotiation, the chief negotiator has
to have a clearly defined mandate and has to be provided with the necessary resources to carry out the negotiation in the best possible manner.
To be effective, the team leader needs to display leadership qualities and
decision making skills as well as being sensitive to other people's culture.
To maintain a working relationship with the other chief negotiator, it is
better for the team leader to let the technical staff handle toxic issues.
Throughout the negotiations, team leaders should concentrate their efforts on the overall strategy while stressing the benefits to be gained by the
other party through persuasion and cooperation.

In case the other party members consist of several engineers and only
one or two financial analysts, it sends a strong signal that the main theme
to be discussed will be technical. Similarly, if the other party is sending senior executives, it indicates the importance they are giving to the
negotiations. Sending junior staff to negotiate with senior executives in
traditional societies can lead to a breakdown in the discussions as it shows
a lack of respect for status. As can be seen, managing negotiations is a demanding task, especially when the discussions take place away from home
base and in different cultures. Some of the main duties and attributes of a
chief negotiator are listed in Figure 12.1.

• Displays strong leadership
• Consults all stakeholders throughout the process
• Projects confidence and enlists the support of senior management
• Contributes to the development of the strategy
• Ensures that the firm's database is consulted
• Focuses on corporate objectives rather than on personalities or individual goals
• Assigns a specific role/task to each team member
• Presents the team as a unified group in front of the other party
• Resolves internal disagreements away from the negotiation table
• Builds a high degree of loyalty among the members
• Manages one or more rehearsals before meeting the other party
• Encourages group consensus and problem solving
• Communicates clearly the strategy and tactics to the team members
• Knows how to control own emotions
• Shows respect of other culture's values
• Displays patience and understanding of others' viewpoints
• Works well away from home base
• Makes sound decisions under stress
• Demonstrates flexibility in changing conditions
• Is open to the point of view of the other party
• Is willing to take calculated risks

Figure 12.1 Attributes of a chief negotiator

As far as the size of the team is concerned, it is better to limit the team between five to ten members for maximum efficiency. Larger teams are known to be difficult to manage and less effective.[4] For complex negotiations requiring ten or more members, it is best to set up subteams, each one responsible for specific issues. Another possibility for keeping large teams to a manageable size is to rely on availability of experts (internal or external) only when required, or to assign people with low priority expertise to be put "on call." To optimize the inputs from experts, they should participate only when their expertise is required to avoid their intervention in areas outside their competencies, which can be detrimental to their own party. Experts with big egos, quick tempers, or acting individually should be excluded from the team. For negotiations calling for a large number of experts, it is advisable to divide the team into groups, subgroups, or task forces to tackle specific/technical issues.

Sending large teams can lead to delays in decision making, encourage dissension among the members, and provide greater opportunities for the other party to detect individual weaknesses. Another important aspect of team management is the need to speak in a single voice and for the group to enter and leave together.

The use of technical committees is recommended when one party needs to take breaks from on-going discussions to prepare counterproposals, or reconsider its strategy due to new information.

Security Issues

When negotiating international deals, particularly away from home base, there are a number of security issues that must be considered, although this applies to any negotiations. Handwritten notes, messages, proposals, counterproposals, and background documents should not be left behind or placed in a waste bin. Special care is required to avoid leaving documents in the photocopier or throwing away bad copies in the nearby waste basket. Although many firms have paper shredders to destroy documents, they are not always available. If documents require reproduction they should be printed away from the negotiation site to avoid potential leaks. Confidential documents should not be taken to the negotiation meeting unless absolutely necessary. In case the documents are essential to the discussions, they should be carried out by the team leader. Besides protecting yourself from leaking information, all these records provide useful reference material for future negotiation and should be fed into the company's database.

Negotiating in another country may need visas, which can often be difficult and time consuming to obtain. In some countries, visas are given only when an invitation has been extended, placing the visiting party in a relatively weak position. Changing the dates of departures may not be possible due to the dates on the visa or due to problems in obtaining seats on flights. Sometimes, information may be leaked away from the negotiation table. For example, a Western firm was negotiating a significant deal with a company from another continent. After several meetings, the Western firm became suspicious about confidential information being passed to the other party. A security check was carried out at the headquarters and at the negotiation site to locate the source of the leak. The investigation did not find any security breach, yet information continued to leak calling for further investigations. With a little bit of luck, the investigators found out that during the ten hour flights, the firm's negotiators chatted with their nearby passengers. What the negotiators did not know was the fact that the other party had booked adjacent seats with their own informants. Having several of their own people on the flights, they were able to gather sufficient information to decipher the other party's upcoming strategy. To avoid information leaks, the chief negotiator should ensure that no members should be left alone with the other team.

Negotiation Site

Where the negotiations take place does influence outcomes. For this reason, both sides may prefer holding the negotiations in their environment to benefit from the "home court" advantage. The benefits from negotiating at the home base include:

- Selecting the site, seating arrangements, logistics
- Having quick access to staff, advisers, and files
- Showing facilities and landmarks
- Controlling the schedule and social agenda
- Benefitting from deadline pressure
- Saving travel expenses
- Avoiding jet lag (if any)
- Gaining a psychological advantage

There are times, particularly when considering doing business with a new firm located in another country and when holding discussions in the other party's environment is advantageous—for checking on the reputation of the firm, inspect their facilities, its manner of operation. For example, a manufacturer of wood furniture exported most of the produce to several major markets and enjoyed a relatively good reputation abroad. The owner of the firm, however, had a reputation for having poor relations with his workers and management. One day while the owner was attending a trade fair in a foreign country, the factory was completely destroyed by fire. As a result, the buyers had to seek another source of supply at the last minute. Had the negotiations been held at the exporter's home base, the buyers would have had a different opinion of the owner and possibly would have refused to deal with him.

If the parties agree to hold the negotiations at a neutral place, it is essential that it really is neutral. For instance, if one negotiator has lived previously at the selected site or speaks the local language, or the firm has a regional office at that location, is the place really neutral? When one party suggests a specific site, it is wise to make sure that other the party has no hidden agenda or unfair advantage. Small and medium enterprises may suggest meeting at nearby hotels to have appropriate space to hold the negotiations. Although hotels may be a more suitable location, the other party should ensure that the selected site does not favor either side. Irrespective of the location, the chief negotiator should encourage a positive atmosphere during the discussions.

Time of Negotiations

In addition to selecting the chief negotiator, team members, and the site, it is equally important to determine the most appropriate time to hold the discussions, particularly in cross-cultural contexts. Different dates may have different meanings in different cultures. For example, suggestion to start the negotiations on the company or the CEO's birthday sends a positive message. Similarly, holding the negotiations on specific dates is considered to bring good luck while other dates may have negative connotations. In a number of cultures, certain days of the year are considered "auspicious" for initiating negotiations or for the signing of contracts.

For instance, the number 7 is viewed as a lucky number in many Western countries. Therefore proposing to start the discussions on that day of the month is likely to be considered favorably. In these cultures, holding negotiations on the 13th of the month is to be avoided, particularly if it is a Friday, as it could bring bad luck. In Russia, 6 is considered a lucky number. In China, 8 is viewed as extremely lucky as it is associated with wealth and prosperity. In Korea and Vietnam, 4 is considered as unlucky, while in Japan 4 and 9 are associated with bad luck. In addition, there are religious days considered as holidays when business is put on hold. In view of the importance given to numbers in various cultures, it is equally valuable to have the number of team members corresponding to a lucky number prevailing in the counterpart's culture. The same applies to pricing as it is better to round up the last digit to fit the lucky number in that culture.

Summary

How a chief negotiator manages the team can make or break a negotiation. Negotiations are stressful, particularly in international deals requiring the expertise in a wide range of specialized fields. Managing negotiators require rigorous selection of the team members. To control the process, the chief negotiator must be given a clear mandate, obtain the full backing from higher authority, display people skills, maintain discipline, and control the discussions throughout the process. Carrying out internal negotiations before meeting the other party is critical to achieve the intended goal. The worst case scenario to avoid is when the chief negotiator is carrying two negotiations simultaneously, one with his or her own team and the other with his or her counterparts. Companies setting up cross-cultural and cross-functional teams with a strong leader have a competitive edge over other organizations when negotiating complex deals in the global economy.

After concluding a negotiation, the team leader should explain in detail the agreement to all the people expected to be involved in the implementation. That is the time to have a reality check, when implementers may discover that negotiators made too many concessions to get the deal resulting in potential problems when it comes to delivering. That is when most of the difficulties arise. Problems are not like fine wines—they do not get better over time. In the end, it is how the team negotiates that will distinguish it from the competition and open new possibilities for developing personal and business relationships.

CHAPTER 13

Developing an Organizational Negotiating Capability

Negotiation is a core organizational competency.
—Hallam Movius and Lawrence Susskind

Negotiating business deals are becoming increasingly sophisticated and complex, calling for the adoption of an institutional negotiating mindset. To avoid negotiating outcomes that create unnecessary difficulties, negotiators take an integrated institutional framework instead of the ad hoc, short-term, case by case approach. The need to improve the efficiency of organizations negotiating capabilities has been the subject of research in the past decade.[1] As negotiations are becoming more demanding, business executives having access to an in-house organizational culture and capability can look forward to limit risks while negotiating mutually beneficial outcomes.

To build, develop, and maintain an organizational negotiating culture, management commitment is essential. Despite management willingness to build its own organizational negotiating capability, negotiators tend to abandon the institutional approach by switching to an ad hoc style based mainly on competitive tactics. By failing to consider the overall benefits, these firms are likely to face difficulties in the implementation phase, resulting in endless problems, additional costs, and lower profits over the life of the agreement. A successful negotiation reflects not only an excellent preparation but how well the agreement is implemented.

To reach superior and sustainable outcomes, negotiators take a long-term view and expand the number of issues to be negotiated by focusing on common/complimentary interests. In most negotiations, decisions are based on both tangible benefits (economic gains) and intangible ones (noneconomic). Lately, intangibles have become increasingly valuable, particularly in knowledge based industries as well as in highly competitive markets and in traditional societies as they can make the difference between reaching a deal or not. In most relationship-oriented cultures, negotiators may be willing to consider taking a business risk but will be reluctant to risk a relationship. In case negotiators do not have an existing relationship with their counterparts, they can rely on the services of intermediaries.

As mentioned above, a shift from treating negotiation as a spontaneous activity to a collective and coordinated undertaking is starting to take hold. This is particularly beneficial to enterprises doing business in emerging economies where past experiences, trust, and personal ties play a dominant role in reaching agreement. Adopting the institutional approach requires the full commitment of all stakeholders throughout the negotiation process including the postnegotiating phase.

A 2009 benchmark study of the world's largest organizations by Huthwaite International and the International Association for Contract and Commercial Management (IACCM) shows that 80 percent of the responding firms had no formal negotiation process. Moreover, only half of the companies had a system for cross organizational interface. Concerning negotiation planning tools, nearly three out of four firms did not have them. With regard to authority approval from higher management, no more than 50 percent of the firms had formalized it. As far as training is concerned, only one-third of the firms had their employees receiving some sort of training or retraining, mostly of a general nature. To be effective however, training has to reflect employee needs and has to be linked to corporate objectives while taking into account the competitive environment the firm is operating in.

When it came to measuring the performance of their negotiations, over 80 percent of organizations had no established procedures for evaluation. Finally, the survey found that those firms having set up an organizational

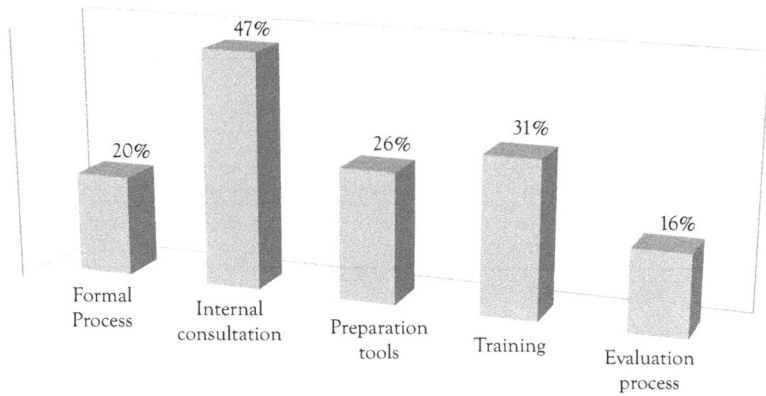

Figure 13.1 Organizations having an in-house negotiating capability

Source: Adapted from "Improving Corporate Negotiation Performance: a Benchmark Study of the World's Largest Organizations", *Huthwaite International & International Association for Contract and Commercial Management*, 2009, UK.

negotiating capability registered significant improvements in net income, while those firms without a formal negotiation process experienced a drop in profitability. Figure 13.1 below illustrates the areas where corporations have introduced an organizational negotiating capability.

The above findings point out that business executives having access to an organizational negotiating capability achieve higher outcomes. In other words, negotiation is not just an individual capability but an organizational one.[2] Organizations experiencing high staff turnover or operating in rapidly changing and competitive business environments would benefit from having an internal negotiating culture and capability.

Comparison of Negotiation Processes

To highlight the major differences between ad hoc negotiations and institutional ones, Figure 13.2 compares these two approaches in terms of setting objectives, preparation, interaction, and postnegotiation/implementation phases.

As success in any negotiation depends on the quality of its preparation, it becomes essential for organizations, particularly those competing globally, to build an in-house negotiating culture and capability. To do so, management sets up an organizational infrastructure that recognizes

Process	Ad hoc Approach	Institutional Approach
Setting objectives	Objectives improvised on a case by case basis	Aimed at optimizing corporate interests
Preparation	Insufficient time allocated	Time made available
	Limited information available	In-house database consulted
	Based on individual capabilities	Based on corporate capability
	Team selected ad hoc	Team selected based on qualifications
	Only own interests and tangible issues considered	Common/complementary interests including both tangible and intangible issues considered
	Team hardly has time to rehearse	Team rehearsals carried out to remove any unexpected issues/ internal conflicts
	Limited number of issues considered	Multiple options developed
	BATNA is not known or estimated lightly	Own BATNA developed and the other party's BATNA estimated
	No internal "buy in"	Cross organizational consultations carried out to reach consensus
	No formal approval process	Higher authority involved throughout the process
Interaction	Often relies on competitive tactics	Problem solving strategies adopted
	Mostly reactive	Proactive behavior stressed
	Seeks quick results with short time outlook	Both short- and long-term implications considered
	Concedes easily and too much to close rapidly	Concessions traded when necessary and reciprocated
	Pricing dominates discussions	Nonprice and intangibles discussed to expand ZOPA
	Fails to consult others	All stakeholders consulted
Post negotiation/ implementation	Irregular feedback	Systematic debriefings held
	Training is "one off"	Training based on needs and priorities
	Not concerned with implementation unless when problems arise	All parties concerned with implementation informed

	No time for review, must move on to other priorities	Time allocated for review as part of process and monitoring system put in place
	Evaluation carried out sporadically	Evaluations carried out regularly
	Lessons learned not recorded	Lessons learned are stored in database

Figure 13.2 A Comparison of ad hoc and institutional negotiation approaches

Source: Adapted from D. Ertel (1999), "Turning Negotiation into a Corporate Capability," *Harvard Business Review*, May/June, p.68.

negotiation as a strategic core competency coupled with a culture of problem solving and relationship building.[3] Furthermore, it would be helpful for negotiators to prepare contingency plans (having a strong plan B) in case the original one does not meet the parties' interests. As preparing for successful negotiations can represent as much as 80 percent of time it takes to complete a negotiation (excluding post negotiations), negotiators should be allowed to devote all their energy to the task ahead and receive full support from senior management. Preparation consists of multiple tasks that include among others, developing a strategy, planning options and alternatives, setting an agenda, identifying concessions to be traded, finding out the other party's interests, priorities, and its BATNA, estimating one's own BATNA, analyzing competition and taking into consideration competitive pressures and how the agreement will be implemented. By establishing a core negotiating capability, organizations provide their executives with access to the latest market information, references to past negotiations, the firm's position vis-à-vis competition, technical expertise, and the time needed to design appropriate strategies and tactics. This calls for organizations setting up and maintaining an up to date centralized database. Although having access to a database is a significant advantage to organizations, most negotiators fail to utilize it.[4]

The institutional/integrated approach differs from the traditional ad hoc negotiation model where competitive strategies and short-term benefits prevail. This is best illustrated by the fact that negotiators have access to over one hundred different competitive tactics but only twenty cooperative ones. In relationship-oriented cultures where business deals cannot be discussed openly unless there is a relationship, negotiators need to take whatever time is necessary to establish a relationship based on mutual trust. This is particularly relevant for those firms seeking business opportunities in Brazil, Russia, India, and China (BRIC), and in other emerging markets where relationship matters most. Experience shows that when negotiators are concerned with preserving the relationship, they tend to leave money on the table. However, in the long run, these suboptimum agreements can become a source of additional benefits from repeat orders, expanding business opportunities or referrals, thereby contributing further to their relationship capital.

Insufficient preparation and the lack of an organizational negotiating capability lead to poorly negotiated outcomes. For instance, in international business, as many as 70 to 80 percent long-term agreements have to be renegotiated at one time or another due to unexpected problems or unforeseen market conditions. Concerning negotiations dealing with mergers and acquisitions, over half of all agreements fail within three years. There are many reasons for these failures including the overemphasis on financial returns, underestimating the dangers of excessive debt, neglecting common synergies, and lacking cultural sensitivity. An example of a failed merger is the Chrysler-Daimler, where Chrysler was negotiating a merger while Daimler was seeking an acquisition.[5]

Structuring In-house Negotiation Capability

By setting up an in-house negotiating capability and promoting best practices, organizations improve substantially their chances of reaching mutual gains that are not only profitable but sustainable. Negotiating global deals require both sides to invest in developing a working relationship and enhance their reputation as world-class organizations. The main elements of an in-house corporate negotiation culture and capacity include the elements shown in Figure 13.3.

Designing an Evaluation System and In-house Database

In an organizational negotiating culture, each negotiation completed or failed is the subject of a systematic feedback to record the lessons learned.

Make the negotiation function a strategic component of the organization core values
Set up a centralized database on past negotiations, competition, and business environment
Link negotiation goals to corporate objectives
Consider both short- and long-term implications
Identify both tangible and intangible issues and benefits
Focus on problem solving strategies, techniques, and solutions
Develop specialized training programs based on company/individual needs
Introduce an implementation mind set among the negotiators
Review compensation policies to reward long-term results based on performance metrics
Establish a monitoring system of ongoing agreements
Emphasize internal consultations throughout the entire negotiating process
Obtain the full backing of all stakeholders before starting as well as during and post negotiations/implementation
Have a rigorous selection process in appointing the chief negotiator and team members
Develop a strong plan B in case the original strategy fails to meet the other party's interests
Leave the door open in the event of a breakdown or an impasse in the discussions
Identify the lessons learned and the way to replicate them in future dealings
Foster an in-house negotiating culture including best practices

Figure 13.3 Main responsibilities of an in-house organizational negotiating capability

During debriefings, both the chief negotiator and team members share their experiences with management and implementers, whether they are positive or not as sometimes more can be learned from past mistakes than from successful negotiations. These debriefings have to take place shortly after concluding a negotiation and documented before important information is forgotten. Another advantage of having these debriefings is to let management and the people responsible for implementation know how the discussions progressed, which were the key issues creating difficulties, and how major objections were resolved. On the basis of these discussions, executive summaries are prepared, distributed to all the concerned parties, and entered into a centralized database. Good record keeping is essential, particularly for renegotiating contracts or when having to deal with the interpretation of the various clauses during the implementation phase.[6] To be of relevance, evaluations have to be specific and factual, and provide advice on how to avoid future pitfalls. This information is most valuable to new negotiators as well as useful for markets characterized by stiff competition, organizations experiencing high staff turnover, and when negotiating complex deals. The rational for setting up evaluation procedures is not only to improve its negotiating capability, but to develop best practices and enhance the organizational institutional memory. Typical questions to be completed soon after a negotiation are listed in Figure 13.4.

Depending on the company's structure and commitment, this list can be elaborated further by seeking more detailed information from past negotiations. What is important for organizations is to recognize the importance of having an effective feedback system that contributes to its institutional memory on a regular basis.

Evaluations may be carried out either by the internal section responsible for evaluation, a special task force, or by an independent evaluator. Generally, evaluations are confidential and not available to the public. There are exceptions, however, when negotiations between multinationals are analyzed for the development of case studies. An example of a case study was the negotiation between Renault and Nissan during an 18 months period in 1998 and 1999. With 15 years of joint operations, the agreement has proved successful for both parties, mainly because Renault's

Was the preparation sufficient to carry out the negotiations successfully? If not, what should have been done?
Did the team leader control the agenda and the process?
Could the team have created more value?
Which party did better and why?
Which party made more concessions?
How did the team handle threats, if any?
Did the team have sufficient background information to convince the other party?
Has the team discussed in detail how each party will implement the agreement?
Was the database helpful? How could it be improved?
What lessons, if any, were learned from this negotiation?
What should the organization do to improve its negotiating capability?
What should the organization do differently next time?

Figure 13.4 Typical evaluation questions

Focus on common long-term goals, complementary interests, and respective capabilities
Prepare extensively, continuously, and jointly as well as internally
Consider new forms of relationship
Behave not only as a negotiator but as a prospective partner
Manage the influence of the other party's no-deal alternative
Assess the quality of an outcome by its effects as well as its content

Figure 13.5   Renault- Nissan negotiation highlights

Source: Stephen E .Weiss. Negotiating the Renault-Nissan Alliance; Insights from Renault's Experience in *Negotiation Excellence: Successful Deal Making,* Benoliel, 2011.

management paid special attention to Nissan's concerns about keeping its identity after the agreement. The analysis of the Renault-Nissan negotiations has led to the recommendations listed in Figure 13.5.[7]

Implementation Phase

For world-class negotiators, reaching agreement is not the end of the discussions but the beginning of a business relationship. Having negotiated a deal is pointless if it cannot be implemented successfully. To reduce risk of noncompliance during implementation, experienced negotiators consider the following key issues throughout the negotiation process:

Generally, preparing well, acquiring negotiation know-how, improving communication skills, and learning from past mistakes increase negotiating power. However, effective negotiators never stop learning from their past experiences.

Create incentives for each party to honor its obligations
Discuss with the counterpart how to overcome potential problems
Identify and brief the people in charge of implementation
Establish procedures to handle conflicts
Plan a transitional period to allow each party to learn how to work together
Hold regular meetings to evaluate implementation
Set up an early warning system to identify problems
Consider sanctions for noncompliance if necessary
Contribute to the database during the length of the contract
Keep all stakeholders informed on the progress of the implementation of the agreement

Summary

Negotiating agreements that do not create difficulties during implementation, particularly in multiyear and complex global deals, are the exception rather than the rule, requiring greater attention to details and constant monitoring. Generally, long-term agreements encounter numerous problems that can be resolved without being confrontational when the parties consider problem solving a joint undertaking due to mutual interests and existing relationships. This requires a shift in negotiating strategies, from an ad hoc approach to an institutional one, and a change of perspectives, from short-term to long-term. This also requires adopting a global implementation mindset. An agreement that satisfies both parties is not only the best guarantee to counter competitive threats but can generate greater profits over the long-term and strengthen the business relationship. Finally, experienced negotiators know that the people involved in implementation want a workable agreement and not problems. World-class negotiators committed to building an in-house negotiating capability and applying best practices are likely to negotiate mutually rewarding and sustainable outcomes while improving the bottom line. In the end, executives adopting an implementation mindset, having access to an organizational negotiating capability, and respecting diverse cultural values can make the difference between success and failure. In other words, successful negotiators possess the following:

- Communication skills
- People skills
- Decision making skills

Effectively combining these three skills are most likely to lead to superior outcomes. For this reason, negotiation is considered more of an art than a science.

PART 5

Miscellaneous Topics

CHAPTER 14

Negotiating Intangibles

The value of intangibles is what the buyer is willing to pay and can be priceless.

—Anonymous

In today's highly competitive globalized economies, intangibles are becoming an important comparative advantage. In fact, in most businesses, intangibles play an increasing role and are likely to grow in the near future. Too often, negotiators focus on trading tangibles, as they can be easily measured, while neglecting intangibles. Tangibles refer to property, equipment, accounts, receivables, cash, prepaid expenses, copyrights, patents, etc. Intangibles are nonphysical in nature and harder to quantify.[1] Intangibles consist of brand, business models, customers' loyalty, designs, employees' motivation and retention, goodwill, R&D, software, trade mark, trade secrets and trust, etc. as elaborated in Figure 14.1.

Intangibles also refer to negotiators' behavior when their underlying psychological motivations may directly or indirectly influence the negotiation.[2] Intangibles are relevant in any negotiation, particularly for complex, long-term business deals, in intensive knowledge-based industries, in services, with start-ups, or in cross-cultural contexts. Over the years, intangibles have increased in importance vis-à-vis tangibles. As shown in the Figure 14.2 below, between 1978 and 2015, intangibles assets have increased from 15 to 85 percent of S&P 500 market value. The rise of intangibles is likely to grow faster than tangibles as a result of the Internet revolution and globalization.

Negotiators planning their future negotiations need to explore the type of intangibles that can influence their decisions. The importance of intangibles can vary from one firm to another and from one negotiator to another calling for extra time during preparatory phase.

Related to the firm	Related to the negotiator
Brand/image	Attentive listener
Business model/processes	Reputation
Certification/credentials	Status
Copyright/patent	Title
Customer lists, customer satisfaction	Testimonials
Customers' loyalty and high retention	Trustworthy
Employees' morale/motivation	Well connected
Goodwill	Reliable
Intellectual property rights	People oriented
Information (proprietary)	Knowledgeable
Market share/position/marketing rights	Consensual
Management commitment	Experienced
Recognition	Shows interest in others
Research and development	Persuasive
Reputation	Prepares well
Software	Views problems from other side viewpoint
Trade mark/logo/label	Think outside the box
Trade secrets	Patient
Unpatented technology	Communicates clearly

Figure 14.1   Short list of intangibles*

*All the above can have either a positive or negative impact on any negotiations

Nature of Intangibles

There are two main types of intangibles: hard and soft, as depicted in Figure 14.3.

The distribution mix between tangibles and intangibles depends on the type of business and issues being discussed as well as the context. In the case of a manufacturing firm, its tangible assets, consisting mainly of plant and equipment, are likely to be greater than its intangibles. The opposite mix is expected for an Internet start-up where its value is mostly made up of intangibles.

Hard intangibles consist of assets having potential economic value such as market exclusivity, underdeveloped patents, intellectual property rights, and brand recognition. Soft intangibles refer to the firm's reputation, management commitment, customer's mailing list, adhering to

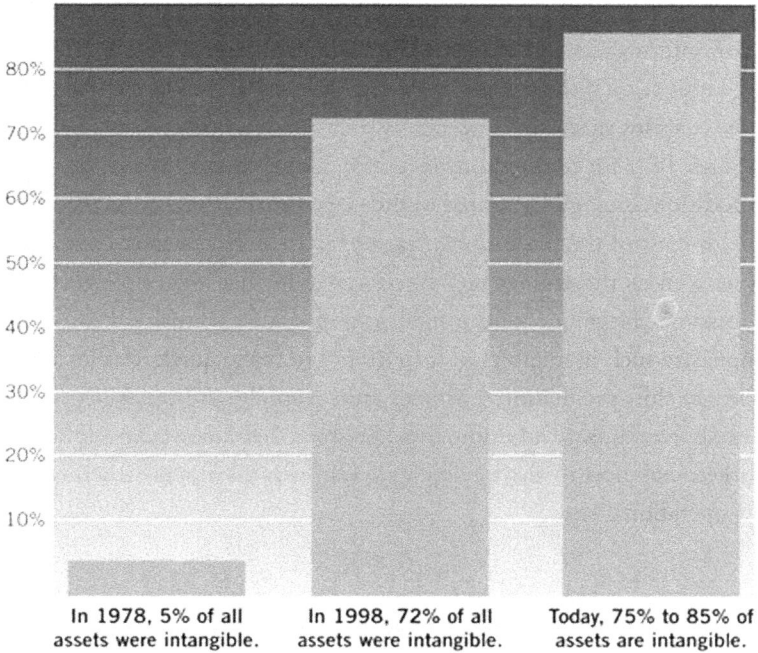

In 1978, 5% of all assets were intangible.	In 1998, 72% of all assets were intangible.	Today, 75% to 85% of assets are intangible.

Figure 14.2   The Growing significance of intangible assets

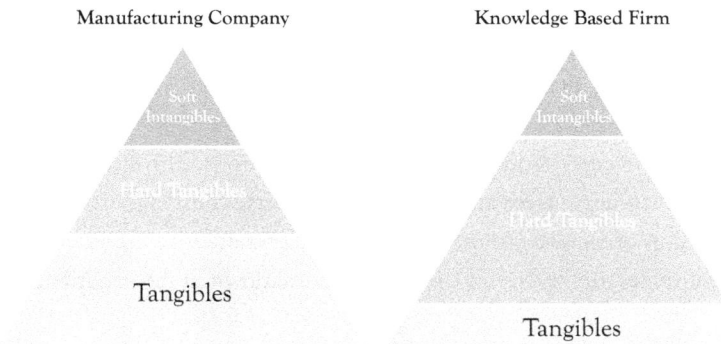

Figure 14.3   Hard and soft intangibles for different firms

corporate social responsibility principles, testimonials, and trust among others. Intangibles are also derived from the negotiator's personal attributes, behavior, and experience.

Of all intangibles, trust among the parties is essential to greater sharing of information and reducing the transaction costs. Trust is critical in any negotiation if the parties are to engage in value creation. In fact, trust is the basis for successful agreements particularly in relationship-oriented cultures. In these cultures, buyers prefer to deal with someone they trust. In addition, intangibles related to the negotiator's behavior, such as being able to control the discussions, fear of failure, need to look competent, to be seen as the winner and so on can influence the outcome of the discussions. Negotiators from small and medium enterprises (SMEs) can emphasize such intangibles as their ability to make quick decisions, flexibility to shift production schedules rather rapidly, and capability to produce shorter runs. In addition, they can stress their knowledge of the local market, closeness to their customers, lean organizational structure, and low operational costs.

Impact of Intangibles

Intangibles can influence the negotiations either positively or negatively. For instance, negotiators representing firms which have a poor image in the market place or have been forced to recall products due to poor quality, or those firms which are facing financial instability, incurring high management turnover, or experiencing frequent labor conflicts are negotiating from a vulnerable position vis-à-vis their counterparts. Similarly, firms losing market share due to increasing competition, experiencing technology obsolescence, having a low retention of customers, and/or declining profits place their negotiators in relatively weak positions. This list can be expanded when negotiators are dealing across diverse cultures, particularly in relationship-oriented cultures, where failure to acknowledge the other party's cultural values can lead to an impasse or a breakdown in the negotiations.

Intangibles and Negotiator Background

Although all negotiators consider tangibles, and to some extent intangibles, experienced negotiators stress both of them to reach mutually beneficial outcomes. With regard to intangibles, negotiators can be grouped into the following four categories:

- Inexperienced negotiator
- Task-oriented negotiator
- Relationship-oriented negotiator
- Global minded negotiator

The relationship between the four types of negotiators is illustrated in Figure 14.4.

Inexperienced negotiators consider mainly tangible issues, usually based on their own interests. This approach is frequently used in short-term transactions of low value where negotiators look for quick results even if the outcome fails to maximize value and/or leads to the negotiations breaking down. In such cases, preparation is insufficient, not much information is exchanged, and the results are likely to be suboptimal.

Task-oriented negotiators stress value claiming (the substantive issues) at the expense of value creating and building rapport with their counterparts. In these negotiations, trust among the parties is less important to reach agreement and concessions tend to be mostly tangibles in nature. Task-oriented negotiators can be more effective when dealing in certain cultural environments, where the market is highly competitive and at times dominated by large firms.

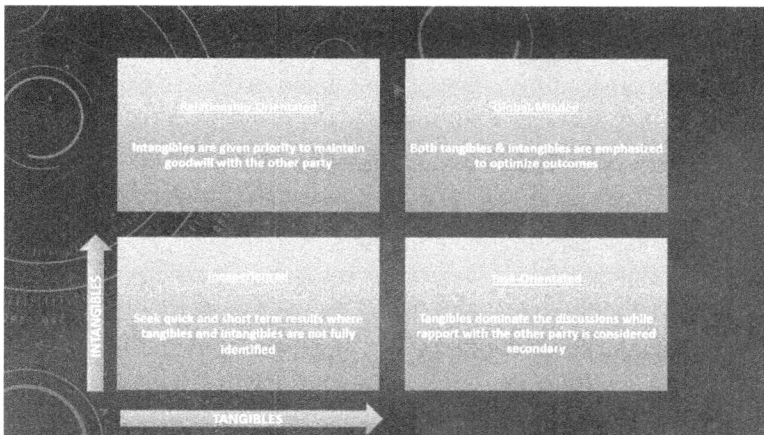

Figure 14.4   Types of Negotiator – Tangibles & Intangibles Matrix

Relationship-oriented negotiators emphasize rapport and trust when dealing with their counterparts. To them, trust is essential to achieve success. In most cultures, the presence of a healthy relationship is a must if the negotiations are not only to take place but conclude. Concessions contain tangibles benefits and a substantial number of intangibles. This type of negotiator is most effective when negotiating services, with SMEs owners, and in multicultural environments where the human factor plays a critical role. In situations where relationship-oriented negotiators are dealing with task-oriented counterparts, they have to be careful not to concede too many concessions (particularly tangibles) for the sake of maintaining harmony with the other party.

Global minded negotiators invest a great deal of time preparing and interacting with the other party. By being global-minded, negotiators seek to have a "big picture" of all the issues, thus enabling them to create and then claim value based on their counterparts interests and priorities. Tangibles as well as hard and soft intangibles are given high priority. Throughout the negotiations, information is shared, creativity is encouraged, and rapport is promoted. This type of negotiator is more suitable for negotiating high-value transactions and long-term contracts. By taking a comprehensive view of the negotiations, global minded negotiators are in a better position to obtain agreements that are mutually beneficial and can be implemented without major difficulties.

Trading Intangibles

Trading intangibles does influence the negotiations process and outcome. Furthermore, by including intangibles in the discussions, the zone of potential agreement (ZOPA) is expanded when negotiators explore their respective priorities, interests, and underlying needs. For example, in relationship-oriented cultures, a negotiator's reputation and trust are essential not only for the meeting to take place but for the discussions to progress. As intangibles have different values to different negotiators, it becomes easier to trade them once the wants and interests of the parties are known. This assumes that both parties trust each other and are willing to trade intangibles that do not cost them very much but are highly valued by the other party and vice versa.

An example illustrating the trading of intangibles took place between the owner of a small retail outlet and a large regional one. The owner decided to sell his business due to approaching retirement age, declining profits, and increasing competition. The buyer made an opening offer that seemed reasonable. However, the owner refused it without giving any justification. Despite receiving better offers (the last one representing a premium over the economic value of the retail outlet), the owner still hesitated to accept the offer. By now, the buyer thought that the owner was not interested in the sale. Instead of making a further offer or withdrawing from the negotiation, the buyer switched strategy by turning his attention to the owner's background, his hobbies, what he would do with his time if he sold the business, and other personal questions until he had a clear understanding of the seller's underlying interests. From these discussions, it became clear that the retail outlet was more than a business to the owner—it was a lifetime achievement. Besides, he did not wish to severe his ties with its long-term customers and loyal employees as some had been with the firm for decades. In the end, the buyer shifted from a task-oriented strategy to a global-minded one by repackaging the offer that contained not only a fair price for the business but a clause that committed the new owner to hire the senior employees of the small retail outlet. In addition, the owner was given a consulting role for an initial period of three years in the new organization with the possibility of an extension.

As the above example shows, intangibles can have greater value to owners of SMEs as they are emotionally attached to their business. Often, owners of SMEs may not be objective or conscious of their firm intangibles while concentrating all their attention on tangible issues. When buyers negotiate with SMEs, they consider both economic and noneconomic benefits. For instance, owners selling their firm may be offered such intangibles as consultancies, an advisory role, an honorary title, the opportunity to keep in touch with their long time and loyal customers, maintaining the name of the firm, keeping the firm facility in the same location, as well as protecting the employee rights and benefits. These and many other intangibles allow the negotiators to discuss multiple options besides economic values that could bring them closer to agreement.

Intangibles and Future Outlook

Negotiating is more than reaching an agreement. It is an opportunity for each party to work together toward a common objective. Often, it is the lack of trust, the absence of a working relationship, and poor communications among the parties that result in conflicts. For example decisions made by the automobile manufacturers giving preference to economic aspects at the expense of intangibles have a negative impact on their profits. The replacement of defective parts, the payment of fines, legal expenses, and damaged reputation could have been avoided by including intangibles and tangibles during the negotiations. By considering suppliers as partners and developing long-term working relationships based on trust and common interests, problems caused by defective parts would not have reached such proportions. A firm that works closely with suppliers by encouraging innovation and sustaining quality improvement processes can expect fewer problems during the life of the agreement.

An example illustrating the role of negotiating intangibles took place recently between Avis and Zip car.[3] Avis agreed to acquire Zipcar for $12.95 per share in cash, a 49 percent premium over the closing price on 31 December 2012. For both companies, the negotiated agreement brought access to each other's intangible assets. By purchasing Zipcar, Avis obtained an immediate entry into the growing market of car sharing, a list of 760,000 customers, a brand identity, a proven business model, a modern reservation system, and rights to parking spaces in selected locations. As far as Zipcar is concerned, it obtained Avis' large fleet of diverse brands, increased utilization of its cars, access to airport locations, and an international network of customers.[4] As car rental and car sharing is partially complementary rather than competitive, the transaction could prove to be a strategic decision provided Avis maintains Zipcar corporate culture and business model. Recent mergers and acquisitions show differences between reality and expectations on the part of the negotiators, where decisions are not made solely on facts but on potential intangible benefits.

Summary

It is no secret that negotiating profitable and sustainable business deals require a thorough understanding of each party's needs and an accurate knowledge of the context in which the discussions are taking place. To do so, negotiators explore tangibles as well as intangibles. In a globalized economy, where e-commerce is revolutionizing business practices, intangibles are becoming essential for enterprises to remain competitive. By developing an appropriate mix between tangibles and intangibles, global-minded negotiators are able to optimize outcomes by expanding the fixed pie through creative solutions.

CHAPTER 15

Negotiating on the Internet

E-launch business activities often have to be carried out in an order that may seem totally illogical.

—Bill Gates

In today's new economy, the Internet is changing the way business is carried out and is fast becoming an important channel of communication. It offers a wide range of business opportunities and challenges for enterprises, particularly those firms seeking new markets. Exporters, importers, suppliers, buyers, and agents are increasingly using the Internet to carry out their business transactions thanks to lower communication costs, reliability, and expediency.[1] As a result of its capabilities, many international executives have started to rely on the Internet for negotiations.

Although the benefits from the Internet are numerous, inappropriate use can result in costly mistakes. In fact, most negotiations carried out over the Internet fail due to a lack of clear communication resulting in misunderstanding between the parties. As negotiation is about communication, negotiators must take the time to craft clear e-messages. By avoiding a few common pitfalls, negotiators doing business on the Internet can greatly improve their performance and optimize their outcomes.

Merits of Negotiations Over the Internet

Because communicating on the Internet is relatively inexpensive, user-friendly, and timely, it is easy to maintain ongoing contact with the other party. The Internet also provides an effective means for a firm to promote its products or services anywhere in the world. By maintaining a website, firms gain instant exposure and visibility worldwide, generating interest from potential customers.[2] Receiving inquiries on the Internet leads to dynamic interaction with quick exchanges of information. Communicating on the Web permits both parties to rapidly reach the concluding phase of negotiations. However, extra care is needed to determine the buyers' requirements, making offers competitive to improve one's chances of establishing a productive dialogue with the buyer. Similarly, the buyer needs to obtain vital information from the seller before considering concessions and counteroffers. Besides it being a neutral communication medium, the Internet overcomes traditional barriers and allows greater interaction with potential partners on a global scale.[3]

Eliminates Time Zones and Distances

Corresponding on the Internet reduces cultural, organizational, and gender barriers. Obtaining face-to-face appointments with key managers and getting involved in the bid process may be difficult for executives representing lesser-known firms. Thanks to the Internet, however, these same executives can communicate with the intended parties without any barriers.

In the e-economy, any business partner regardless of location, availability, time zone, and position can be easily contacted. This is a tremendous advantage considering how busy today's executives are. Even if executives are unable to contact their counterparts, their messages are getting through. Eventually the targeted person will look at his or her computer screen and respond. Being able to reach business partners on the Internet reduces the need to travel abroad, which is time consuming and costly. Today, buyers and importers seeking suppliers are less concerned with specific geographical locations as long as they believe a firm can be reached through the Internet. This option opens up new business opportunities for firms seeking an active role in global trade. More importantly, it projects an image of modern organizations relying on state-of-the-art technologies.

Reduces the Role of Status

Doing business on the Internet provides opportunities for junior or lower-ranked executives to interact with senior managers. In some countries and business organizations with a well-structured hierarchy, higher-ups may be reluctant to negotiate with junior personnel. In such cases, there will be undue delays, risk of changes in personnel, and/or breakdowns in communication. This problem is greatly reduced when the interaction takes place on the Internet. Generally, people are more inclined to respond to inquiries via e-mail regardless of age or status of the other person. The Internet can be considered as an equalizer in situations where status, position, and age are considered essential in negotiating business deals.[4] This point is particularly significant in markets where culture and tradition play a major role in negotiations. In negotiation situations in which one party is more relationship oriented, the Internet should be used selectively with greater attention paid to crafting clear messages and addressing the other party properly. For example, in more traditional cultures, sending a junior executive to negotiate a contract in which a senior executive represents the other side is a disaster in the making.

Erases Gender Biases

The Internet is an excellent medium that can be used to overcome gender biases in business negotiations where women executives are not expected to hold key managerial positions. In specific geographic regions of the world as well as in certain organizations, women decision makers may face difficulties obtaining appointments with key managers or being invited to participate in negotiations. Doing business on the Internet neutralizes, to a large extent, this gender bias while allowing women executives to negotiate with their counterparts on an equal basis.[5] As the Internet reduces the need to travel, women managers are able to more effectively combine family obligations with their professional responsibilities.

Increases Personal Power

E-negotiations provide new sources of negotiating power to those executives who have difficulty interacting effectively in face-to-face discussions. E-negotiations also reduce the risk of discussions failing due to personality conflicts. By negotiating on the Internet, less-confident executives can gain greater personal power, thereby interacting with the other party on an equal, if not superior, basis.

Another benefit of e-negotiations is the home-court advantage enjoyed by both parties. Negotiating from one's own office offers a number of advantages. Besides being able to save on travel expenses and avoiding recuperating from jet lag, an executive has access to his or her files and staff, and to any other expertise needed to carry out the discussions satisfactorily. Selecting the place for negotiations is no longer a sensitive issue when doing business on the Internet.

Allows Simultaneous Multinegotiations

An important feature of e-negotiation is the ability to carry out several tasks simultaneously, including negotiating with other parties to maximize outcomes. For example, after sending out a message, an executive does not need to remain idle while waiting for an answer. Instead, he or she can undertake other priority tasks. Nothing stops the executive from checking out the competition to see whether his or her most recent offer is competitive. To improve the chances of success, the executive can negotiate simultaneously with other interested parties.

Expands One's Audience through New Technologies

With the introduction of new technologies, it is now possible to communicate on the Internet with video and interactive voice communication. Along with the exploding use of sophisticated mobile phones, digital communication generates greater virtual business opportunities. Using chat rooms and discussions groups, executives can negotiate with one or more parties. However, to ensure its effective use, a moderator is needed to manage the flow of communications. Due to technical and practical reasons, it is preferable to rely on the text channel only. Discussion groups are most useful for finding out what customers think of a product or service, for exchanging information, for finding new supply sources, and for testing the market.

Pitfalls of Internet Negotiations

Executives who rely on the Internet to keep in touch with existing customers and to seek access to new markets should be aware of a number of mistakes inexperienced e-negotiators tend to make. E-negotiations increase risk. Although the Internet provides worldwide opportunities, it also results in greater risks due to competitive forces dominating e-commerce. The ease with which companies can access global markets and do business using the Internet not only expands trading opportunities, but also gives more power to buyers. In other words, buyers and sellers must be extremely careful when corresponding via e-mail with business partners. All that is needed for an importer to switch to the competition for a better offer is receiving an unfavorable or unfriendly reply from an exporter.

Conflict Escalation

A danger of Internet negotiations is that the negotiators may become antagonistic, as it is easier to become less agreeable when not dealing with another party face-to-face. Frequently, due to the absence of interface with the other party, e-negotiations can turn to "take it or leave it" offers—hardly the type of business strategies and tactics suitable for negotiating long-term agreements.[6]

Greater Emphasis on Price

E-negotiations allow an executive to carry out multinegotiations without the knowledge of the concerned parties. E-buyers also negotiate with several sellers to maximize their results. As a result, e-negotiations often reflect a lack of cooperation coupled with more competitive moves centered on a single issue, namely, price.[7] Carrying out simultaneous negotiations with several parties may yield better outcomes, but mainly results in one-time deals. Multiparty negotiations are sometimes used to test the market and to determine whether one's offers are within an acceptable range. Generally, these initial contacts do not develop into full-scale negotiations.

Strategies for Negotiations on the Internet

Negotiating from one's office and exchanging information is an easy and comfortable way to carry out discussions. Reading e-messages on a computer screen and sending replies by e-mail is fast becoming an acceptable practice for business-to-consumer and business-to-business transactions. Unless negotiators take notice of the danger of negotiating on the Internet, they may develop "screen myopia" or "tunnel vision." In other words, negotiators enter an interpersonal game where messages are sent and received from one or more partners to obtain the best deal. After several rounds of exchanges, negotiators tend to become obsessed with winning at all costs and begin to take greater risks while relying on more aggressive tactics. By getting involved in this game, negotiators often fail to consider the context in which the transaction is taking place, do not consult others for advice, and forget the long-term consequences or benefits of their actions.[8] This explains the high failure rate of negotiations on the Internet.

Situations Suitable for E-Negotiations

Negotiating on the Internet should be limited to exchanging information, clarifying key issues, and finalizing specific clauses in an agreement. The Internet is also an excellent medium for preparing arrangements for a forthcoming face-to-face negotiation, such as making travel bookings, finalizing the agenda, selecting the location of the meeting, and agreeing to the number of people participating in the discussions. The Internet is also expedient when negotiating a repeat order or a small transaction that does not justify an investment of time, personnel, and financial resources.

To business executives, the Internet provides up-to-date information about the competition and buyers' technical requirements and offers a plethora of timely marketing intelligence. Companies must know who their competitors are and what buyers are looking for before their employees can reply to e-mail inquiries.

Because communication on the Internet is easy and fast, there is a tendency to respond immediately without taking time to prepare well. Negotiating on the Internet is no different than face-to-face negotiations; both require planning, preparing, displaying patience, understanding people, knowing the needs of the other party, and using persuasive skills and problem solving abilities (the four Ps of negotiations, i.e., preparation, patience, persuasion, and problem solving).

As e-enterprise involves receiving inquiries from parties operating in a borderless world, great care should be given to local business practices, legal aspects, and financial considerations. Payment and security concerns are sensitive issues requiring serious assessments, particularly when requests originate from unfamiliar markets or unknown parties.

Proper Planning for E-Negotiations

An executive should take time to think through the full implications of the negotiations on the Internet before communicating with the other party. Once a message is sent, particularly when it is printed, it can be viewed as a legal or binding document by the recipient. Furthermore, what is written tends to be taken more seriously by the other party and may come back to haunt the executive, especially when the message is of a negative or unpleasant nature. Frequently, people use the Internet to send messages without planning and without assessing the long-term implications of their actions. An inadequately prepared message is likely to be misunderstood, resulting in unproductive communication. A consequence could be that both parties may take positional stands, and instead of seeking common ground, they may concentrate on exploiting their differences.

Too often, a party's main concern is to reply as soon as possible. In fact, numerous e-commerce manuals recommend replying within 48 hours. For some business transactions, 48 hours may be too long, for others, 48 hours may not be long enough. Because many executives consider quickness in decision making a sign of superior management skills, they have a tendency to act rapidly. Acting quickly is easier on the Internet as a person is facing a screen instead of people. What is important is for a company representative to give each incoming and outgoing message full consideration, including assessing the risk over the long term and how the message will affect his or her position with their competition. To avoid being overwhelmed with incoming e-messages, the employee should thoroughly screen all incoming messages and set priorities allowing him or her to reply to genuine inquiries only. If the employee needs more time before replying, he or she can send an interim message.

Negotiators must use common sense and sound business practices to maintain open communication lines with potential clients while taking time to be well prepared for upcoming negotiations.

Combining E-negotiations with Face-to-Face Discussions

To reap the full benefits of e-commerce, negotiators may wish to combine off-line, face-to-face meetings with online communication. Despite all

the advantages of doing business on the Internet, when it comes to negotiations, face-to-face interaction is still preferred by most executives, particularly if the value of the deal justifies it. In more relationship-oriented
cultures, online communication should be restricted to exchanging information, while the main issues are discussed off-line. One danger to be
aware of is the impersonal nature of e-negotiations. Trust and confidence
are difficult to establish and maintain solely on the Internet.[9] This is particularly true in situations where one party is only interested in pricing.
Because of competitive pressures, buyers and sellers limit their exchanges
to offers and counteroffers centered on the single issue of price. This scenario is at the heart of too many negotiations, whether they are held face
to face or over the Internet. For example, sending ultimatums ("this is
my last offer") or other forms of competitive moves tends to dominate
e-negotiations. Although pricing is a key issue in any business negotiation, in the end, it is the firm's reputation as well as its capacity to produce
the required quality and quantity, and deliver timely that influence the
decision. For this reason, each party should take the time to explore in
detail what is required and take the time to develop sound proposals that
can withstand competitive pressures and lead to repeat orders over the
long run.

Cooperative Versus Competitive Approach in E-negotiations

Basically, competitive behavior dominates e-negotiations. Given the fact
that e-negotiations are impersonal, executives are inclined to pay less attention to personal relationships and cooperative strategies. This behavior
is reflected by the wide use of irritants, negative expressions, and aggressive tones in e-communications. Moreover, as e-negotiators do not benefit from observing the other party's body movements, a great deal of
information communicated through nonverbal cues is lost.

In e-negotiations, new technologies have an impact on the way negotiations are carried out, particularly on how fast they take place. Because
e-negotiation is basically an exchange of information between two or
more parties until each party's needs are satisfied, e-messages become the
mainstay of communications. But sending ultimatums or responding
with tit for tat is hardly the best approach for building a lasting business

relationship. In any face-to-face negotiation, there is a mixture of competitive and cooperative strategies, with more collaboration prevailing in the concluding phase.

To ensure success, e-negotiators should avoid being too competitive in the early rounds, as such discussions can lead to a breakdown of communications. E-negotiators must encourage the sharing of information in the early rounds, allowing both parties to reach the closing phase through the exploration of joint solutions.

Pros and Cons of E-Negotiations

The Internet has proven to be an excellent vehicle for business-to-business dealings. It is estimated that 80 percent of the growth in e-commerce will come from business-to-business transactions, mainly from global supply chains. Companies wishing to benefit from supply chains need to be connected with these global firms in order to be in contention for their procurements. The direct linkage between buyers and suppliers is likely to result in a restructuring of commercial distribution channels, with less reliance on intermediaries. As buyers' requirements will be accessible to anyone connected to the Internet, greater competition among suppliers can be expected, resulting in lower prices and reduced profit margins. E-negotiators will need to be well prepared to face the competition and must emphasize their technical capacities, delivery capacities, reputation, and long-term commitment. Finally, despite the benefits of negotiating on the Internet, negotiators should continue to travel to their markets to maintain personal contact with customers and to assess the local business environment. Figure 15.1 provides a selected list of tips for negotiators communicating via e-mail.

Summary

Until e-commerce is fully integrated into the global economy and management is committed to this new form of doing business by restructuring their processes, negotiators should continue face-to-face interaction supported by e-exchanges. However, the Internet has changed

Advantages of communicating via e-mail

- Allows access to a wide range of sources of information
- Allows for more time for reflection and research before responding
- Bypass organizational barriers and overcomes age gap/gender differences
- Empowers shy persons and negotiators with low power or status
- Supplements face-to-face negotiations with more information
- Overcomes geographical location and time zones
- Provides for storage and easy access to information
- Reduces personal hostilities, particularly for those persons who cannot control their emotions
- Useful when the negotiating parties do not want their agents to develop a relationship with the other party

Main disadvantages of using e-mail

- Contributes to a higher rate of impasses
- Conveys limited interpersonal information
- Encourages self-centered behavior
- Leads to the greater use of competitive tactics
- Makes it difficult to develop relationships
- Is a one-dimensional communication medium
- Raises security and privacy issues
- Tends to be impersonal

Key points to remember when communicating on the Internet

- Assume that your e-mail may be read by others
- Better to place important issues at the beginning of the text
- Careful who you copy
- Put in extra effort while drafting in cross-cultural contexts
- Focus on clarity
- Keep messages short
- Will be more difficult to detect deceptive tactics
- Use font size 11 or 12

Best to avoid

- Bundling too many issues in one message
- CAPS
- Colors, particularly blue as it is used to display links
- Emoticons, icons, and smileys
- Words that may have a double meaning

• Colloquialism
• Abbreviations that may not be understood by the other party

Figure 15.1 Useful tips for e-negotiators**

** The above tips for e-negotiators are developed from Claude Cellich's book review in the Journal of Euromarketing, Volume 23, Number 3, July-September 2014 for the book E-Negotiations; Networking & Cross-cultural Business Transactions by Harkiolakis, Nicolas with Halkias, Daphene and Abadir, Sam (2012). Gower Publishing, Surrey

the competitive landscape. It has given more power to buyers and has provided greater business opportunities to suppliers, importers, and exporters, regardless of time zones and distances. Thus, negotiations on the Internet are more competitive, impersonal, and adversarial, often resulting in negotiation failures. With e-commerce stimulating competition, firms engaged in business-to-business trade face greater price pressures, higher client turnover, and unpredictable markets conditions.

E-negotiation is no panacea to business-to-business deals, but if used effectively, it can lead to better agreements. Failing to do so, e-negotiators may find themselves without business deals, as other parties switch to the competition with a simple click of the mouse. By and large, e-negotiations are best for negotiating repeat business, taking and confirming orders, initiating trade leads, testing the market, clarifying specific points, obtaining additional information, providing after-sales service, giving details about shipping and deliveries, communicating with existing customers, checking the competition, and preparing for face-to-face negotiations. But e-negotiation success requires sending well-crafted e-messages, considering long-term implications, consulting others before replying, carefully reviewing messages before sending them, being selective when replying, refraining from using negative/irritating expressions, adopting more cooperative strategies, avoiding discussing pricing issues from the outset, and avoiding developing "screen myopia."

CHAPTER 16

Overcoming the Gender Divide in Global Negotiation

A woman with a voice is by definition a strong woman.
—Melinda Gates

Traditionally, it has been held that when men and women negotiate against one another, men derive a better deal. It is because women tend to be more intuitive, people oriented, and patient, while men are aggressive, assertive, and dominant. But these stereotype notions may not be true when you see highly qualified women in positions of authority in the modern world. Although they may project a picture of acceptance, giving, and empathy, when it comes to negotiating, they can be tough and aggressive. It all depends on how one prepares ahead of time to negotiate. As has been said, "Chance favors the prepared mind." Women who prepare themselves will fare better in negotiation than those who don't.

The Gender Divide

There are six main differences that distinguish women from men negotiators: (1) Women want to feel and empathize but men want to prioritize, (2) women want to talk about problems before solving them while men go directly looking for solutions, (3) women notice subtleties among people better than men, (4) women say what they feel and move on to other matters while men tend to hold on to their emotions longer, (5) women feel bad when they are not liked but men feel bad when they don't solve problems, and (6) men and women have different body languages.[1]

Generally, women have different negotiating styles from men—mainly in displaying patience, listening carefully, seeking everyone's opinions, and trying to build consensus with the other parties. By showing interest in other people and focusing on the relationship, a team consisting of men and women executives may have a competitive advantage when negotiating in relationship-oriented cultures. Moreover, women have been found to be less receptive to unethical or deceptive tactics than men.[2]

When comparing the different characteristics of women and men negotiators, men tend to do better at the cost of long-term benefits and lasting relationship.[3] Competitive strategies and adversarial tactics are more suited for one time transactions. For long-term business deals and repeat business, cooperative strategies are more effective than competitive ones, which are more in line with women's preferred negotiating styles.[4] By using a "softer" approach, women negotiators should prove to be more successful as they view negotiations not just as a business activity but as an interpersonal transaction where relationship plays a crucial role.

Women tend to	Men tend to
Be people oriented Focus on building relationships Talk about problems	Be task oriented Focus on reaching agreement Give priority to solving problems
Adopt more cooperative tactics Concede more easily and too quickly Ask fewer questions	Use more competitive tactics Resist making concessions and do so reluctantly Ask a lot of questions
Be patient Be good listeners Use more words/qualifiers	Be impatient Be poor listeners, often interrupting Use few words/forceful and direct language
Talk about other issues Be better at reading nonverbal cues Be emotional	Concentrate on one issue at a time Poor readers of body language Repress emotion
Be intuitive Consult others/seek consensus Talk to build rapport	Be analytical/rational Make quick decisions and then inform others Talk to show knowledge/skills
Be better at understanding others Adopt a conciliatory attitude Seek acceptance	Be too self-centered to fully understand others Adopt a winning attitude Seek respect

Figure 16.1 **Major differences between men and women negotiators**

In other words, the key difference is due to the fact that women have dual roles when negotiating, one being issue-related and the other, relationship-related. By having two goals in mind, women are in a better position to apply collaborative strategies where success depends to a large extent on how the relationship dimension is handled. This assumes, however, that women negotiators know how to counter manipulative ploys, are willing to apply adversarial tactics when needed, are convincing in asking for concessions, and resist conceding too quickly. Figure 16.1 summarizes some of the key differences between men and women negotiators.

The Cultural Divide

The above observations need to be somewhat modified when negotiating in cultures where the role of men and women are different and clearly defined. Hofstede identified five cultural dimensions common to all cultures with different intensity. These cultural categories consist of power distance, individualism versus collectivism, uncertainty avoidance, masculinity versus femininity, and short-term/long-term orientation.[5] Masculinity pertains to societies in which men are supposed to be assertive and expected to seek material success. On the other hand, femininity refers to cultures where both men and women are supposed to be more modest and concerned with the quality of life. For example, masculinity cultures value self-assurance, independence, task orientation and self-achievement. Femininity cultures value cooperation, nurturing, service to others, relationships and consensus.

Negotiators from masculinity cultures are best suited for competitive strategies and adversarial tactics, which often leads to win-lose or lose-lose solutions. On the contrary, femininity cultures value cooperation, relationships, patience, and showing concern for the other party's welfare. This favors collaborative strategies of the win–win type. In countries where women are not fully represented in executive positions, foreign women negotiators will be considered a foreigner first and will be less likely discriminated against than local women negotiators. Women negotiators doing business where gender equality is yet to be attained should emphasize their company's importance, their position in the organization, and should display confidence. Furthermore, a personal introduction or a letter of support from senior management can help overcoming initial resistance from male negotiators.[6]

On the basis of his research, Hofstede classified 53 countries according to their masculinity culture. The countries with the highest index are Japan, followed by Austria, Venezuela, Italy, Switzerland, Mexico, Ireland, Jamaica, Great Britain, and Germany. Femininity cultures include Thailand, Portugal, Chile, Costa Rica, Denmark, Netherlands, Norway, and Sweden.

It is possible to group countries by languages. For instance, German-speaking countries (Austria, Germany, and Switzerland) are mainly masculinity cultures while English-speaking countries (Australia, Canada, Great Britain, Ireland, United States, and New Zealand) are moderately masculinity cultures. Latin countries (France, Spain, and some Spanish-speaking countries) are both masculinity and femininity cultures. Nordic countries (Denmark, Finland, Norway, and Sweden) and the Netherlands are mainly femininity cultures. That explains why many more women are in executive positions in the Nordic countries than elsewhere. Although not exhaustive, such a list is a valuable tool for preparing negotiations in these countries. It is also a fundamental indicator for selecting the team members and team leader.

The Corporate Culture

Corporate culture plays a growing role in business negotiation. Over time, most companies develop their own corporate culture with its corresponding set of values, rules, and policies. Knowing in advance companies policies concerning recruitment and promotion of women to executive positions will help both men and women negotiators identifying what the other side's behavior is likely to be and develop appropriate strategies and tactics. For example, will the other party be led by a women executive or will the team consist of both men and women negotiators? If a company has no clear policy for the advancement of women employees and the negotiating team is all male, it is sending a strong message about its position about gender equality. As each negotiation is rather unique, it is critical to select team members who are both qualified technically and sensitive to cultural diversity, including gender differences.

Managing the Gender Divide

It is well known that preparing for a negotiation is a time consuming and difficult task, particularly in an international context. Successful cross-gender global negotiations are complex and challenging, and are becoming more common place than being the exception. To overcome being stereotyped, women should establish their credentials from the start and present their offers in a clear, brief, and direct language without introducing nonbusiness essential details that may confuse the other party.[7] Figure 16.2 provides hints for negotiators to handle the gender divide.

Studies have shown that women place greater emphasis on relationships by talking about family or personal matters.[8] This reflects the tendency to adopt a relationship negotiating style. Men, on the other hand, tend to prefer the competitive negotiating style. By doing so, they get straight to the point when negotiating

Getting Ready to Negotiate Across the Gender Divide

Dealing with cross-gender negotiations in an international context requires much more preparation than traditional ones. The key to success is to take the time to obtain the maximum information about the other party and to prepare accordingly. In addition, negotiators need to know the national and corporate cultures of the other party, company's policy

---

Hints for women negotiators dealing with men executives
- Start discussing business issues early on
- Project self-confident image
- Show that one is knowledgeable about the issues to be discussed
- Let the other party know that one has the authority to get the deal done
- Avoid being too emotional
- Stay away from competitive tactics that can be interpreted as threats

Hints for men negotiators dealing with women executives
- Improve listening capability
- Show more patience and understanding
- Use a language that is less direct/aggressive
- Display greater flexibility in discussing the various issues
- Avoid relying too much on confrontational tactics
- Be respectful and professional

Figure 16.2 Hints for cross-gender negotiations

towards women equality, past negotiation behavioral style, composition of the team, and the overall context in which the negotiation will be taking place. Having collected this information, the strategy can then be developed, appropriate tactics identified, and team members selected on the basis of their technical and social competencies including gender sensitivity. If the other party is expected to include women executives in their team, it would be wise to appoint a women negotiator in one's own team. In addition, male members should be briefed on cross-gender negotiations and, if time permits, mock sessions should be planned before meeting the other team. According to experienced executives, there is no such thing as an international business negotiation but only an interpersonal business negotiation, where both social and technical competencies are essential to reach optimum results.

Summary

Men negotiators operating in the global marketplace are increasingly interacting with women executives. As more women are moving into senior positions with negotiation responsibilities, overcoming the gender divide is critical for both men and women alike. Until recently, the literature on negotiation has largely ignored the characteristics of women negotiators. Recent research, however, shows that women negotiators can do as well as men if not better due to their ability to listen, read nonverbal signs, consult others, and adopt cooperative moves. As one of the most frequent obstacles in reaching an agreement is misunderstanding among the parties, women negotiators are ideally suited for addressing this problem by taking the time to understand people, discovering the other person's underlying interests while establishing trust and credibility, and encouraging social harmony.

CHAPTER 17

Strategies for Small Enterprises Negotiating with Large Firms

The less powerful parties tend to be creative than more powerful ones.
—Stuart Diamond

In recent years, the trend among large firms has been to merge, form alliances, or outsource to remain competitive in the global marketplace. Large firms, by contracting out value-added activities to smaller external suppliers create greater contacts between large and small enterprises. Due to their size and resources, larger firms tend to obtain more favorable agreements in dealing with smaller ones. Experience shows, however, that negotiators from smaller enterprises, when entering discussions, can improve their outcomes not only by being well prepared but also by being prepared to walk away from potentially unprofitable deals. One of the major weaknesses of smaller firms is to allow the bigger party the control of the negotiating process in the faint hope of getting sizeable contracts.

Larger companies, being well aware of this, encourage smaller firms in the illusion of securing substantially lucrative future business by making them accept major and immediate concessions in current deals. Unfortunately, these future orders might not materialize, or if they do, might easily turn out to be unprofitable for the small firm that has been persuaded into giving away too many concessions. In the long term, these small companies may go out of business due to financial insolvency. There are exceptions, however; for example, a small firm to win recognition in the marketplace wishes to associate itself with a world class leader. In this case, the objective of the negotiation is to reach a deal in order to claim a well-known firm as its client. Whatever the objectives of the smaller firms are, it is important for them to overcome their relatively weak position vis-à-vis the larger party by developing appropriate strategies. This chapter examines strategies which smaller firms may employ to strengthen their bargaining position.

Success Strategies for Smaller Enterprises

Discussed here are strategies that help small businesses in negotiations successfully.

Preparation is the most crucial element in any negotiation. The more complex the deal, the more complex the preparation.[1] This is an area where executives from smaller firms have difficulty mainly due to factors such as having access to few qualified support staff, a lack of information, expertise shortcomings, and, finally, having no clear objectives. As a result, when entering into discussions with larger partners, smaller firms find themselves in a weak position right from the start. To compensate for their lack of preparation, they start making unilateral concessions because of a lack of sufficiently valid arguments to support their proposals. Being prepared means knowing what the other party's needs are, the risks involved, the type of concessions to be traded (by creating and claiming value), and one's position vis-à-vis the competition, and having an alternative plan.

Another advantage of being well prepared is when the more powerful party comes in badly prepared. It is common for large firms to keep their best negotiators for complex business deals, therefore leaving the negotiations with smaller businesses to less experienced junior managers. There are times when at the last moment large firms also send in their senior executives without adequate preparation. This reflects the attitude of large enterprises of not taking their negotiations seriously with smaller firms.

When negotiators enter into discussions pressurized by limited time, they lose control of the negotiation process leading to less than optimum decisions. On the other hand, executives with plenty of time use the clock to their advantage by simply displaying patience.

A golden rule among professional negotiators is if you don't have time to negotiate, don't enter into the discussions. Otherwise you run the risk of negotiating against yourself.

To do well in any negotiation, the party which is ready with prepared options and alternatives is likely to do better regardless of its size. The executive walking into a negotiation with multiple options gains bargaining power. For instance, a small firm having several enterprises as potential clients is better placed both to protect its bottom line and to resist making unnecessary concessions. At times, even with limited options, one may find oneself in control of the discussions as long as the other party is not aware of how strong or weak one's position is. Frequently, the smaller firm is intimidated by the larger firm and fails to face contentious issues and clarify key elements. This is often due to insufficient technical expertise to master all the essential points in the negotiation. Hiring experts on a short term basis is an effective way of overcoming deficiencies. The more options one develops, the greater the chances of reaching one's goals and protecting profit margins. One particular danger to avoid is having one major client accounting for the bulk of the revenue. Unless one has a unique product, service, or technology not available anywhere else, this stops one from negotiating effectively.

Find Out How Important the Deal is to the Large Firm: Determine Your Bargaining Leverage

Most importantly, before contacting the larger party, the smaller firm must find out how important the deal is to the larger enterprise. The importance of the deal will determine which strategy and tactics the smaller firm needs to develop. According to the 80/20 principle, 20 percent of the number of items purchased by a large firm accounts for about 80 percent of the total budget.[2] The remaining 80 percent of the items represent only 20 percent of the expenditure. As a result, the smaller firm must find out whether its product or service is marginal or part of the core business of the larger party. Most firms want to deal with core products or services because of the potential size of the business. However, the terms and conditions for core products are highly demanding. Moreover, the competition is at its most severe. This calls for detailed preparation and taking a long-term approach in order to develop a sound business relationship. Even if an offer is marginal to the other party and unappealing to others, a new business opportunity may present itself where competition is less fierce.

Associate Yourself with Recognized Organizations: Become a Recognized Player

To increase their negotiating power, smaller firms seek to associate themselves with better known enterprises who already enjoy international status. Furthermore, it is essential in today's market for smaller firms to obtain certification from recognized standard organizations. For instance, large enterprises that outsource part of their requirements insist on doing business only with firms that are certified as having ISO 9000. In the case of food products and pharmaceuticals, the USFDA certification is essential because of its international recognition. Similarly, firms attaining the appropriate European Union standards are allowed to do business in any of the member states. With the enlargement of the EU to 25 members, smaller firms can now access a bigger market than ever before. Relying on a world-renowned inspection agency to guarantee that the goods being shipped are in accordance to the pro-forma invoice adds bargaining strength.

Select Large Firms in Difficulty: Get Your Foot in the Door

Probably the most demanding negotiation for a small firm is obtaining the first order from a larger enterprise. Once you are doing business with larger partners, you are taken more seriously in the global marketplace. Although representatives of larger enterprises seek the best deal, they might, when having major difficulties, be more flexible and understanding with new suppliers. For example, when a firm is going through a time of crisis that makes current suppliers nervous about continuing doing business with it, it is the time for a new supplier to begin negotiations with the firm. Moreover, preparations on the part of the large enterprise may be less than adequate because of inside dissentions that hinder the effective management of daily operations. In these circumstances, a small firm could well negotiate a deal that would have been impossible under normal conditions.

Identify Individual Units Within the Larger Firm: Build Your Network

When considering doing business with a larger firm, it is advisable to identify single units within the organization.[3] Generally, large corporations can consist of numerous divisions, departments, or separate companies in which they have a controlling interest. As more and more organizations decentralize and give greater decision making authority to their managers, a smaller firm must identify the right contacts in order to create a better chance for itself. The aim is for the small firm to negotiate with the people from the larger organization who actually deal with the product. Often, large, successful companies establish small, autonomous divisions and units to stimulate individual initiative, internal entrepreneurship, and risk-taking.[4] In addition, it is important to be sure that these people have decision making authority. If case decisions are made by committees or by other senior executives, smaller companies can save time by providing the relevant information that committee members of the larger firm will require to conclude a deal. Another important point for smaller firms is to find out the extent of the other party's decision making authority. For example, suppose a smaller firm is negotiating an order worth $1.5 million, but the larger firm's representative only has the authority to negotiate deals up to $1 million. Thus, any orders above that amount must be approved by a committee of senior executives. If the small firm splits the order into smaller amounts that fall within the authority of the representative, the deal can be concluded without having to wait for a committee decision. For example, the smaller firm can propose a trial order worth $300,000 to be followed by two orders of $600,000 each. By doing this one concludes the negotiation with the counterpart without further discussions or delay.

Involve the Real User or Decision Maker in the Discussion: Be a Problem Solver

A typical situation that smaller firms find themselves in when dealing with large parties is that they have to negotiate with buyers from the purchasing department. Professional buyers must necessarily seek the best conditions from suppliers. These buyers continually negotiate with large numbers of interested firms and therefore are well informed on what is available.

They obtain the best terms by encouraging suppliers to compete among themselves. Usually, the firm with the lowest price that satisfies the required conditions gets the deal. To be seen as such a successful firm, you need to convince the users within the larger firms of your superior technical capability, higher quality standards, management commitment, and any other arguments that place your offer above your competitors. Doing so not only gives added value to your firm, but also helps to develop an ally on the other side. This person will give direct support to your proposal by convincing his or her buyer to award you the deal. Remember, potential users of your product or service are more interested in the technical aspects of your proposal while purchasing executives are mostly concerned with pricing.

Be Ready to Walk: Your Ultimate Power

A source of strength that is often underrated by smaller firms and frequently misunderstood is walking away from a deal that no longer makes sense. In any negotiations, when a deal begins to look unprofitable, you should seriously consider withdrawing from it. Frequently, small companies are faced with technical and capacity limiting problems—they might lack qualified staff or plant facilities that can serve larger orders. This limit is based on a thorough calculation of real potential costs. Having a bottom line coupled with alternatives gives a greater leverage in protecting your interests. Knowing when to walk out of a negotiation gives you greater confidence in advancing the benefits of your proposal as well as being more reluctant to make unnecessary concessions.[5] Moreover, the other party will soon realize that this negotiation will be difficult. You now have two separate scenarios: either the larger firm will consider you as a worthwhile partner, or might decide to end discussions. If the larger party wants to continue, chances are that you will be closer to achieving your goals, or if the negotiations end early, at least you have saved time on a deal that might have eventually turned risky or gone below expectations.

Readiness to Negotiate Successfully

As already seen, a smaller firm can negotiate more effectively with larger firms by planning negotiations more carefully. Better planning and thorough preparation place a smaller firm in control of the negotiating process, advancing its goals, protecting its interests, and reaching more balanced agreements.

To ensure that you are confident of reaching your goals when entering into your next negotiation, complete the table below to test your readiness. If your score is 30 or more, you are ready. On the other hand, if your score is between 25 and 29, you have certain weaknesses which need to be addressed. A score below 25 indicated serious flaws in your strategies, calling for a postponement of negotiations until you improve your position or select other firms that may be more compatible with your goals. In the example given in Figure 17.1 below, the firm with a score of 19 is not ready to conduct a successful negotiation.

Your Strategies	Ratings*					Remarks
Be well prepared	1	2	③	4	5	Fairly ready
Find out importance of the deal	1	②	3	4	5	Going after marginal orders
Associate yourself with recognized organizations	1	2	3	4	⑤	Meeting international standards
Select large firms in difficulty	1	2	3	4	⑤	Willing to take the risk
Identify individual units	1	②	3	4	5	Not dealing with the right people
Involve the real user	①	2	3	4	5	But without much success
Be ready to walk away	①	2	3	4	5	Can't afford losing the deal
Total score	19					You are not ready

*1 is the lowest score, while 5 is the highest score

Your road map		
Green	Score of 30 or more	Go ahead with the discussions
Yellow and blinking	Score of 25 to 29	Your preparations need improvement
Red and flashing	Score below 25	You are not ready. Reconsider your strategy, improve your preparations, and develop other options before meeting the other party.

Figure 17.1 Testing your readiness to negotiate with larger firms

Summary

Many small enterprises benefit from the opportunities opened up by larger firms from subcontracting and outsourcing. This can be a lucrative business for the companies involved. Moreover, doing business with larger supply chains can be a highly effective strategy for firms seeking to be more integrated in international trade. But there are many pitfalls for smaller firms, who, by definition, are likely to be the weaker party in business negotiations. This chapter suggests a series of strategies to strengthen the capacity of small businesses to negotiate more effectively.

CHAPTER 18

Negotiating Via Interpreters

Interpretation is both an art and a science and to many a passion.

—Anonymous

Business executives negotiating with counterparts unable to speak the same language can count on the services of interpreters. Even if they have a working knowledge of the other party's language, when it comes to negotiating international business deals, particularly complex ones, it is best to rely on professional interpreters to overcome the language divide. Too often, when cross-cultural business negotiations fail, the reason is frequently poor communications and misunderstanding among the parties. For instance, when Mr. Sato, Chairman of Toyota Motor Sales met Roger Smith, Chairman and CEO of General Motors, the language barrier made the visit "bewildering" in Smith's words.[1]

The main distinction between the interpreter and the translator is oral versus written translation. Furthermore, translators have more time to refer to dictionaries and reference materials, and if need be consult language experts.[2] Consequently, translators can revise their translation over and over again until they are satisfied with the end product before submitting it to the interested party. Language interpretation is much more difficult than language translation as it is highly demanding and stressful. The strain and tension is further aggravated as negotiation is itself a stressful process and even more so when negotiating in a highly global competitive environment.

Types of Interpretation

Negotiators have the choice of simultaneous or consecutive translation. Generally, simultaneous interpretation is used in diplomacy, the United Nations and its specialized agencies, the European Commission as well as international and national conferences. Simultaneous translation demands language expertise, a high level of concentration and the ability to manage constant pressure throughout the discussions. In addition, it calls for special physical arrangements, sophisticated audio equipment, and technical support personnel, requiring significant financial investment, particularly if a second or third interpreter is needed. The other type consists of consecutive interpretation, which is more common in business negotiations. Concerning consecutive interpretation, negotiators have two options to choose from, either the short or long interpretation. The first option (short interpretation) is called "liaison interpreting." Consecutive interpreting always refers to the long consecutive type of interpretation, with note taking. Consecutive interpretation actually means more than just providing a summary. The interpreter (unless the client wishes summaries) is required to reproduce the whole speech (with all the details). From the outset, negotiators have to decide with the interpreter what type of translation would be most suitable. As consecutive interpretation slows the negotiation process, and even more so if both parties exchange information through their respective interpreters, more time needs to be planned. On the other hand, it could be an advantage to slow down the discussions as negotiators have extra time to think about how to reply while the interpreter is translating the previous statement. This strategic advantage benefits both parties.

Interpretation Requirements

To avoid misunderstandings or misinterpretation, negotiators have to speak slowly and then pause after completing a phrase or statement to allow the interpreter to translate what has been said. It is important for interpreters to pay special attention to the negotiator's speech pattern, voice variations, and pronunciation. In a number of languages, the interpreter has to rely on several words or sentences to convey the intended meaning. Because English is a more direct language, particularly in business, a statement in English will require at least 25 percent additional words to express the same message in French, Spanish, Russian, and many other languages as there are no specific equivalent words.

When negotiating with Japanese executives, interpretation is increasingly complex due to cultural factors and language structure. For example, when communicating with Japanese negotiators, interpreters have to overcome social factors and language syntax as well as handling periods of silence or lack of disagreement that can be mistaken for agreement. In addition, Japanese has several grammatical structures for communicating respect and power distance while English has only a few words for differentiating status.[3] With regards to Chinese, the same words in English may have different interpretation when translated in Chinese, making translation even more difficult.[4] In eastern Asian cultures, language tends to be indirect, where the message is communicated not only with words but with nonverbal cues and the social context. In Asia, silence is considered a part of communication, is highly appreciated, and long pauses between speakers expected. For instance, Japanese have a high tolerance for silence.[5] In these cultures, communication tends to favor politeness, cooperative, and conciliatory behaviors. In Anglo-Saxon cultures where communications are direct, negotiators tend to adopt more competitive behavior and favor persuasion and arguments. As it may take more words and time for interpreters to translate, negotiators should not become impatient or assume that the interpreters are deviating from the original statement. This is particularly relevant when negotiations take place in cultures where time is considered a precious commodity that should not be wasted.

Interpreters' Qualifications

Interpreters not only know how to listen but to understand what is being said and find the right words in another language. When negotiating with the help of interpreters, the negotiating parties should speak in short sentences, rely on plain words, and not interrupt. Lastly, when a negotiator speaks, he or she should address the other party, not the interpreter, particularly in traditional and relationship-oriented cultures as this could be interpreted as a lack of respect to the other negotiator. Moreover, there is a tendency to speak to the person sitting on the opposite side of the table who is fluent in your language, thereby ignoring the other team members including even the team leader, which in many cultures is considered disrespectful.[6]

When hiring interpreters, negotiators need to determine their competencies and experience from independent and reliable sources. This is best done by contacting the embassy/consulate for their advice as they are likely to maintain a list of approved interpreters. Chambers of commerce, trade associations, or multinational banks are also excellent contacts for identifying professional interpreters.[7] Ideally, the interpreter should have travelled frequently to the host country to remain up to date with the latest economic realities, political changes, and social developments. Although negotiators have access to a large pool of people with language skills, qualified interpreters are in short supply. To avoid unpleasant surprises, it is advisable to stay away from inexperienced interpreters, particularly when negotiating complex or sensitive business deals. Whenever possible, hire interpreters familiar with the other party's culture and industry as well as ongoing business practices, as illustrated in Figure 18.1.

If you have a large pool of interpreters to choose from, avoid those with high pitched, hoarse, stressful, or monotone voices. To have access

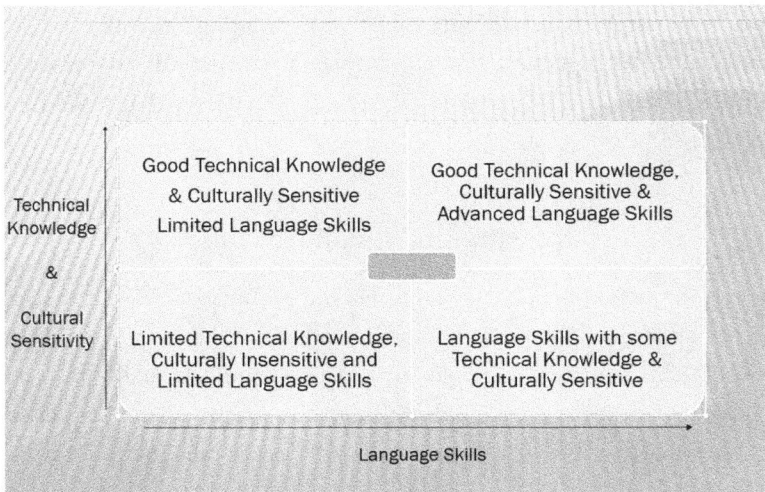

| Technical Knowledge & Cultural Sensitivity | Good Technical Knowledge & Culturally Sensitive Limited Language Skills | Good Technical Knowledge, Culturally Sensitive & Advanced Language Skills |
| | Limited Technical Knowledge, Culturally Insensitive and Limited Language Skills | Language Skills with some Technical Knowledge & Culturally Sensitive |

Language Skills

Figure 18.1 Technical, cultural, and language expertise matrix

to experienced interpreters, they should be contacted early on to ensure their availability instead of waiting till the last minute.

Involving Interpreters

Before the discussions actually begin, negotiators ought to hold one or more briefings with the interpreter to explain the nature of the deal, what you want in the way of translation, and why you want it. For example, make your requirements clear if you want everything to be translated or if you would rather have summaries. At times, your choice will depend on whether the negotiations are mainly technical and without major problems as both parties are near agreement, or difficult and require more time, plenty of patience, and persuasive arguments. To optimize the quality of their interpretation, brief the interpreters as early as possible about the upcoming negotiations, particularly the key issues that will be discussed, allowing them to consult background documents, carry out research to familiarize themselves with the issues to be negotiated, and the technical terms that are likely to be referred to. Advance preparation by interpreters is essential to the success of any business negotiation when the participating negotiators do not share a common language.

In the event you have prepared a written text to be read during the negotiations, make sure to provide an advance copy to the interpreter to familiarize himself or herself even if it is at the last moment, as it will be greatly appreciated. In relationship-oriented cultures, the interpreter's input can go beyond interpretation by transmitting emotions, motivation, and speech variation of the negotiator. Actually, professional interpreters, independently of the culture, should take all these aspects into consideration. An experienced interpreter not only translates what the negotiator is saying but is able to adapt the verbal and nonverbal messages to the cultural context.[8] Their role is to protect their own teams from confrontational conduct and even advise the team how to counter adversarial tactics.[9]

When negotiating with interpreters, it is better to speak clearly and pause after each statement to give the interpreter time to translate, whether it is liaison interpreting (short passages) or consecutive interpretation(longer passages). Each statement should be planned carefully so that it can be easily understood as well as ensuring that it does not contain abbreviations, slang, idioms, local expressions, double negatives, and words having several meanings. It is equally important to pronounce correctly the names of the party, places, dates, and figures. Moreover, avoid proverbs, sophisticated metaphors, and references to political events unless you are absolutely sure that it will not confuse or offend the other party. Special attention must be given to metaphors as they are culture oriented and can easily lead to misunderstanding and poor interpretation. Both interpreters and negotiators need to ask for clarifications, or repeat intricate or important statements when they have doubts about their meanings. As interpretation is difficult, stressful, and extremely tiring work, it is suggested that the interpreter be consulted for the judging the pace of discussions and planning breaks. To avoid mistakes by the interpreter, discussions should not go beyond a certain number of hours. Simultaneous interpretation of 30 minutes followed by 30 minutes breaks is the norm in most international conferences. In consecutive interpretation, more flexibility concerning breaks is possible, including the duration. For instance, a six-hour-day of interpretation is made up of frequent breaks and may require a second interpreter.

At times when negotiations near the deadline, there is a tendency for negotiators to speak faster and faster causing interpreters to fall behind in the translation and making unnecessary mistakes. To avoid these types of situations, negotiators can ask for more time to close the deal. However, they need to consult the interpreters to determine whether they are physically able to continue.

Interpreters as Facilitators/Mediators

There are times when interpretation is not really needed, but one or both sides insist on interpreters for reasons other than language translation, usually when anticipating highly emotional/conflicting situations or contentious/toxic issues, or to gain more time in preparing their responses. On other occasions, the interpreter is expected to play a role of go between or to act as a facilitator/mediator. For example, some time ago, one of the authors was assigned to accompany a trade delegation of Asian exporters of essential oils to meet French importers in Paris. His role was to do the interpretation from French into English as the French buyers were reluctant to negotiate in English. At the beginning of the discussions, he was doing the interpretation for both sides but found it increasingly difficult to do so as each side started to accuse the other of unfair business practices. As the discussions were getting more confrontational, he tried to interpret what was being said in a more neutral tone and less conflicting language. This approach did not help as the French importers without waiting for the interpretation started to reply directly to the accusations in English. From then on, he became a spectator rather than an interpreter, and finally a mediator. According to the Asian exporters, they were being paid low prices for their products. To them, low prices called for low quality essential oils. On the other hand, the French buyers were paying high prices as they needed fine quality ingredients for producing perfumes. The problem came from agents who profited from the situation by promising the importers quality oils while buying a mixture of various qualities at bottom prices, which created problems in the production of high priced perfumes. In the end, both exporters and importers realized the nature of the problem and came to the conclusion that it was best for them to deal directly, bypassing intermediaries.

Considering Interpreters as Team Members

To benefit fully from the interpreters' expertise, negotiators need to get to know the interpreters. Besides holding briefings concerning the upcoming discussions, it is most helpful to share common interests and experiences to build a working relationship and develop trust. In case the negotiator is accompanied by one or more experts, the interpreter should meet the other team members as well. During the discussions, it is most likely that these team members will be called upon to express their views, making it essential for the interpreter to become familiar with their speech patterns, enunciation, and technical terms. These briefings are necessary if one wants to integrate the interpreter in the negotiating team. By considering himself or herself a part of the team, the interpreter may provide additional useful information about the other party and the cultural context. However, make sure that the interpreter does not get involved in the negotiations and remains neutral.

Effective Interpretation

In a negotiating team, it is advisable to include a member who can speak the language of the other party. This member can notice any discrepancies in the translation and eventually help the interpreter with technical issues. However, if during the negotiations such a person finds the interpretation is incorrect, he or she should avoid interrupting the interpreter, but instead, write a brief note clarifying the problem and giving it to the interpreter. In addition, the interpreter can help the team members with their requirements if travelling to a country where their language is not spoken widely. Generally, interpreters are not available outside official function as interpretation is demanding and exhausting. In the event the interpreter is available to join the team at its social functions, it can reinforce the team spirit and solidarity. It is worth remembering that interpretation is highly strenuous, requiring plenty of recovery time. Do not be surprised if the interpreter declines the invitation, unless his or her presence is needed and included in the contract. Whether the invitation is accepted or refused, it will be appreciated a lot by the interpreter.

Language Knowledge

That a negotiator or a team member is conversant in the other party's language should be mentioned before the discussions begin. If you do not want to do it in a formal way, you can have your bilingual team member say a few words in the host language at the beginning of the discussions. Withholding this information from the other party may be considered unethical and can lead to suspicion, a lack of trust, or even a break in the negotiations. For example, a North American consulting firm went to the Middle East to present a project for constructing a hospital. One of the engineers was fluent in Arabic having lived in the region as a teenager. Although the discussions were carried out in English, the local representatives spoke among themselves in Arabic in side conversations. This happens often as team members switch to their native language as they find it easier and more convenient to discuss issues among themselves. Furthermore, they may believe that the foreigners do not understand their language. During these conversations, information concerning weaknesses of the project was picked up by the visiting team thanks to its own Arabic speaker. As a result of this new information, the consulting firm presented a modified design that included most of their objections which allowed the discussions to move forward. To avoid any loss of face or embarrassment by the other party, the bilingual team member was excluded from further discussions in case the other party found out that their conversations were being listened to without their knowledge.

In the event you intend to record the negotiations, your request should be made as soon as possible, even before meeting the other party. The interpreter must also be asked if he or she agrees to be recorded. It helps if your request is supported with valid justification. If the request is refused, it is better to drop it as it may lead to suspicion or jeopardize the discussions.

Whenever possible, negotiators making an effort to acquire some basic vocabulary of the host language can help develop a friendly working relationship. Being able to speak a few words in the host language even with a foreign accent can break the ice. However, it is not recommended to inject words from a third language as it may lead to confusion. By letting the other parties know that you are trying to learn their language is not only a sign of respect for their culture but a commitment to the negotiations. By learning a language, negotiators not only acquire linguistic skills, but equally important, are gaining a better understanding of the other party's behavior and thinking process, as there is a close link between language and culture. An excellent example of how language has an influential role in discussions is that of the discussions between Renault, the French automobile manufacturer, and Nissan of Japan. In early 1999, during the identification of possible synergies, Renault's executive vice president Carlos Ghosn and 50 Renault researchers began to take daily Japanese classes to improve their understanding of Japanese culture and language.[10] After 18 months of discussions, the negotiators agreed to an alliance that has proved to be mutually beneficial for both parties.

Summary

Effective communication is at the heart of any negotiation, particularly in cross-cultural ones. Communication between negotiators becomes more complicated when they belong to different cultures and do not speak each others' language. Although English has become the lingua franca of business, not all negotiators have a proficiency level sufficient to negotiate it. In view of the rapid expansion of global trade, business executives will be increasingly dealing with foreign counterparts. To overcome the language barrier, negotiators can rely on professional interpreters to communicate and interact with their foreign counterparts.[11] Negotiators can optimize the interpreter's expertise by referring to best practices for interpretation as listed in Figure 18.2.

DOs

- Hire your own interpreter instead of relying on the other party's interpreter.
- Choose interpreters having language skills but also possess cultural sensitivity and business exposure.
- Contact your embassy/consulate, chambers of commerce, trade associations, or local translators associations for their list of approved interpreters
- Give preference to candidates who have traveled extensively to the host country.
- Brief them well in advance about your requirements and type of translation wanted.
- Prepare a set of working documents for the interpreter to get acquainted with the nature of the negotiations.
- Use these briefings to get accustomed to each other's speech, voice intonation, diction, accent, and speech pattern.
- Speak slowly in short sentences, be explicit and repeat/rephrase key points, and be careful when pronouncing names.
- Keep your language simple, avoid slang, colloquialisms, abbreviations, and local expressions.
- Wait until the interpreter is finished translating what you just said before continuing.
- Break complex issues into simpler and smaller parts.
- Take frequent short breaks.
- Direct your conversation towards the chief negotiator, not the interpreter.
- Observe the other party's body language when your interpreter is translating.
- Have the interpreter meet your team members as a part of briefing.
- Hire a second interpreter for long complex negotiations.

DON'Ts

- Rely on the other party's interpreter.
- Call on people having limited language skills for difficult negotiations.
- Interrupt the interpreter while your statement is being translated.
- Make any negative comments to the interpreter, especially in front of the other party, and avoid doing it in front of your own team when it is not necessary.
- Show irritation or give away body language different from what is being translated.
- Use words that have several meanings, double negatives, or long complicated sentences.
- Read your statement unless an advance copy has been to your own team and interpreter.

KEEP IN MIND

- Interpretation increases negotiation costs.
- Negotiations require more time, particularly if both parties need interpretation.
- Interpretation is rated as one of the most stressful job in the world.
- Relying on interpreters can delay the development of working/personal relationships with the other party.
- Interpreters can influence the outcome of negotiations, particularly in relationship-oriented cultures.
- Jokes don't travel well across borders and cultures.
- Adapt your speech pattern, vocabulary, and voice to avoid misunderstanding.

Figure 18.2 Best practices for negotiators relying on interpretation

Notes

Chapter 1

1. Rudd and Lawson (2007).
2. This and the following section draw heavily from Phatak and Habib (1996), pp. 30–38.
3. Baelman and Davidson (2010), pp. 15–20.
4. "Ultimatum for the Avon Lady" (1998), p. 58.
5. Moran (2011).
6. Jain (2008), pp. 161–162.
7. Deardorff (2009).
8. Thompson (2009), pp. 31–52.

Chapter 2

1. Taylor (1871), p. 1.
2. Hall (1977), p. 16.
3. Lewicki et al. (2001), pp. 196–200.
4. Ricks (1998), p. 11; Dinker et al. (1998), pp. 337–345.
5. Foster (1992), p. 281.
6. Herbig and Kramer (1992), pp. 287–298.
7. Hall (1973); Sebenius (2002), pp. 76–89.
8. Hofstede (1980).
9. Sebenius (2002), pp. 76–89.
10. Oliver (1996).
11. Salacuse (2005), pp. 1–6.

Chapter 3

1. Kale (1999), pp. 21–38.
2. Weiss (1994), pp. 51–61.
3. Herbig and Kramer (2001).
4. Gregersen, Morrison, and Black (1998), pp. 21–23.
5. Jandt (1985).
6. Foster (1992), chap. 8.
7. Allred (2000), pp. 387–397.

Chapter 4

1. Lewicki, Saunders, and Minton (2001), chap. 2.
2. Acuff (2008).
3. Lewicki et al. (2001).
4. Salacuse (1991).
5. Jain (2004).
6. See Fisher and Ury (1991).
7. Thompson (1998). Also see Thompson (2008).
8. Kublin (1995).
9. Graham (1986), pp. 58–70. Also see Avruch (2004), pp. 330–346.
10. Black and Mendenhall (1993), pp. 49–53.
11. Hendon, Hendon, and Herbig (1996).
12. U.S. Purchasing Professionals (1993).

Chapter 5

1. Lewicki, Saunders, and Minton (2001), pp. 67–68.
2. Cialdini (1993).
3. Eyuboglu and Buja (1993), pp. 47–65.
4. O'Quin and Aronoff (2005), pp. 349–357.
5. Thompson (1998), pp. 38–42.

Chapter 6

1. Koch (1998).
2. Jensen and Unt (2002).
3. Ghosh (1996), pp. 312–325.
4. Olekalns, Smith, and Walsh (1996), pp. 68–77.
5. Gruder and Duslak (1973), pp. 162–174.
6. Pruitt (1994), pp. 217–230.
7. Koch (1998).

Chapter 7

1. Pechter (2002), pp. 46–50.
2. The discussion on pricing factors draws heavily from Jain (2008), chap. 13.
3. Jain (2008), chap. 13.

4. Lester (2005), p. 8.
5. Narayandas, Quelch, and Swartz (2001), pp. 61–69.

Chapter 8

1. Moran and Stripp (1991).
2. Riley and Zeckhauser (1983), pp. 267–289.
3. Foster (1992).
4. Ghauri (1986), pp. 72–82.
5. Graham (1986), pp. 58–70.
6. Campbell, Graham, Joliber, and Meissur (1988), pp. 49–62.
7. Axtell (1993).

Chapter 9

1. Salacuse (1991).
2. Blackman (1997), pp.98–102
3. This section draws heavily from Salacuse (1991).
4. Salacuse (1991).

Chapter 10

1. Rudd and Lawson (2007), chaps. 4 and 6.
2. Discussion in this chapter draws heavily from Lewicki, Saunders, and
3. Moran, Harris, and Moran (2011), pp. 52–54.
4. Lewicki, Saunders, and Minton (1997), pp. 124–127.
5. Hendon, Hendon, and Herbig (1996), pp. 63–64.
6. Kublin (1995), pp. 119–125.
7. Klopf (1991), p. 197.

Chapter 11

1. Habeeb (1988).
2. Banks (1987), pp. 67–75.
3. Berten, Kimura, and Zartman (1999).
4. Cross (1996), pp. 153–178.
5. Druckman (1983).

Chapter 12

1. Thompson (1998).
2. Brett, Friedman and Behfar (2009).
3. Mannix (2005).
4. Kramer (2001).

Chapter 13

1. Ertel (1999); Ertel and Gordon (2007); Movius and Susskind (2009).
2. Movius (2007).
3. Movius and Susskind (2009).
4. Ertel and Gordon (2007).
5. Benoliel (2011).
6. Kramer (2001).
7. Weiss (2011).

Chapter 14

1. Nurn and Tan (2010), pp.360–371.
2. Lewicki, Barry and Saunders (2010).
3. Dyer and Chu (2003).
4. Ro (2013).

Chapter 15

1. McGrath and Hollingshed (1999).
2. Sproull and Keisler (1991).
3. Silkenat, Aresty, and Klosek (2009).
4. McGrath and Hollingshed (1999).
5. McGuire, Keisler, and Siegler (2001), pp. 917–930.
6. Dorlet and Morris (1995).
7. Kramer (1995), pp. 95–120.
8. Thompson (1998), pp. 264–265.
9. Arunchalan and Dilla (2003), pp. 258–290.

Chapter 16

1. Anderson (1994).
2. Lewicki and Robinson (2000), pp. 665–692.
3. Herring (1996).
4. Lewis (2001).
5. Hofstede (1991).
6. Katz (2006).
7. Adler and Izraeli (1994).
8. Babcock and Laschever (2003).

Chapter 17

1. Cohen (2002).
2. Koch (1998).
3. Watkins (2002).
4. Collins and Porras (1994).
5. Dawson (1995).

Chapter 18

1. Weiss (1987), pp.23–37.
2. Ferraro and Briody (2013).
3. Rudd and Lawson (2007).
4. Fang (1999).
5. Yamada (1997).
6. Cavusgil, Ghauri and Aklcal (2012).
7. Salacuse (1991).
8. Ting-Toomey (1999).
9. Trompenaars and Hamden-Turner (1999
10. Weiss (2011)
11. This chapter contains valuable comments by Yury Obozny and Jenny Sigot Müller

References

Achebe, C. (1959). *Things fall apart*. New York, NY: Ballantine.

Acuff, F. (1993). *How to negotiate anything with anyone anywhere*. Chicago, IL: AMACOM.

Adler, N. J., Gehrke, T. S., & Graham, J. L. (1987). Business negotiations in Canada, Mexico and the United States. *Journal of Business Research 15* (October), 411–430.

Allas, T., & Georgiades, N. (2001). New tools for negotiators. *The McKinsey Quarterly* (2), 8–97.

Allison, G. (1971). *Essence of decision: Explaining the Cuban missile crisis*. Boston, MA: Little, Brown.

Altany, D. (1998). Wise men from the east bearing fights. *International Management (UK) 37*(5), 67–68.

Arrow, K., Mnookin, R., Ross L., Tversky A., & Wilson, R. (1995). *Barriers to conflict resolution*. New York, NY: Norton.

Auster, E. R., & Sirower, M. (2002). The dynamics of merger and acquisition waves: A three–stage conceptual framework with implications for practice. *Journal of Applied Behavioral Science 38*(2), 216–244.

Avruch, K. (2004). Culture and Negotiation Pedagogy, *Negotiation Journal 16*(4), 339–346.

Axtell, R. (Ed.). (1985). *Do's and taboos around the world* (3rd ed.). New York, NY: John Wiley & Sons.

Axtell, R. (1998). *The do's and taboos of body language around the world*. New York, NY: John Wiley & Sons.

Axtell, R., & Lewis, A. (1997). *Do's and taboos around the world for women in business*. New York, NY: John Wiley & Sons.

Babcock, L., & Laschever, S. (2003). *Women don't ask: Negotiation and the gender divide*. Princeton, NJ: Princeton University Press.

Babcock, L., & Laschever, S. (2008). *Ask for it: How women can use the power of negotiation to get what they really want*. London: Piatkus.

Baker, J. A. (1995). *The politics of diplomacy: Revolution, war and peace: 1989–1992*. New York, NY: G. P. Putnam & Sons.

Banks, J. C. (1987). Negotiating international mining agreements: Win-win versus win-lose bargaining. *Columbia Journal of World Business 22*(4), 67–75.

Banthin, J. (1991). Negotiating with the Japanese. *Mid-Atlantic Journal of Business 27*(April), 79–81.

Barnum, C., & Wolniansky, N. (1989). Why Americans fail at overseas negotiations. *Management Review 78*(10), 55–57.

Bennett, D. C., & Sharpe, K. E. (1979). Agenda setting and bargaining power: The Mexican state versus transnational corporations. *World Politics 32*(1), 57–89.

Benoliel, M. (Ed.). (2011). *Negotiation Excellence: Successful Deal Making.* Singapore: World Scientific Publishing, p. 3.

Berton, P., Kimura, H., & Zartman, I. W. (Eds.). (1999). *International negotiation: Actors, structure, process, values.* New York, NY: Bedford/St. Martin's.

Bilder, R. B. (1981). *Managing the risks of international agreement.* Madison: University of Wisconsin Press.

Billings-Yun, M. (2010). *Beyond deal making.* San Francisco, CA: Jossey-Bass.

Bird, A. (2001). Using video clips in the classroom. *AIB Insights 2*(2), 20–22.

Black, J. S., & Mendenhall, M. (1989). A practical but theory-based framework for selecting cross-cultural training methods. *Human Resource Management 28*(4), 511–539.

Black, J. S., & Mark Mendenhall. (1993). Resolving conflicts with the Japanese: Mission impossible. *Sloan Management Review 34*(3), 49–53.

Boyer, B., & Cremieux, L. (1999). The anatomy of association: NGOs and the evolution of Swiss climate and biodiversities policies. *International Negotiation 4*(2), 255–282.

Boyer, M., Starkey, B., & Wilkenfeid, J. (1999). *Negotiating a complex world.* New York, NY: Rowman and Littlefield.

Breslin, J. W., & Rubin, J. Z. (1991). *Negotiation theory and practice.* Cambridge, MA: Program on Negotiation at Harvard Law School.

Brett, J., Adair, W., Lempereur, A., Okumura, T., Shikhirev, P., Tinsley, C., & Lytle, A. (1998). Culture and joint gains in negotiation. *Negotiation Journal 14*(1), 61–86.

Brett, J. M. (2001). *Negotiating globally.* San Francisco, CA: Jossey-Bass.

Brunner, J. A., & Wang You. (1988). Chinese negotiating and the concept of face. *Journal of International Consumer Marketing 1*(1), 27–43.

Bryan, R. M., & P. C. Buck. (1989). The cultural pitfalls in cross-border negotiations. *Mergers and Acquisition 24*(2), 61–63.

Burt, D. N. (1984). The nuances of negotiating overseas. *Journal of Purchasing and Materials Management 20*(Winter), 2–8.

Burt, D. N. (1989). The nuances of negotiating overseas. *Journal of Purchasing and Materials Management 25*(1), 56–64.

Cai, D. A., & Drake, L. E. (1998). The business of business negotiation: Intercultural perspectives. In M. E. Roloff (Ed.), *Communication yearbook 21* (pp. 153–189). Newbury Park, CA: Sage.

Casse, P. (1991). *Negotiating across cultures.* Washington, DC: United States Institute of Peace Press.

Cavusgil, S., Ghauri, P., & Aklcal, A. (2012). *Doing business in emerging markets,* 2nd ed. Thousand Oaks, CA: Sage Publications.

Cellich, C. (1991). Negotiating strategies: The question of price. *International Trade FORUM* (April–June), p. 12.

Cellich, C. (1997). Closing your business negotiations. *International Trade FORUM 1,* 16.

Cellich, C. (1997). Communication skills for negotiation. *International Trade FORUM 3,* 25.

Cellich, C. (2000). Business negotiations: Making the first offer. *International Trade FORUM 2,* 15.

Cialdini, R. B. (1984). *Influence: The psychology of persuasion.* New York, NY: William Morrow.

Cohen, H. (1980). *You can negotiate anything.* Secaucus, NJ: Lyle Stuart.

Cohen, R. (1993). An advocate's view. In G. O. Faure & J. Z. Rubin (Eds.), *Culture and negotiation* (pp. 30–31). Thousand Oaks, CA: Sage.

Cohen, S. (2002). *Negotiating skills for managers.* New York: McGraw-Hill.

Collins, J., & Porras, J. (1994) *Building to last.* New York: Harper Business Essentials.

Contractor, F. J., & Lorange, P. (1988). *Cooperative strategies in international business.* Lexington, MA: Lexington Books.

Copeland, M. J., & Griggs, L. (1985). *Going international.* New York, NY: Random House.

Covey, S. (1989). *The 7 habits of highly effective people.* New York, NY: Simon & Schuster.

Craver, C. (2002). *The intelligent negotiator.* New York, NY: Prima Venture.

Cutcher-Gershenfeld, J., & Watkins, M. (1997). *Toward a theory of representation in negotiation.* Presented at the Academy of Management, Boston, MA.

Dawson, R. (1995). *Roger Dawson's Secrets of Power.* Franklin Lakes, NJ: Career Press.

De La Torre, J. (1981). Foreign investment and economic development: Conflict and negotiation. *Journal of International Business Studies 12*(2), 9–32.

Dietmeyer, B. (2004). *Strategic negotiation.* Chicago, IL: Dearborn Publishing.

Drake, L. E. (1995). Negotiation styles in intercultural communication. *The International Journal of Conflict Management 6*(1), 72–90.

Druckman, D. (1983). Social psychology and international negotiations: Processes and influences. In R. F. Kidd & M. J. Saks (Eds.), *Advances in applied social psychology* (Vol. 2, pp. 51–81). Mahwah, NJ: Erlbaum.

Dupont, C. (1996). Negotiation as coalition-building. *International Negotiation 1*(1), 47–64.

Dussauge, P., & Garrette, B. (1999). *Cooperative strategy: Competing successfully through strategic alliances.* Chichester: John Wiley & Sons, Chichester.

Dyer, J., & Chu, W. (2011). The determinants of trust in supplier-automaker relations in the US, Japan and Korea: A retrospective. *Journal of International Business Studies 42*, 35–47.

Elashmawi, F. (2001). *Competing globally.* Boston, MA: Butterworth Heinemann.

Elgstrom, O. (1994). National culture and international negotiations. *Cooperation and Conflict 29*(3) 289–301.

Ertel, D. (1999). Turning negotiation into a corporate capability. *Harvard Business Review* (May-June) p. 68.

Ertel, D., & Gordon, M. (2007). *The point of the deal.* Boston, MA: Harvard Business School Press.

Fang, T. (1999). *Chinese business negotiating style.* Newbury Park, CA: Sage Publications.

Faure, G. O. (1995). Nonverbal negotiation in China. *Negotiation Journal 11*(1), 11–18.

Faure, G.O. (1998). The China Quarterly. *Negotiation Journal 74*(2), 137–148.

Faure, G. O. (2003). *How people negotiate.* Dordrecht, The Netherlands: Kluwer Academic.

Faure, G. O., & Rubin, J. Z. (Eds.). (1993). *Culture and negotiation.* Newbury Park, CA: Sage.

Ferraro, G. & Briody, E. (2013). *The cultural dimension of global business,* (7th ed.). Upper Saddle River, NJ: Pearson.

Fisher, G. (1980). *International negotiations: A cross-cultural perspective.* Chicago, IL: Intercultural Press.

Fisher, R., & Brown, S. (1989). *Getting together: Building relationships as we negotiate.* New York, NY: Penguin Books.

Fisher, R., & Shapiro, D. (2005). *Beyond reason: Using emotions as you negotiate.* New York, NY: Viking.

Fisher, R., Ury, W., & Patton, B. (1991). *Getting to YES: Negotiating agreement without giving in* (2nd ed.). New York, NY: Penguin Books.

Fisher, R., Kopelman, E., & Schneider, A. (1994). *Beyond Machiavelli: Tools for coping with conflict.* Cambridge, MA: Harvard University Press.

Frances, J. N. (1991). When in Rome? The effects of cultural adaptation on intercultural business negotiations. *Journal of International Business Studies 22*(3), 403–428.

Gesteland, R. (2005). *Cross-cultural business behavior.* Copenhagen, Denmark: Copenhagen Business School Press.

Ghauri, P. N. (1986). Guidelines for international business negotiations. *International Marketing Review 3*(3), 72–82.

Ghauri, P. N. (1988). Negotiating with firms in developing countries: Two case studies. *Industrial Marketing Management 17*(1) (February), 49–53.

Ghauri, P. N., & Usunier, J. C. (Eds.). (2003). *International business negotiations.* Amsterdam: Pergamon.

Gosling, L. A. P. (1990). Your face is your fortune: Fortune telling and business in Southeast Asia. *Journal of Southeast Asia Business 6*(4), 41–52.

Graham, J. L. (1985). The influence of culture on the process of business negotiations: An exploratory study. *Journal of International Business Studies 16*(1), 81–96.

Graham, J. L. (1986). Across the negotiating table from the Japanese. *International Marketing Review 3*(3), 58–70.

Graham, J. L. (1993). Business negotiations: Generalizations about Latin America and East Asia are dangerous. UCINSIGHT University of California Irvine GSM (Summer), 6–23.

Graham, J. L., & Herberger, R. A. (1983). Negotiators abroad: Don't shoot from the hip. *Harvard Business Review* (July–August), 160–168.

Graham, J. L., Kim, D., Lin, C. Y., & Robinson, M. (1988). Buyer-seller negotiations around the Pacific Rim: Differences in fundamental exchange processes. *Journal of Consumer Research 15*(1), 48–54.

Graham, J. L., Mintu, A. T., & Rodgers, W. (1994). Explorations of negotiation behaviors in ten foreign cultures using a model developed in the United States. *Management Science 40*(1), 72–95.

Graham, J. L., & Sano, Y. (1990). *Smart bargaining: Doing business with the Japanese* (2nd ed.). Cambridge, MA: Ballinger.

Greenhalgh, L. (2001). *Managing strategic partnerships: The key to business success.* New York, NY: Free Press.

Griffin, T. J., & Daggatt, W. R. (1990). *The global negotiator: Building strong business relationships anywhere in the world.* New York, NY: Harper Business.

Gross, S. H. (1988). International negotiation: A multidisciplinary perspective. *Negotiation Journal 4*(3), 221–232.

Guittard, S. W., & Sano, Y. (1989). *Smart Bargaining: Dealing with the Japanese.* New York, NY: Harper & Row.

Gulbro, R., & Herbig, P. (1996). Negotiating successfully in cross-cultural situations. *Industrial Marketing Management 25*(3), 235–241.

Gunia, Brian, Brett, Jeanne & Nandkeolyar, Amit (2014). Trust me, I'm a negotiator: Diagnosing trust to negotiate effectively, globally. *Organizational Dynamics 4*(1), 27–36.

Habeeb, W. M. (1988). *Power and tactics in international negotiation.* Baltimore, MD: Johns Hopkins University Press.

Hall, E. T. (1959). *The silent language.* Greenwich, CT: Fawcett.

Hall, E. T., & Hall, M. (1987). *Hidden differences: Doing business with the Japanese.* Garden City, NY: Anchor Books/Doubleday.

Hall, E. T., & Hall, M. (1990). *Understanding cultural differences: Germans, French and Americans*. Yarmouth, ME: Intercultural Press.

Hampden-Turner, C., & Trompenaars, F. (2000). *Building cross cultural confidence*. New York, NY: John Wiley & Sons.

Harris, P. R., & Moran, R. T. (1991). *Managing cultural differences*. Houston, TX: Gulf Publishing Company.

Hendon, D. W., Hendon, R. A., & Herbig, P. (1996). *Cross cultural business negotiations*. Westport, CT: Quorum Books.

Herbig, P. A., & Kramer, H. E. (1992a). The dos and don'ts of cross-cultural negotiations. *Industrial Marketing Management 20*(2), 1–12.

Herbig, P. A., & Kramer, H. E. (1992b). The role of cross-cultural negotiations in international marketing. *Marketing Intelligence and Planning 10*(2), 10–13.

Hobson, C. (1999). E-negotiations: Creating a framework for online commercial negotiations. *Negotiation Journal 15*(3), 201–218.

Hofstede, G. (1991). *Cultures and organizations*. London: McGraw-Hill Europe.

Hofstede, G. (1994). *Culture's consequences*. London: Sage.

Hofstede, G., & Usunier, J. C. (1996). Hofstede's dimensions of culture and their influence on international business negotiations. In P. Ghauri & J. C. Usunier (Eds.), *International business negotiations* (pp. 137–153). Oxford: Pergamon.

Ikle, F. C. (1982). *How nations negotiate*. New York, NY: Harper and Row.

Jensen, K., & Unt, I. (2002). *Negotiating partnerships*. New York, NY: Prentice-Hall.

Kale, S. H., & Barnes, J. W. (1992). Understanding the domain of cross-national buyer-seller interactions. *Journal of International Business Studies 23*(1), 101–132.

Kapoor, A. (1975). *Planning for international business negotiations*. Cambridge, MA: Ballinger.

Katz, L. (2006). *Negotiating International Business*. Charleston, SC: Booksurge.

Kemper, R., & Kemper, D. (1999). *Negotiation*. Metuchen, NJ: Literature Scarecrow Press.

Kennedy, G. (1987). *Negotiate anywhere!* London: Arrow Books.

Kennedy, R., & Raiffa, H. (1992). Structuring and analyzing values for multiple-issue negotiations. In P. H. Young (Ed.), *Negotiation analysis* (pp. 131–151). Ann Arbor: University of Michigan Press.

Kersten, G., & Noronha, S. (1999). Negotiation via the World Wide Web: A cross-cultural study of decision making. *Group Decision and Negotiation 8*(3), 251–279.

Klein, G. (1998). *Sources of power: How people make decisions*. Cambridge, MA: MIT Press.

Klotz, J. M. (2000). *Going global: Power tools for international business deals*. Toronto: Global Business Press.

Koch, R. (1998). *The 80/20 Principle: the secret to success by achieving more with less*. New York, NY: Doubleday.

Kremenyuk, V., & Sjostedt, G., (Eds.) (2000). *International economic negotiation: Models versus realities*. Cheltenham, Gloucestershire, UK: Edward Elgar.

Latz, M. (2004). *Gain the edge*. New York, NY: St Martin's Press.

Lax, D., & Sebenius, J. (2006). *3-D negotiation*. Boston, MA: Harvard Business School Press.

Lax, D. A., & Sebenius, J. K. (1986). *The manager as negotiator*. New York, NY: Free Press.

Lewicki, R., & Hiam, L. (2006). *Mastering business negotiations*. San Francisco, CA: Jossey-Bass.

Lewicki, R., Saunders, D., & Minton, J. (1993). *Negotiation* (3rd ed.). Burr Ridge, IL: McGraw-Hill.

Lewis, R. (1996). *When cultures collide*. London: Nicholas Brealy Publishing.

Lewis, R. (2003). *The cultural imperative*. London: Nicholas Brealy Publishing.

Li, X. (1999). *Chinese-Dutch business negotiations*. Amsterdam: Rodopi.

Low, P. (2010). *Successfully negotiating in Asia*. New York, NY: Springer.

March, R. M. (1985). No no's in negotiating with the Japanese. *Across the Border* (April), 44–50.

March, R. M. (1991). *The Japanese negotiator*. Tokyo: Kodansha International.

Mautner-Markhof, F. (Ed.). (1989). *Processes of international negotiations*. Boulder, CO: Westview Press.

McCall, J. B., & Warrington, M. B. (1990). *Marketing by agreement: A cross-cultural approach to business negotiation (2nd ed.)*. New York, NY: John Wiley & Sons.

Min, H., & Galle, W. (1993). International negotiation strategies of U.S. purchasing professionals. *Journal of Supply Chain Management 29*(3), 40–50.

Mintzberg, H. (1990). Strategy formation: Schools of thought. In J. Fredrickson (Ed.), *Perspectives on strategic management* (pp. 105–235). New York, NY: Harper Business.

Mnookin, R. (2000). *Beyond winning*. Cambridge, MA: Harvard University Press.

Mnookin, R., & Susskind, L. (Eds.). (1999). *Negotiating on behalf of others*. San Francisco, CA: Sage Publications.

Moran, R. T., & Stripp, W. G. (1991). *Successful international business negotiation*. Houston, TX: Gulf Publishing Company.

Moran, R. T., Harris, P. R., & Moran, S. V. (2007). *Managing cultural differences*. Burlington, MA: Elsevier.

Movius, H., & Susskind, L. (2009). *Build to win: Creating a world-class negotiating organization*. Boston, MA: Harvard Business Press.

Nurn, C. W., & Tan, G. (2010). Obtaining intangible and tangible benefits from corporate social responsibility. *International Review of Business Research Papers 6*(4), 360–371.

Parker, V. (1996). Negotiating licensing agreements. In P. Ghauri & J.-C. Usunier (Eds.), *International business negotiation* (pp. 3–20). New York, NY: Elsevier.

Pearlstein, S. (2013). How Avis will ruin Zipcar. *Washington Post*, January, 2.

Pfeiffer, J. (1988). How not to lose the trade wars by cultural gaffes. *Smithsonian* *18*(10), 145–156.

Pye, L. W. (1992). *Chinese negotiating style: Commercial approaches and cultural principles*. New York, NY: Quorum Books.

Quinn, J. (1992). Strategic change: "Logical incrementalism." In H. Mintzberg & J. Quinn (Eds.), *The strategy process: Concepts, contexts and cases* (pp. 96–104). Englewood Cliffs, NJ: Prentice Hall.

Raiffa, H. (1982). *The art and science of negotiation*. Cambridge, MA: Belknap Press of Harvard University Press.

Raiffa, H. (with Richardson, J., & Metcalfe, D.). (2002). *Negotiation analysis: The science and art of collaborative decision-making*. Cambridge, MA: Belknap Press.

Raiffa, H., Richardson, J., & Metcalfe, D. (2002). *Negotiation analysis*. Boston, MA: Harvard University Press.

Ro, S. (2013). Zipcar is Getting Acquired by Avis. *Business Insider*, January, 2

Roemer, C., Garb, P., Neu, J., & Graham, J. L. (1999). A comparison of American and Russian patterns of behavior in buyer-seller negotiations using observational measures. *International Negotiation 4*(1), 37–61.

Rosegrant, S., & Watkins, M. (1996). Sources of power in coalition building. *Negotiation Journal 12*(1) 47–68.

Rubin, J., & Sander, F. (1991). When should we use agents? Direct v. representative negotiation. In J. W. Breslin & J. Rubin (Eds.), *Negotiation theory and practice*. Cambridge, MA: Program on Negotiation Books.

Rubin, J. Z., & Faure, G. O. (1993). *Culture and negotiation*. San Francisco, CA: Sage.

Salacuse, J. W. (1991). *Making global deals: Negotiating in the international marketplace*. Boston, MA: Houghton Mifflin.

Salacuse, J. W. (2005). Negotiating the top ten ways that culture can affect your negotiation. *Ivey Business Journal 69*(4), 1–6.

Salacuse, J. W. (2008). *Seven secrets for negotiating with government*. New York, NY: AMACOM.

Saunders, H. (2007). We need a larger theory of negotiation: The importance of pre-negotiating phases. *Negotiation Journal 1*(3), 249–262.

Schuster, C., & Copeland, M. (2006) *Global business practices: Adapting for success*. Cincinnati, Ohio: South-Western Educational Publishing.

Sebenius, J. (1991). Negotiation analysis. In V. A. Kremenyuk (Ed.), *International negotiation: Analysis, approaches, issues* (pp. 203–215). San Francisco, CA: Jossey-Bass.

Sebenius, J. (1992). Negotiation analysis: A characterization and review. *Management Science* 38(1), 18–38.

Sebenius, J. (1996a). *Introduction to negotiation analysis: Structure, people, and context.* Boston, MA: Harvard Business School Publishing.

Sebenius, J. (1996b). Sequencing to build coalitions: With whom should I talk first? In R. Zekhauser, R. Keeney, & J. Sebenius (Eds.), *Wise choices: Decisions, games, and negotiations.* Boston, MA: Harvard Business School Press.

Sebenius, J. (1998). Negotiating cross-border acquisitions. *Sloan Management Review 39*(2), 27–41.

Shell, G. (1999). *Bargaining for advantage.* New York, NY: Viking.

Silkenat, J., & Aresty, J., (Eds.) (1999). *The ABA guide to international business negotiations.* Chicago, IL: ABA.

Stein, J. G. (Ed.). (1989). *Getting to the table: The process of international pre-negotiation.* Baltimore, MD: John Hopkins University Press.

Stoever, W. A. (1981). *Renegotiations in international business transactions: The process of dispute resolution between multinational investors and host societies.* Lexington, MA: Lexington Books.

Subramanian, G. (2010) *Negotiations.* New York, NY: W. W. Norton & Co.

Taylor, E. B. (1871). *Primitive culture.* London: John Murray.

Thompson, L. (1998) *The mind and heart of the negotiator.* Upper Saddle River, NJ: Prentice Hall.

Thompson, T. (2008). *The truth about negotiations.* Upper Saddle River, NJ: Pearson.

Ting-Toomey, S. (1988). Intercultural conflict styles: A face-negotiation theory. In Y. Kim & W. Gudykunst (Eds.), *Theories in intercultural communication.* Beverly Hills, CA: Sage.

Trompenaars, F., & Hampden-Turner, C. (1998). *Riding the waves of culture* (2nd ed.). London: Nicholas Brealey Publishing.

Tung, R. L. (1984a). *Business negotiations with the Japanese.* Lexington, MA: Lexington Books.

Tung, R. L. (1984b). Handshakes across the sea: Cross-cultural negotiating for business success. *Organizational Dynamics 23*(3), 30–40.

Tung, R. L. (1984c). How to negotiate with the Japanese. *California Management Review 26*(4), 62–77.

Tung, R. L. (1989). A longitudinal study of United States-China business negotiation. *China Economic Review 1*(1), 57–71.

Unt, I. (1999). *Negotiations without a loser.* Copenhagen, Denmark: Copenhagen Business School Press.

Ury, W. (1991). *Getting past no: Negotiating your way from confrontation to cooperation.* New York, NY: Bantam Books.

Usunier, J. C. (1996). Cultural aspects of international business negotiations. In P. Ghauri and J. C. Usunier (Eds.), *International business negotiation* (pp. 93–118). New York, NY: Elsevier.

Watkins, M. (2002). *Breakthrough Business Negotiation*. San Francisco,CA: Jossey-Bass.

Weiss, S.E. (2011). The Renault-Nissan alliance negotiations. In C. Cellich & S.C. Subbash Jain, *Practical solutions to global business negotiations*. New York: Business Expert Press

Weiss, S. E., & Tinsley, C. H. (1999). International business negotiation. *International Negotiation 4*(1), 1–4.

Wolf-Laudon, G. (1989). How to negotiate for joint ventures. In F. Mautner-Markhof (Ed.), *Processes of international negotiations* (pp. 179–190). Boulder, CO: Westview Press.

Yamada, H. (1997). *Different games, different rules: Why Americans and Japanese misunderstand each other*. New York, NY: Oxford University Press.

Zartman, I. W. (1989). Prenegotiation: Phases and functions. In J. Stein (Ed.), *Getting to the table: The processes of international prenegotiation*. Baltimore, MD: John Hopkins University Press.

Zartman, I. W., & Berman, M. (1982). *The practical negotiator*. New Haven, CT: Yale University Press.

Zartman, I. W., & Rubin, J. Z. (2000). *Power and negotiations*. Ann Arbor: University of Michigan Press.

Index

OTHER TITLES IN THE INTERNATIONAL BUSINESS COLLECTION

Tamer Cavusgil, Georgia State; Michael Czinkota, Georgetown; and Gary Knight, Willamette University, *Editors*

- *Assessing and Mitigating Business Risks in India* by Balbir Bhasin
- *The Emerging Markets of the Middle East: Strategies for Entry and Growth* by Tim Rogmans
- *Doing Business in China: Getting Ready for the Asian Century* by Jane Menzies and Mona Chung
- *Transfer Pricing in International Business: A Management Tool for Adding Value* by Geoff Turner
- *Management in Islamic Countries: Principles and Practice* by UmmeSalma Mujtaba Husein
- *Burma: Business and Investment Opportunities in Emerging Myanmar* by Balbir Bhasin
- *Global Business and Corporate Governance: Environment, Structure, and Challenges* by John Thanopoulos
- *The Intelligent International Negotiator* by Eliane Karsaklian
- *As I Was Thinking....: Observations and Thoughts on International Business and Trade* by Michael R. Czinkota
- *A Strategic and Tactical Approach to Global Business Ethics, Second Edition* by Lawrence A. Beer
- *Innovation in China: The Tail of the Dragon* by William H.A. Johnson
- *Dancing With The Dragon: Doing Business With China* by Mona Chung and Bruno Mascitelli
- *Making Sense of Iranian Society, Culture, and Business* by Hamid Yeganeh
- *Tracing the Roots of Globalization and Business Principles, Second Edition* by Lawrence A. Beer

Announcing the Business Expert Press Digital Library

Concise e-books business students need for classroom and research

This book can also be purchased in an e-book collection by your library as

- *a one-time purchase,*
- *that is owned forever,*
- *allows for simultaneous readers,*
- *has no restrictions on printing, and*
- *can be downloaded as PDFs from within the library community.*
-

Our digital library collections are a great solution to beat the rising cost of textbooks. E-books can be loaded into their course management systems or onto student's e-book readers. The **Business Expert Press** digital libraries are very affordable, with no obligation to buy in future years. For more information, please visit **www.businessexpertpress.com/librarians**. To set up a trial in the United States, please email **sales@businessexpertpress.com**.

.

www.ingramcontent.com/pod-product-compliance
Lightning Source LLC
Chambersburg PA
CBHW060336200326
41519CB00011BA/1949